D0474161

Fine Homebuilding
on
Remodeling

Fine Homebuilding®
on
Remodeling

The Taunton Press

Library of Congress Cataloging-in-Publication Data

Fine homebuilding on remodeling.
    p.   cm.
    "A Fine homebuilding book."
    Contains articles from Fine homebuilding magazine.
    Includes index.
    ISBN 1-56158-051-1 (pbk.)
    1. Dwellings — Remodeling — Miscellanea.   I. Fine Homebuilding.
TH4816.F55.S39   1993   93-12675
   643'.7 — dc20   CIP

Taunton
BOOKS & VIDEOS
for fellow enthusiasts

Cover photo: Mark Feirer

First printing: June 1993

Printed in the United States of America.

A FINE HOMEBUILDING Book

FINE HOMEBUILDING® is a trademark of The Taunton Press, Inc.,
registered in the U.S. Patent and Trademark Office.

The Taunton Press, Inc.
63 South Main Street
Box 5506
Newtown, Connecticut
06470-5506

C O N T E N T S

INTRODUCTION

Remodeling can add years to the useful life of a house. Instead of looking for a new home every time our needs change, we can save money (and memories) by adding on, adapting and modernizing the homes we already own. And we'll enhance the value of our property in the bargain.

To get the job done, home remodelers, whether seasoned professionals or serious amateurs, need wide-ranging skills and knowledge. That's why remodeling articles have been so popular with *Fine Homebuilding* magazine readers over the years, and why we've pulled together the best of these articles for the first time in this volume. You'll find articles here that clearly explain the tested techniques of expert craftsmen and the novel design ideas of well-known builders. You'll see and read how to make over a kitchen or bath, convert a garage or attic, add floors or wings, and restore a classic house. Whatever your remodeling needs, you'll find a wealth of inspiration and information here.

—Jon Miller, Associate Publisher

A footnote with each article tells you when it was originally published. Product availability, suppliers' addresses and prices may have changed since the article first appeared.

After. The remodel replaced the attic with a cruciform master-bedroom suite capped by a cupola that serves as a private retreat. Outside, the old, painted shingle siding was replaced by new cedar clapboards garnished with decorative shingles and sunbursts.

Going up

This speedy remodel added a master-bedroom suite

By Michael J. Crosbie

When Doug Haney and Susan Mitchell bought their house in 1984, it was two stories high, with a squat hipped roof and gray shingle siding—a rather conventional, turn-of-the-century place (photo facing page). It had, however, undergone a series of significant renovations that considerably improved the interior. Coupled with a secluded site having a seasonal view of the Connecticut River, the open, bright first-floor was a major selling point.

Unfortunately, the rest of the house was cramped. On the first floor, a stuffy little kitchen

was a sorry counterpoint to the large, light-filled living areas. Upstairs were three small bedrooms and a single bath. Compounding the problem, Haney ran his computer business at home, and Mitchell brought her banking job home two days a week; they shared the smallest bedroom as their home office. Adding on to the house presented problems. Although the wooded site was secluded, property lines were tight. The boundary to the east was just 12 ft. from the house, and the septic system made the west end of the site unbuildable. The land sloped away to the north,

and to the south the house butted the driveway. The pristine nature of the house's square plan also discouraged bump-outs. Going up seemed the only alternative.

A three-story solution—Initially the couple hoped the attic space could be converted into a master-bedroom suite simply by popping a few dormers into the roof, a concept that was studied by the architectural firm I work for. Bob Harper was partner-in-charge of the project, Susan Edler-Wyeth was project architect, and the design team

From *Fine Homebuilding* (April 1992) 74:46-49

included Tracy Davis, William Eagan and me. We quickly determined that the 8-in-12 pitch of the roof wouldn't supply the headroom needed for a simple conversion.

The solution was to tear off the roof and to build a third story (photo left). The addition would include four dormers to accentuate the existing square plan. An 11-in-12 roof pitch and a higher eave would allow on the third floor much of the spaciousness and sunlight that Haney and Mitchell enjoyed on the first floor.

The cruciform plan of the addition (drawing below) would be perfect for accommodating a sleeping area, a sitting area, a dressing area and a master bath complete with a whirlpool tub. Each space would occupy its own quadrant, with the four quadrants arranged around a central stair and a chimney.

We added to the design something the clients hadn't requested but that appealed to them instantly—a cupola above the third floor, accessible by a ladder. The cupola would offer a very private retreat and, with windows on three of its four sides (the fourth containing the chimney), panoramic views of the town and the river.

The transformation would be completed by pulling off the existing painted shingle siding and installing clapboards over the entire house and most of the addition. The clients initially wanted to re-side the house with unpainted shingles, but the likelihood of uneven weathering dissuaded them. The sharp lines and crisp edges of clapboard siding presented a viable alternative.

Beating the weather—Haney and Mitchell planned to occupy the house during construction, conducting business as usual. Tearing off the roof to build the addition would place them and the existing interior of the house at the mercy of the weather. Fortunately, Triangle Building Associates, Inc., the local builders who tackled the addition, devised a clever plan that minimized the risk.

Conceived by Harper and Russell Smith, Triangle's hands-on president, the plan was to remove the existing roof and frame enough of the addition to support reinforced polyethylene tarps—all in one day. The strategy was pretty straightforward: Prefabricate the walls for the addition on site and then use a crane to lift off the existing roof and raise the prefabricated components into place. The crane would remove the old roof in large chunks. Prefabrication (all of it done on site) would take about a week, and the crane would complete the lifting in one day at a cost of $750.

The repetitive nature of the addition's elements—four equal dormers with a square cupola on top—made prefabrication a snap. All exterior walls were framed with 2x4s spaced 16 in. o. c. and sheathed with ⅝-in. plywood. A square opening framed into each of the dormer sidewalls would give the carpenters easy access to the outside corners of the addition for framing small hip roofs between the dormers. The 2x8 rafters for the dormers were also precut, and eight ladders were assembled to serve as the gable-end roof overhangs. A simple 2x4 cage was framed for supporting the cupola, and finally, the cupola

Before. **When the Haney-Mitchell's bought their conventional turn-of-the-century house, it had plenty of room in its living areas but lacked a real master bedroom. Photo by Doug Haney.**

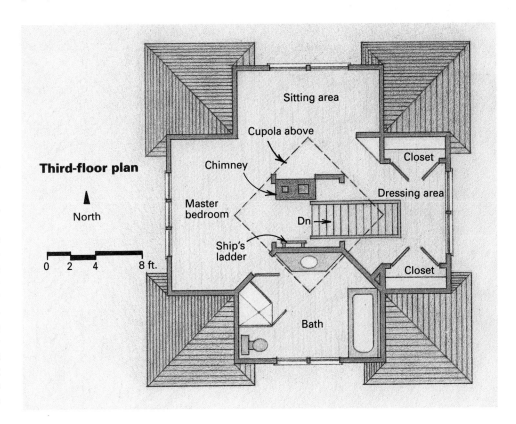

Third-floor plan

North

0 2 4   8 ft.

Sitting area

Cupola above

Chimney

Closet

Dressing area

Master bedroom

Dn

Ship's ladder

Closet

Bath

floor was framed with 2x8 joists spaced 16 in. o. c. and decked with ¾-in. plywood.

Meanwhile, Triangle's crew removed the existing shingle siding on the house and then covered the exposed sheathing with Tyvek housewrap. The crew also dismantled the existing single-flue, brick chimney down to the smoke chamber of the first-floor fireplace. This chimney would later be replaced by a double-flue chimney (where one flue serves a furnace and the other a fireplace) that would extend through the cupola roof.

With the chimney out of the way, a new floor was built in the attic. Originally, the idea was to sister new floor joists to existing joists to beef up the structure, but Smith was worried that the plaster in the second-floor ceilings might crack in the process. Instead, a new floor of 2x8 joists decked with ¾-in. plywood was built on top of the attic floor. Because the roof was supported at its perimeter by beams raised about 6 in. above the existing attic floor, the new floor could butt into the beams without bumping into the existing rafters. Once the roof was torn off, a 2x4 plate

Craning day. To limit exposure of the existing interior, a crane lifted the old roof off and then hoisted the prefabricated walls of the addition onto the new third-floor deck (photo above). The addition was sealed tightly enough to resist a heavy downpour that night. Photo by Doug Haney.

Shaping the cornice. The coved cornice of the cupola was achieved by cutting curves in a series of 2x10 blocks, nailing the blocks to the eaves and then nailing 1x3 strips of T&G Western red cedar horizontally to the blocks.

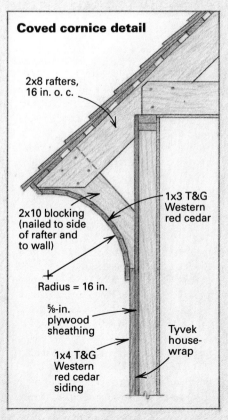

Coved cornice detail

2x8 rafters, 16 in. o. c.

2x10 blocking (nailed to side of rafter and to wall)

Radius = 16 in.

⅝-in. plywood sheathing

1x4 T&G Western red cedar siding

1x3 T&G Western red cedar

Tyvek house-wrap

would be nailed to the tops of the beams to bring them flush with the new subfloor. To compensate for raising the floor, Triangle added one riser to the existing third-floor stair.

Off with its roof—To everyone's relief, the morning of lift-off dawned with a clear sky. Now it was time to put the grand plan to the test.

Smith describes his strategy for removing the roof as "the soft-boiled-egg routine—take off the top and then peel away the rest." Smith's crew used reciprocating saws to make a number of cuts in the roof. This produced nine separate roof sections: the peak, four hip sections and four midsections (which included two small dormers). Where necessary, temporary 2x4 bracing was installed in the attic to shore up the roof. With the cuts completed, holes were cut in each section to allow a cable to be threaded through.

Smith hired Bombaci Tree Experts and Crane Service of Essex, Connecticut, to do the lifting. Their heavy lifter is a 12-ton capacity, 105-ft. long telescoping crane planted in the chassis of a Ford F-800 truck. The crane lifted the peak off first, then worked its way counterclockwise around the roof to remove the hips and the midsections. When lifting the eight bottom sections, the crane operator gently rocked each one to loosen the nails at the plate line. This method, as opposed to ripping the sections straight up, minimized stress on the walls below and helped prevent the interior plaster from cracking. Upon removal, each roof section was placed neatly next to a dumpster, cut into smaller pieces and deposited. The entire process took about an hour.

With the roof off, Smith's crew quickly nailed 2x4 plates to the tops of the perimeter beams and laid out the deck to ensure proper alignment of the prefabricated parts. When hoisting the prefabricated components, the crane worked its way from the back of the house toward the front to avoid collisions. The east gable wall was raised, positioned and nailed down, then braced to the deck until its two sidewalls were installed. Next, the supporting cage for the cupola was installed directly over the stairwell on the third floor. That done, the north dormer was installed, followed by the south and west dormers.

With the dormers up, the prefabricated cupola floor was lifted and placed on top of the cage and rotated 45° so that its doubled rim joists were supported at midspan by the corners of the cage. The four cupola walls were then hoisted and installed (photo left). The cupola's load is transferred down through the cube to the balloon-framed walls of the existing stairwell. These walls extend to the first floor where they're supported by double 2x10 beams that rest on Lally columns bolted to the basement slab.

With the cupola walls up, Smith's crew nailed up temporary 2x ridge beams to support a reinforced polyethylene tarp. It was secured with nylon rope just as storm clouds appeared on the horizon. Sure enough, it rained hard and steady that night, but only a tiny amount of water trickled into the house.

Diamonds and sunbursts—The rest of the framing was completed quickly. For visual interest, the clapboard siding was installed 2½ in. to the weather below the first-floor window sills and 4½ in. to the weather up to the tympanums (triangular tops) of the four gable walls. The tympanums are filled with clapboard sunbursts (for more on making sunbursts, see *FHB* #51, p. 14). Three of the gable ends are fitted with two 6-ft. high, double-hung windows. The west gable end, however, has three 2-ft. high awning windows placed high in the wall for privacy in the bedroom. To balance the gables visually, a 4-ft. by 6-ft. square of decorative shingles was nailed up directly beneath the awning windows.

The cupola is finished with 1x4 T&G Western red cedar siding, installed vertically. Three of the cupola walls have identical awning windows, while the northwest wall (adjacent to the chimney) harbors a 3-ft. square field of decorative shingles. The cupola's singular feature, however, is its coved cornice (photo and drawing facing page). The cornice was built by cutting 16-in. radius curves into a series of 2x10 blocks, nailing the blocks to the eaves and then nailing 1x3 strips of T&G Western red cedar to the blocks. Compound miters were cut at the corners and trimmed with a ¼-in. by ¾-in. strip of plain molding.

The understated color scheme for the exterior is patterned after that of a nearby house. (The

Twisting in the bedroom. **The core of the addition is occupied by the main stairwell and a two-flue chimney that twists and corbels from the first-floor fireplace to the cupola before exiting through the cupola roof. At the top of the stair, a shop-built ship's ladder ascends to the cupola. When not in use, the ladder is pressed against the wall.**

painter suggested a different color for every piece in the gable fans—an option the clients politely refused.)

Interior with a twist—The most dramatic feature of the third-floor interior is the new chimney, which rises straight up to the third floor from the first-floor fireplace, then twists 45° to the cupola roof while simultaneously corbeling 20 in. to the northwest (photo above).

This massive leaning tower would demand more of brick and mortar than gravity alone would allow. According to structural engineer Jim Norden, a backbone of steel was a must. This backbone would consist of four lengths of #5 rebar routed through an 8-in. by 12-in. concrete-filled channel. Originating on the east side of the fireplace, the channel would follow the convex side of the chimney through the roof, placing the steel in tension to counteract the leaning mass of the chimney. Norden also called for the addition of an 8-in. concrete-block wall on the east side of the fireplace to help counterbalance the load.

Mason Stan Bates worked out the construction details. He tied the chimney base to the fireplace by scooping out the rubble on the east side of the smokebox, inserting the bottom ends of the rebar (which were bent to right angles) into the resulting pocket, then filling the pocket with con-

crete. Bates worked with 8-ft. long rebar throughout, overlapping the joints a minimum of 24 in. and lashing them with tie wire. From the third floor up, the outside of the fireplace is a frogged composition shale brick (a frog is an indentation in the surface of a brick that interlocks with mortar) laid with high-bond strength, type S mortar.

Bates added 22.5° of the twist in the third floor and the second 22.5° in the cupola. Laying up the twisted chimney turned out to be almost as simple as laying up a straight one. Bates just ran four strings (one at each corner) from the rectangular opening in the third floor to the rectangular opening in the cupola floor. Aligning the ends of each course with the strings guaranteed the proper degree of twist in the chimney.

Bates used strings in the cupola, too. When the chimney reached the cupola ceiling, it was snug against the northeast wall. At the top Bates bent the rebar and embedded it in the chimney cap.

A chimney like this one deserves a special accent. Bates installed two decorative clay chimney pots on top (Superior Clay Corp., P. O. Box 352, Uhrichsville, Ohio 44683; 614-922-4122) that echo the shape of the gables below. □

Michael J. Crosbie is an architect with Centerbrook Architects in Essex, Conn. Photos by Bruce Greenlaw except where noted.

Growing Up in Minnesota

Jacking up the garage roof cuts the cost of a new addition

by Steven Jantzen

In March 1989, work at the office was slow. As a structural engineer and architect, I dreamed about adding a studio to our house—a place where I could relax and pursue hobbies while escaping the demands of our new baby. The most logical place for an addition was above our attached double-car garage, next to the master bedroom.

In April, I drew up plans and estimated the cost to determine the project's feasibility. My wife, Janis, indulged me this last home-improvement adventure only after I assured her that my construction methods were safe, my design sound, the cost per square foot within our means and, finally, that I could do all the work myself within a reasonable time frame.

Convincing her that my methods would work wasn't easy; I planned to cut the existing roof off the garage, raise the roof 9 ft., and then finish the new studio under it. Lifting would be accomplished by framing the front and back walls of the studio on the garage slab (framed a little short of their finished length so they'd fit inside the garage), positioning them upright just inside the existing front and back walls, and then jacking up the two studio walls and the roof, using simple hydraulic jacks (top drawing, facing page). Later, the two lifting walls would be aligned directly above the corresponding garage walls and framed to their finished lengths.

In retrospect, the plan worked well. Our 624-sq. ft. addition (photos above) was completed at a cost of about $11 per sq. ft. as opposed to the typical $45 per sq. ft. for new construction in our area. Truth is, though, there were times during construction when the project made me a little nervous.

Digging in—Before construction could begin, I needed to inspect the existing garage foundation to make sure it would support the weight of the addition. I accomplished this by digging a hole 6 ft. deep next to the foundation using a post-hole digger fitted with a pair

To cut costs, the author jacked up the existing garage roof 9 ft., then built the studio addition under it.

of 2x2 extension handles. Surprisingly, I failed to reach the footing, but I at least determined that the foundation walls extended well below the frost line. Instead of digging deeper, I calculated that even a 12-in. wide footing would have adequate bearing to support the weight of the addition. Nevertheless, my guess is that there's at least an 18-in. wide footing supporting the block walls.

My next step was to pile into the house all the junk stored in the garage. That done, I removed the 3/8-in. drywall and most of the fiberglass insulation from the garage ceiling, removed the garage-door opener and track, and rerouted the electrical wiring in the ceiling. Finally, I neatly stacked all the building materials on the garage slab where they wouldn't interfere with the roof-jacking process.

Now I was ready to work outside. In mid-May, I started a 2½-week-long vacation by removing the siding and roof overhangs from the house directly above the garage and cutting off two narrow sections of the garage eaves next

to the house. This would allow the garage roof to be raised straight up, unimpeded.

The garage roof was detached from its supporting walls by removing the soffits at the eaves and tearing off the cedar shakes covering the gable-end top plates, then prying apart the double 2x4 top plates with flat bars and cutting the nails with a reciprocating saw. In the process, I worked my way past a nest of robins perched on a lantern about 12 in. below the soffit. I banged away right next to four baby birds, who apparently couldn't have cared less. The parents scolded me, however, and during the course of the job, the birds eventually flew away, one by one.

The jacking strategy—After a week of preliminaries, I was ready to jack up the roof. The lifting procedure gave me the chance to test my architectural, structural and builderly prowess (not to mention my nerve).

Using values given in the building code, I determined that two standard shear walls consisting of 2x4 studs spaced 16 in. o. c. and sheathed with 25/32-in. fiberboard would suffice as the lifting walls. The theoretical amount of stress exerted on these walls during jacking would equal almost exactly the amount allowed by code. Because the code contains a built-in safety factor and I would only be subjecting the walls to a temporary load, I figured that would not be a problem. It was crucial, though, that I faithfully follow the prescribed nailing pattern for the sheathing to achieve the required shear value of 175 lb./sq. ft. That meant spacing the nails 3 in. o. c. at the perimeters of the fiberboard and 6 in. o. c. in the field. A 3-ft. long 4x4 beam placed between each jack and the bottom plates of the walls would help distribute the load.

The addition of four sets of 2x4 diagonal "X" bracing would tie the two lifting walls together, and the trusses would be temporarily nailed to the top plates of the lifting walls, creating a rigid frame out of the entire roof/wall

From *Fine Homebuilding* (April 1991) 67:64-66

Lifting the roof

To raise the garage roof, the author framed a portion of the front and back walls of the studio inside the garage, braced them diagonally, cut the roof free, and then jacked up the two walls and roof using four hydraulic jacks in combination with wood and concrete blocks. Next, he framed the new studio floor, installing a pair of steel I-beams to support the new floor joists. One lifting wall was then braced diagonally to the floor, and the roof jacked up slightly above the opposite wall, allowing that wall to be moved out to the floor's perimeter and nailed down. The roof was then lowered and nailed to the top plate before the process was repeated to reposition the opposite lifting wall.

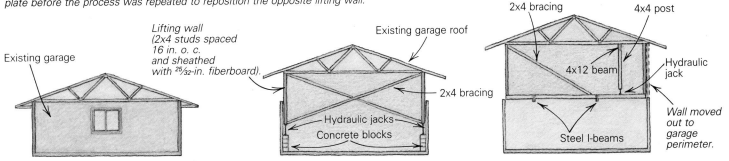

Existing garage

Lifting wall
(2x4 studs spaced
16 in. o. c.
and sheathed
with ²⁵/₃₂-in. fiberboard).

Existing garage roof

2x4 bracing

Hydraulic jacks

Concrete blocks

2x4 bracing

4x4 post

4x12 beam

Hydraulic jack

Wall moved out to garage perimeter.

Steel I-beams

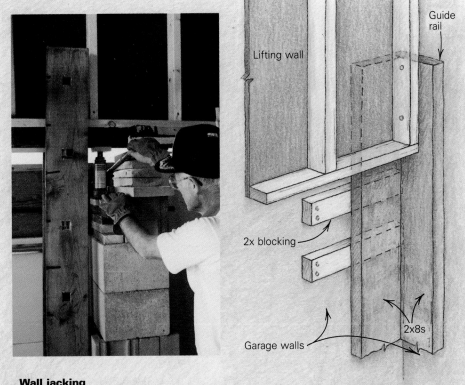

Guide rail

Lifting wall

2x blocking

Garage walls

2x8s

Wall jacking

Jacking was accomplished with the use of hydraulic jacks resting upon wood and concrete blocks (photo above). An adjustable stand (left in photo) was used to support the lifting walls while the concrete blocks were periodically restacked with alternate rows crisscrossed for added stability. During jacking, the walls were steered by vertical guide rails that leaned against the ends of the lifting walls and were contained by wood blocking nailed to the inside corners of the garage. Once a lifting wall cleared the corner blocking, as shown in the drawing above, the guide rails were raised and nailed to the walls to maintain contact with the blocking.

Floor-framing detail

¾-in. T&G plywood

Gap prevents floor joists from shrinking below top of I-beam.

2x8 blocking

2x8 floor joists, 16 in. o. c.

2x10s ripped in half

⅜-in. bolt

½-in. plywood

The studio's floor joists are supported by a pair of 26-ft. long steel I-beams.

structure. On paper, everything looked good. Even the building inspector thought the whole idea was "pretty gutsy."

An uplifting experience—Janis' parents, Gerald and Arlene, arrived on the very afternoon I was to begin jacking up the walls. They were both supposed to help Janis around the house, but Gerald wound up helping me (for days, in fact). That same afternoon I called a friend from church, Paul, and he came over to help.

Our first challenge was to raise the two lifting walls high enough to slip a pair of hydraulic jacks and 4x4 beams underneath each one. We tried using 1-in. thick steel pry bars for

that purpose, but they lifted the walls only 6 in. high and then started bending and forcing the walls out of alignment. Paul suggested using a hydraulic automobile jack on wheels instead. I called a nearby store that was open late that evening. They just happened to have one, so I bought it. We used the car jack to realign the walls and raise them high enough to fit beneath them four small jacks (borrowed from co-workers at my office) and their accompanying 4x4 beams. Two of the jacks were rated at two tons, one at five tons and one at eight tons, but four 2-ton jacks would have sufficed.

My system called for the use of the hydraulic jacks in conjunction with concrete blocks

and 2x wood blocks. To begin, we jacked up one wall about 3 in., stacked several 2x blocks next to each jack and then lowered the jacks all the way down so that the wall rested on the blocks. Each jack was then propped up on an adjacent pile of wood blocks so the process could be repeated (photo above). We jacked up the two walls alternately in this way, making sure one was never more than 1½-in. higher than the other. Whenever a stack of wood blocks reached a height of 8 in., we replaced it with a concrete block, orienting its cores vertically for maximum compressive strength.

Twice we used an adjustable stand to support the walls while we restacked the concrete blocks with the alternate rows crisscrossed for added stability. The simple stand consisted of two vertical 2x8s spaced about 5 in. apart by a pair of plywood gussets. A matched series of square holes cut through the 2x8s accommodated a short length of 1¼-in. steel tubing upon which the walls rested. The stand also served as a sort of safety net during jacking.

I leaned an 8-ft. long vertical, L-shaped guide rail (made out of a pair of 2x8s) against both ends of the lifting walls. These rails were contained by 2x blocking nailed to the inside corners of the garage. This prevented the lifting walls from jumping off their hydraulic jacks and assured clearance for the garage-door springs, electrical panel and wall furnace. Once the lifting walls cleared the corner blocking (bottom left drawing, previous page), the guide rails were nailed to them to maintain contact with the corner blocking and keep the lifting walls on track. At the end of each working day, I nailed the guide rails to the corner blocking temporarily to anchor the structure against possible high winds.

Steeling the floor—The jacking process continued until the lower plates of the lifting walls were 9 in. above the top plates of the garage walls, which took two days. That placed the peak of the garage roof more than 2 ft. above that of the house. It also gave Gerald and me the clearance we needed to raise two steel I-beams for the floor into position, with the help of two neighbors and a block and tackle.

I used steel I-beams to support the floor joists because they could be sized easily to span the garage without the need for intermediate columns. I purchased the I-beams—a W12x16 and a W12x19—at a local scrap yard (amazingly, they had just what I needed). The beams measure 4 in. wide, about 12 in. deep and about 26 ft. long. The flanges of the W12x16 are ¼ in. thick, while those of the W12x19 are ⅜ in. thick. Consequently, the former weighs

16 lb./lf while the latter, which is designed to carry a bigger load, weighs 19 lb./lf.

The I-beams cost about 75% less than new ones. Their only flaws were a few shallow saw kerfs cut in the flanges. I calculated that these kerfs reduced the strength of the beams by only 3% and designed the floors accordingly.

Before raising the I-beams, we bolted ledgers built up out of ½-in. plywood and 2xs to both sides of them using ⅜-in. hex-head bolts spaced 4 ft. o. c., resting the bottoms of the ledgers on the bottom flanges (bottom right drawing, previous page). These ledgers would support 2x8 floor joists, the tops of which would be notched around the top flanges of the I-beams and extend about ⅝ in. above them, ensuring that shrinkage over the years would not create a ridge in the floor. Framing the floor in this way also raised the I-beams as high as possible for maximum headroom in the garage below. The I-beams bear on triple-2x4 columns in the existing garage walls.

Once the I-beams, floor joists, rim joists and blocking were in place, we glued and nailed down a ¾-in. T&G plywood subfloor, blocking the two lifting walls up off the floor joists where necessary to allow installation of the plywood beneath them.

Jockeying for position—Now we could finally reposition the two lifting walls to the perimeter of the floor. To accomplish this, we diagonally braced one of the walls to the floor, removed the four sets of X-bracing between the two walls, and then jacked up the roof above the opposite wall using hydraulic jacks, 4x4 posts and a 4x12 beam. The unbraced wall was then moved out, nailed to the subfloor and diagonally braced to it. Finally, the roof was lowered and the trusses nailed to the top plates. We repeated the process for the opposite wall.

During this portion of the project, Gerald helped me for eight straight days, from sunup to after sunset. On the eighth day, a post fell

over and hit his forearm. Janis and I took him to the emergency room, and though nothing was broken, he had a bad bruise and a puncture wound. Gerald's arm was put into a sling, which he wore like a badge of courage, proud at age 65 to have survived his first construction work.

Much of our physical exertion and emotional trepidation during this period was generated by the constant threat of rain, thunderstorms, hail and high winds. We spent more than an hour each night tacking up polyethylene sheeting over the walls and an hour each morning taking it back down. We even spent an hour in the basement during a tornado warning. Luckily, we somehow escaped the brunt of the weather.

Going it alone—I framed the remaining walls by myself. That included demolishing a portion of one lifting wall to make way for a screened porch, and cutting temporary framing out of the pair of rough window openings in the opposite wall. I also lengthened the ends of both lifting walls.

Next I turned to the roof. Because the back part of the garage roof was now higher than the adjacent roof of the house, I had to add a new overhang to the garage roof. Roofing this overhang was tricky because it required that the new shingles be woven into the old ones. The front side of the garage roof worked out to be just 2 in. higher than the adjacent roof (photo below). Ideally, this portion of the roof would have finished out flush, but that would have sacrificed 2 in. of headroom inside the addition. I'm 6 ft. 5 in. tall, so that was out of the question.

To weatherproof the 2-in. step, I bent galvanized step flashing into a "Z" shape so that it would slip beneath the shingles on both roofs. The flashing is concealed behind a length of 1x2 cedar trim. Finishing up the roof, I installed ridge and soffit vents to inhibit moisture build-up in the attic.

The existing garage-door header was underbuilt. Consisting of a double 2x14 spanning 16 ft., it had sagged in the middle about 1 in. and had long horizontal splits in it that indicated shear failure. To straighten and reinforce it, I tore off its existing fiberboard sheathing, jacked up the header in the middle until it was reasonably straight, and then nailed ¾-in. plywood over it. For extra support, I replaced a 3-ft. wide horizontal strip of fiberboard sheathing directly above the header with ¾-in. plywood. This effectively created a 16-ft. long partial box beam that incorporates a rim joist and a portion of the new studio wall. Finally, I nailed a few truss plates over the plywood seams, but I doubt they're necessary.

I installed handrails for the porch, and my father helped me nail up the new exterior siding. The exterior was stained by the end of October. Next on the list—finishing the interior. □

The garage roof ended up about 3 ft. above the adjacent roof of the house in the back and about 2 in. above it in the front. In the back, the author added an overhang along the rake of the garage roof, which died into the ridge of the house. Up front, the 2-in. step was weatherproofed by installing Z-shaped galvanized step flashing that slipped beneath the shingles of both roofs. The flashing is concealed behind 1x2 cedar trim.

Steven Jantzen is a registered structural engineer and architect in Plymouth, Minnesota. Photos by the author.

East elevation before

East elevation after

North elevation before

North elevation after

Razing the Roof

Until this new second-story was dried in, the old roof defended against the weather

by Jon H. Thompson

When Louis LeLaurin and his wife Flo asked me to design an upstairs addition for their San Antonio, Texas, bungalow, it came as no surprise. Several years before, Louis (a bachelor at that time) had hired my architectural firm to redesign the same 40-year-old house into a living space that would be acceptable to his future wife. Though the house was structurally sound, it originally possessed neither charm nor character. In the process of designing that remodel, I established a theme for the exterior that better reflected its traditional surroundings.

But of utmost importance, I designed in an opportunity to add a second story should Le-

Laurin need it. Now the biological clock was ticking, and the LeLaurins were ready for that second-story addition. My first reaction was simply to add a child's room and bath upstairs. But after reviewing my preliminary sketch, the clients decided they wanted their own bedroom to be on the same floor as their child's. So I drafted a larger addition that contained a master bedroom and bath with a walk-in closet, two children's bedrooms and an additional half-bath (bottom drawing, next page). The addition would extend to the back wall of the house, but it would be set back from the front to minimize its visual impact from the street (top photo, p. 17).

Primary concerns—The initial remodel was straightforward structurally, but the addition was a different story. For one thing, I couldn't just add another story onto the house without first considering the loadbearing capabilities of the house. The existing foundation and framing would demand careful evaluation before we could proceed. Second, leaving a house roofless during the construction process, even if only for a few days, can have serious repercussions. I understood this problem because of a third-story addition I had recently designed. The builder extended the new studs up through holes cut in the existing roof, flashing each stud with building felt,

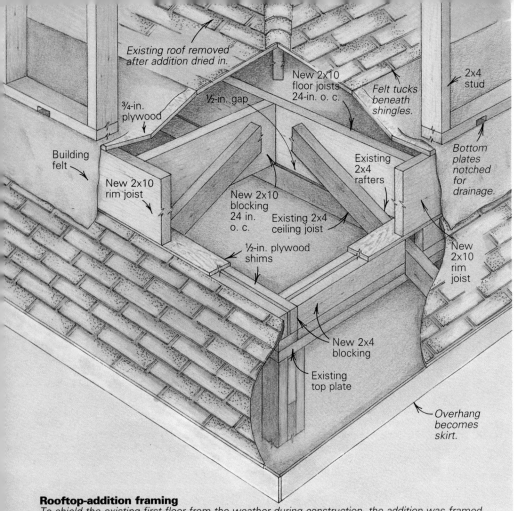

Rooftop-addition framing
To shield the existing first floor from the weather during construction, the addition was framed and dried in before the existing roof was torn off. This was accomplished by removing a 16-in. wide strip of the existing roof deck just inside the building line and slipping new floor joists through the openings to support a temporary weatherproof catwalk, and later, the new subfloor. Once the addition was dried in, rafters were cut off just below the subfloor and the tails nailed to floor joists or blocking to help support the skirt. The rest of the old roof was sliced up with a circular saw and tossed overboard.

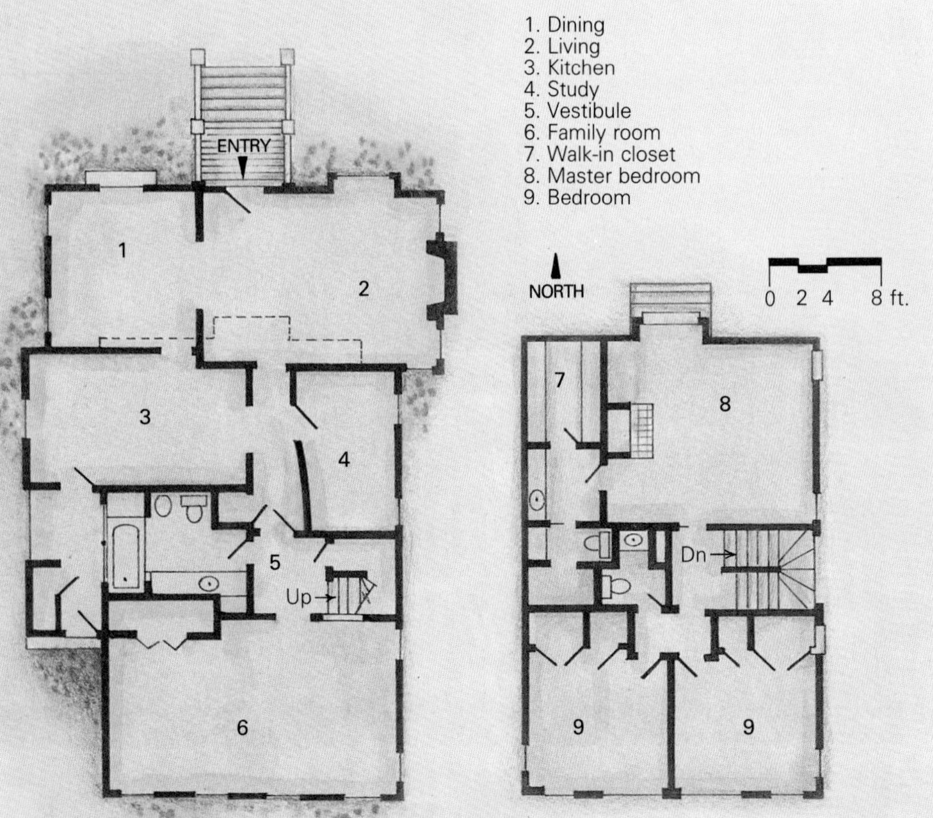

Labels on illustration:
- Existing roof removed after addition dried in.
- New 2x10 floor joists 24-in. o. c.
- Felt tucks beneath shingles.
- 2x4 stud
- ½-in. gap
- ¾-in. plywood
- Building felt
- New 2x10 rim joist
- New 2x10 blocking 24 in. o. c.
- Existing 2x4 rafters
- Existing 2x4 ceiling joist
- Bottom plates notched for drainage.
- ½-in. plywood shims
- New 2x10 rim joist
- New 2x4 blocking
- Existing top plate
- Overhang becomes skirt.

Existing first-floor plan

ENTRY

1. Dining
2. Living
3. Kitchen
4. Study
5. Vestibule
6. Family room
7. Walk-in closet
8. Master bedroom
9. Bedroom

NORTH

0 2 4 8 ft.

Up→
Dn→

New second-floor plan

then framed and dried in the new roof before cutting away and discarding the old roof below it. The approach worked in that the lower floors suffered no water damage during construction, but the process was tedious and provided no level platform from which carpenters could frame the new structure.

Some builders I've spoken to simply tear off the old roof and work 16-hour shifts until the new addition is framed and dried in, cursing each cloud that appears on the horizon. Others patch the gaping hole with the heaviest plastic sheeting they can find, then frame above the suspended wading pool. Everyone has horror stories of the inevitable deluge. In one case, replacement of a buckled oak floor and waterlogged drywall in the existing lower story cost as much as the addition—and the uninsured builder paid for it. For the LeLaurin addition, I was determined to develop a framing procedure that would be simple and dependable (more on that later).

Carrying the load—Before completing the final design, I showed a plan and some photographs of the existing pole-and-beam foundation to a structural engineer, Bob Harper, who earned his license through practical experience. The foundation consisted of unmilled juniper (around here it's called cedar) poles resting on concrete pads buried 3 ft. to 4 ft. in the ground. The poles supported 3x8 girders, which in turn supported the floor joists. At Harper's request we excavated around a post to make sure it was still sound, which it was. That didn't surprise me because the juniper, ubiquitous in central Texas, was once used extensively for fence and foundation posts because of its density and high resin content.

Harper figured that the wall framing could handle the upper-story addition, but recommended reinforcing the foundation. His plan called for 2x8s to be sistered to each side of the interior girders that bisected the house lengthwise, with a pair of posts and concrete piers added near the middle of the span that would ultimately support the new ridge up top. He also suggested that double 2x8s or 2x10s be bolted to the inside of the perimeter girders, depending on the span (typically about 6 ft.) and the loads above.

The proposed front wall of the addition would load a girder that originally carried only floor joists and a partition. Here, Harper suggested sandwiching the existing 3x6 girder with a pair of Micro = Lam LVL (laminated-veneer lumber) beams (Trus Joist Corporation, 9777 W. Chinden Boulevard, P. O. Box 60, Boise, Idaho 83707). LVL is one of Harper's favorite problem-solvers in wood-frame construction because it often performs the same tasks as a steel beam, yet can be cut and nailed like lumber.

Where the new 2xs and LVL butt into the existing juniper poles, they would bear on pressure-treated 3x8s bolted vertically to either side of the poles; the 3x8s would extend all the way down to the concrete pads.

Drawings: Michael Mandarano

Matching up the exteriors—The design of the addition repeats the bungalow motif of the earlier remodel and reflects its thematic elements—gable windows, window seats, wainscoting and skylights. To integrate the new addition, the original "waterfall" wood siding (similar to clapboard siding, except that two courses are molded into each board) was continued up to a water table that forms the sill for several of the new windows (photo below). Above the water table, a frieze of cedar shingles accentuates horizontal lines and reduces the apparent mass of the second story.

I originally designed this frieze to use #2 cedar shingles, but the builder was also asked to include a price using Shakertown prefabricated cedar siding (Shakertown Siding, P. O. Box 400-S87, Windlock, Wash. 98596). Although shingle siding is durable and attractive, it is labor-intensive and requires care in laying out the coursing. The Shakertown product, in contrast, has shingles glued to a plywood panel that nails up like siding. The panels are applied horizontally in 8-ft. lengths of single or double shingle courses, and the shingles on each panel extend beyond the bottom edge and one side edge to lap adjacent panels. Because of lower labor costs, the prefab panels were chosen. The builder liked the easy installation, the owner liked the price, and I liked the look.

The skirt formed by the original roof overhang serves a functional purpose as well as an aesthetic one. It provides protection for the lower windows and back door while emphasizing horizontal lines that mask the height of the addition. Knee braces similar to those under the front window box support the skirt. The new roof is a simple hip with two gable dormers. One dormer is centered on the front of the house and has a window seat below it; the other illuminates the stairwell and breaks up the long expanse of wall along the drive.

Keeping the lid on—The method I devised for framing the addition called for the removal of a strip of the existing roof deck to expose the top plate of the existing walls (top drawing, facing page). A circular saw was set so that the blade cut only through the asphalt roofing and the decking—in this case lx shiplap—leaving the rafters intact. The first cut was made just a hair outside the plate line and the second cut about 16-in. inside the plate line (blind cuts like this are hard on saw blades). This strip of decking was then pried off to expose the rafters and top plate. The resulting gap allowed carpenters to slip the new 2x10 floor joists through.

The joists were installed ½ in. above the existing 2x4 ceiling joists to discourage sound transmission between the first and second floors and to leave room for wiring. As usual there were no rim joists in the ceiling that would serve to support the floor framing. So double 2x4 blocking was installed over the top plates between the rafters. Plywood shims were then nailed to the tops of the

The new second story, which contains a master bedroom and walk-in closet, two smaller bedrooms and one and one-half baths, is set back from the front of the house to limit its visual impact. The addition extends to the back wall of the house. The author designed the bungalow-style front porch as part of an earlier remodel.

To blend the new with the old, the "waterfall" siding was extended up to a water table that does double duty as a sill for several of the new windows. The overhang of the original roof serves as the skirt, which, along with the cedar shingles up top, accentuates the horizontal and reduces the apparent mass of the addition. The gable dormer above the driveway breaks up the long wall visually while lending formality to an interior stairwell.

blocking to lift the floor joists the required ½ in. The shims also raised the joists just high enough to allow the 2x10 rim joists to clear the existing rafters. Some of the new floor joists were supported at midspan by an existing bearing wall, while others were attached with joist hangers to a Micro=Lam beam installed at midspan.

The exposed outdoor portion of the floor framing was then decked with a strip of glue-nailed ¾-in. T&G plywood, which became the subfloor upon which the second-story walls were framed. Also, this created a cat-walk that greatly aided the framing crew while they worked up there. It's my guess that the catwalk made the crew a lot more receptive to my framing system.

The system was more involved on the side of the hip roof where the new joists ran parallel to the existing top plate. Even with the joists spaced 24-in. o. c., the first inboard joist bumped into the underside of the rafters, requiring a large notch to be cut in each rafter for clearance. Because the roof would soon be removed, this notch was of little structural consequence. Also, 2x10 blocking was installed 24-in. o. c. between the first joist and the rim joist to support the catwalk and the second-story walls.

To waterproof the catwalk temporarily, a strip of heavy building felt was tucked under the shingles above, draped across the cat-walk and folded over the rim joist, lapping the overhang below. The bottom plate for the new walls was then nailed on top of the felt; notches every four feet allowed any rainwater to escape. Nails securing the bottom plate were the only penetrations through the felt. When the existing rafters were torn out later on, the rafter tails were left in place and tied to the new floor joists so that the original overhang became the roof skirt.

The front of the addition intersects an existing gable roof. Here, carpenters notched the existing rafters where necessary to clear the new floor joists. When it came time to frame the walls, the carpenters cut a slice out of the roof decking up the rake and then parallel to the ridge (just below the ridge) to allow the new studs to fit through. The openings were weatherproofed with building felt.

Though my floor-framing system sounds complex, it was accomplished in a day, from cutting the strip of decking off the old roof to drying in the new platform. The roof was never left open overnight, and from that point on, the crew could sleep late on Saturdays no matter what the weather.

My firm has now completed its third upstairs addition using this technique. In each case the procedure met initial resistance from the builder because of the apparent increase in framing time. However, the builders soon discovered that the only major increase in labor—cutting away the perimeter strip of roof deck, notching the rafters and installing the roofing felt—is cheap insurance when the first blue norther blows in

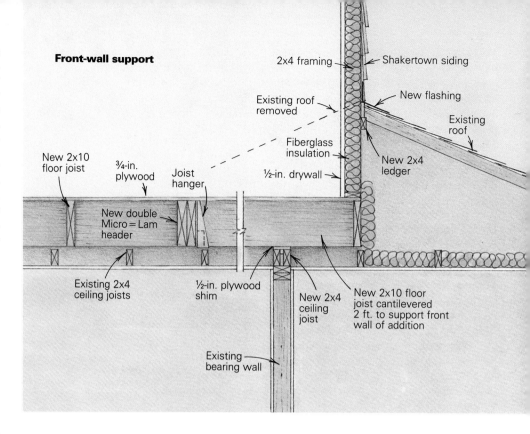

Front-wall support

2x4 framing — Shakertown siding
Existing roof removed — New flashing
Existing roof
Fiberglass insulation
½-in. drywall — New 2x4 ledger
New 2x10 floor joist
¾-in. plywood
Joist hanger
New double Micro=Lam header
Existing 2x4 ceiling joists
½-in. plywood shim
New 2x4 ceiling joist
New 2x10 floor joist cantilevered 2 ft. to support front wall of addition
Existing bearing wall

on a Saturday night before the upper framing has been dried in.

Roof ventilation—The shell of the upper addition was framed in the usual way. I called for cathedral ceilings to give the addition the feel of a large converted attic and to add interest to rectangular rooms. To compensate for the absence of tie beams, we needed a structural ridge beam. Another Micro=Lam, supported at the ends by bearing walls, did the job. The loads were transferred all the way down to the pair of concrete footings added to the foundation.

One concern with a cathedral ceiling is ventilation. I use 2x8 or 2x10 rafters (depending on the span) with 6 in. of fiberglass-batt insulation and a continuous air space above. A 1-in. hole is cut through the top of each hip rafter to allow air to circulate up the hip ridge. For earlier projects, I used hip or pancake vents to evacuate the air, but these clutter the roof. To preserve the simple massing of the LeLaurin's hip roof, I called for ridge vents (Air Vent Inc., 4801 N. Prospect Rd., Peoria Heights, Il. 61614) on the main and dormer ridges, matched with a continuous vent in the soffit. The ridge vents feature a baffle on each side to deflect wind-driven rain, and a glass-fiber filter inside the vent to keep out insects. Once installed, the vents are almost unnoticeable.

After the upper framing was completed and the addition was dried in with rigid sheathing and building felt, we disposed of the original roof. We diced it into manageable sections with circular saws and tossed it overboard, with the rafters cut just below the tops of the new floor joists (photo, p. 15). It might seem to have made sense to install the new joists alongside the existing rafters and nail the rafter tails directly to them to help support

the skirt. But the layout of the original rafters wasn't exact, and the procedure would have been more trouble than it was worth. Where the rafter tails weren't nailed directly to the joists, they were either nailed to 2x10 headers installed between the joists or they were face nailed through spacer blocks to the joists.

A cantilevered floor—The rest of the construction was unremarkable—with one exception. The front of the addition, for aesthetic and drainage reasons, corresponds with the original ridge running parallel to the front of the house. The ridge is 2 ft. forward of a load-bearing wall on the first floor, requiring that the new floor framing be cantilevered beyond the load-bearing wall by that distance to support the new front wall.

The cantilever was accomplished by first installing a double Micro=Lam header parallel to the existing ridge and about 15 ft. back from it (drawing above). Joists were then hung from the header so that their opposite ends rested on the bearing wall and cantilevered out the additional 2 ft. to support the front wall. Once the joists were installed, the remainder of the deck was glued and nailed down.

The gable dormer in the front wall required that a recess be cut out of the front of the existing roof. The sides of the recess were finished off with shiplap siding, and the bottom was flashed with a soldered metal pan.

Links and transitions—Two major concerns in shaping the interior of the LeLaurin addition were links and transitions. The primary link is vertical circulation. For any upper-story addition, the stairs should be located so that they tie in naturally with the flow of traffic. In the LeLaurin addition, stair location was a given—it would displace a portion of the foyer and closet prepared in the earlier remodel (top photo).

This location had been chosen for several reasons. First, it was situated near the addition's midsection to allow easy access to its rooms without the need for space-consuming hallways. Second, it funneled traffic from the private areas upstairs down to the private areas of the first floor. And third, the stairwell brings natural light into the middle of the house, flooding the vestibule with light from above. One wall of the original first-floor closet was torn away, linking the stairwell with the new family room on the first floor so that each is spatially enlarged by the other. This opening is framed by a low arch, a recurring theme throughout the house.

The stair rail in the LeLaurin project received much thought because it was an important element in the house aesthetically. The square balusters were painted white and capped with a cylindrical oak handrail to reflect a simple Craftsman motif.

The simple newel posts consist of 4x4 posts wrapped with clear 1x pine and finished off at the tops with 1x, screen molding and a solid-pine pyramid. The bottom newel post extends through the oak flooring and is anchored to the floor joists, while the landing newel is an extension of the stairwell framing.

A simple wainscot—The stairwell is paneled in simple bas-relief. Constructed of ¼-in. Masonite cut into strips and fastened to the drywall with panel adhesive and finish nails, the wainscot lends low-key formality to the interior. The Masonite is painted with semi-gloss enamel in a color slightly darker than the wall. Masonite is also used over the existing downstairs fireplace and around the new firebox in the master bedroom, where broad strips are glued over the drywall enclosure to suggest masonry coursing (bottom photo).

Throughout the addition, window placement reflects activities in each room. Short windows were installed high up in areas meant for furniture, affording flexibility in interior arrangement and increasing privacy. The large window in the stairwell faces east, filling the upper and lower halls with morning sun. Because of the fierce heat of Texas summer afternoons, there are no windows on the west side of the house, which is buffered by the bathroom and a walk-in closet.

Louis and Flo's infant daughter had to wait to move into her new bedroom. Design and construction delays pushed the move-in date forward by two months (fortunately Louis' father had a house available during construction). In the final analysis, the technique used for the upper-story addition did not affect its design but did safeguard construction, providing peace of mind for the builder, the client and the architect. □

Jon H. Thompson is an architect and an associate professor of architecture at the University of Texas at San Antonio.

Space for the new stairwell was carved out of a foyer and closet on the first floor (photo above). The stair connects the private areas of the first and second floors and draws natural light into the middle of the house. The opening between the stairwell and the foyer is framed by a low arch, a recurring theme in the house. The balustrade consists of simple square balusters capped with an oak handrail. Newels are 4x4s clad with 1x pine and topped with a solid-pine pyramid. Wainscoting was created by gluing and nailing strips of ¼-in. Masonite to the drywall and painting the strips in a color slightly darker than that of the drywall. Upstairs, the window seat in the new master bedroom occupies a gable dormer in the front wall of the addition (photo right). Around the fireplace, broad strips of Masonite glued to the drywall suggest masonry coursing.

Pop-Top Remodel
Recycling a roof saves time and money

by Brian McMahon

Raising the roof. The house in the photo above needed a second-story, so the builder decided to remove and reuse the existing roof. In the top photo, a crane lifts the roof structure from four pick points while men at each corner hold tag lines to stabilize and direct the roof as it's moved.

From *Fine Homebuilding* (February 1992) 72:54-56

As a builder who plies his trade in an area subject to cyclical recessions and unemployment, I have made remodeling my particular area of expertise.

In August of 1990 I was contacted by the Di-Palmas, whose burgeoning family desperately needed more living space. As we discussed plans for a two-bedroom addition to the rear of their ranch-style house, I sensed a lack of enthusiasm about the new floor plan. Their four children loved the existing backyard play area—already modest in size—and the proposed addition promised to reduce it substantially. I wasn't too excited, either, because maneuvering in that area with excavation equipment, concrete trucks and the like would be very difficult and costly. I suggested instead that we go up, not out, to build the needed sleeping quarters.

Initial inspection of the poured-concrete stem wall foundation and carefully framed attic gave me encouragement. In fact, it seemed a shame to throw away all those rafters on perfect 16-in. centers. The ridge beam was still as straight as on the day it was installed, and the roof plywood was topped off with new Timberline shingles. That's when I decided to explore the possibility of recycling a portion of the roof structure. I'd fantasized before about the Jolly Green Giant lending me a hand on a similar project but figured a structural engineer and a crane might be more in keeping with our image.

Feasibility and logistics—The speed with which we could get the house sealed up once we'd cut into the roof would be the critical factor in determining whether the overall concept was feasible. If we could somehow frame the floor in advance, prefabricate the walls and *then* remove and reinstall the roof structure, we could virtually eliminate the threat of water damage to the existing structure (and its inhabitants). I consulted John Witmer, a licensed structural engineer, who reassured me that my scheme to save the roof structure wasn't such a hare-brained idea.

Witmer confirmed that built-up beams, running parallel to the ridge, could be used to lift the roof structure. His calculations indicated that triple 2x12s on each side would be adequate for the lift, and his drawings provided explicit locations for splices and bolts in the beam.

He also added a pair of transverse compression struts, each spaced 10 ft. from the midpoint of the roof structure. The doubled 2x12 struts, reinforced with steel tension rod, would keep the roof from folding inward as it was lifted.

Once Witmer had completed the engineering and the house's owners had accepted the project as feasible, contracts were signed, and I began making preparations for the lift.

Pre-lift preparations—After taking extensive measurements in the attic and ascertaining the locations of the first-floor top plates, I was able to lay out a floor plan for the new second floor. Then my crew prefabricated the exterior

Assembling the second story. Once the old roof was safely on concrete piers in the driveway, the crane lifted prefabricated walls into place. The whole process of removing the roof, assembling the second story and replacing the roof took less than five hours.

walls with window openings, sheathing, and air/moisture barriers in place. The second top plate was left off so we could tie everything together on the day of assembly.

After all eight wall sections (each wall consisted of two sections) were built and stacked safely away from the action, we began work on the house itself. By this time, I had decided to sacrifice the old shingles because of the difficulty of color-matching at the new eaves and over the new gable ends we'd be adding. (The roof, when replaced, would need new overhangs all around.) This reduced the weight of the lift by several thousand pounds. Because all of the engineer's calculations had been based on the premise that the shingles would remain, the subsequent structural work we did in preparation for the lift was overkill. But it provided a huge margin of safety—just the way I like it.

After stripping the shingles from the roof section to be lifted, we removed one course of plywood over both eaves to expose the rafter/ceiling joist intersection. This opening provided access for new 2x8 floor joists, which we sistered to the existing 2x6 ceiling joists using pneumatic nailers to minimize damage to the existing ceiling below. Later on, we'd sever the connections between rafters and joist.

The biggest problem encountered in the second-floor framing was dealing with electri-

cal and plumbing lines that were laced through the existing ceiling joists. We temporarily removed all electrical wiring, then drilled through the new joists and reconnected everything. We gusseted below any notches with 2x scrap.

Framing the floor and preparing the roof structure took about a week, and we had to protect the house from rain in the meantime. We used a 40-ft. by 40-ft. reinforced polyethylene tarp, secured it at the perimeter by tying it to the gutter ferrules and weighed it down with a few dozen strategically placed tires. We all had a few sleepless nights when the wind kicked up, but the temporary covering worked well throughout the project.

After completing the floor framing, we screwed a ¾-in. plywood subfloor to the floor joists. The screws would allow us to remove portions of the subfloor later, if necessary, for plumbing or electrical changes. A 4-ft. wide section of the deck was left unsheathed at the eaves, where the rafters intersected the joists.

The built-up lifting beams were screwed and bolted together in place. This would allow us to disassemble the beams once the roof structure was in place, rather than having to wrestle with a several-hundred pound monstrosity. The lifting beams were attached to the rafters with Teco (P. O. Box 203, Colliers Way, Colliers, W. V. 26035;

Sealed tight to the weather. **A couple of days after the lift, the only remaining hole in the shell was the master-bedroom window, which had been left out so the drywall, furnace and cast-iron tub could be brought in through the opening. Once the window was installed, the exterior could be finished off (photo below). The whole project cost around $50,000 and added 1,000 sq. ft. to the house.**

800-438-8326) metal plates and screws so that the beam wouldn't drop once the roof was set onto the second story and the cables released. The beams were built on 2x4 blocks, spaced every couple of feet, so that lifting cable could be wrapped around each beam at two pick points.

Temporary 2x6 collar ties were added to each pair of rafters to prevent spreading and were fastened to the rafters with 16d duplex nails for later removal.

All of the nails connecting the rafters to the old ceiling joists either had to be removed with a cat's paw or severed with a reciprocating saw. Then we plumb-cut the rafters at the exterior walls, leaving the front porch intact. We tacked the rafters down with 16d duplex nails as a temporary measure to resist wind uplift until the day of the lift.

Liftoff—With all preparations complete, it was nearly a week until we had both an available crane and a dry day. Finally, the day of the lift arrived. Even though it was drizzling in the morning, I decided to take advantage of the break in the weather predicted for the afternoon. The remainder of the week was supposed to be wet, so the die was cast.

The morning was spent removing the tarp, bending and installing flashing, removing the

duplex nails and cutting the roof loose. Some of the crew built concrete-block piers in the driveway, on which to set the roof while the second floor was being assembled. When the crane arrived just before noon, the crew quickly laid plywood and 2x12s on the lawn in an attempt to minimize damage by the crane's tires.

With all our preparations complete, it was time to test the concept. We attached the cables to the lifting beams at the pick points. Tag lines were attached to the corners of the roof structure, though the lack of wind made the lines almost unnecessary. The old roof was lifted off without incident and set down on the concrete-block piers (photo, p. 20). While the new walls

were being lifted into place and tied together (photo previous page), new precut rafter tails were scabbed onto each rafter.

By 4:30 p. m. the old roof had been raised onto the second-story walls. A mixed feeling—of relief and elation—overcame me as I helped guide it into place. My crew and I spent the rest of the day securing the rafters with metal tie-down straps, adding barge rafters at the gable ends, nailing the sheathing and reinstalling the tarp for the evening. The wee hours of the night brought wind and rain once again, but we suffered only minor infiltration where the gable ends hadn't been sheathed yet. Under the circumstances, I was very gratified.

A few days later, we took advantage of the drywall boom truck to lift the furnace, the cast-iron tub and the drywall through the master bedroom's wide front-window opening (photo above). We were buttoned up soon thereafter.

The whole project cost around $50,000, about $10,000 more than the original plan to expand at ground level. Instead of adding just 350 sq. ft. though, we added over 1,000 sq. ft., saved the backyard and improved the appearance of the house.   □

Brian McMahon is a remodeling contractor in Fredonia, N. Y. Photos by author.

Ranch-House Add-Up

Built-up trusses carry the load of a piggyback addition

by April Tome and Peter Siegrist

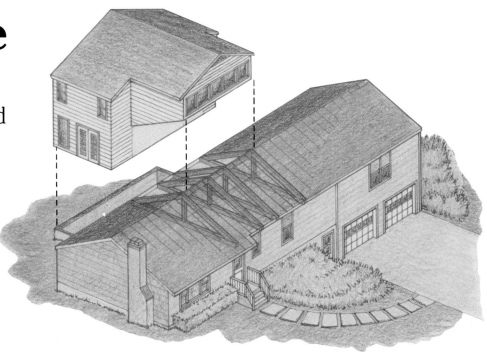

We enjoy exploring unusual solutions to common design problems. One recent example is an addition to a small ranch-style house on a cramped site in Greenwich, Connecticut. Our clients, who had three teenagers and a need for privacy, wanted a 900-sq. ft. two-story addition containing a family room and a master-bedroom suite. One side yard afforded room to build, but a two-story addition attached to the gable end of a ranch house often looks bulky and creates a circulation problem.

An unobtrusive alternative—The 14 ft. of buildable yard behind the house was enough for a ground-floor family room, but 14 ft. couldn't accommodate a master-bedroom suite on the floor above—unless the suite could encroach on the existing roof structure (top drawing). Such a piggyback scheme would solve the problems of space and circulation, but would create new concerns. As with many 1950's tract houses, the structure of this one was on the light side. The bearing walls could carry the load of an addition, but the interior bearing wall parallel to the ridge barely supported the attic, and did not align with the pipe columns in the basement. It could hardly support a second story.

To avoid rebuilding the interior bearing wall—thus disturbing our clients, who needed to remain in the house during construction—we had to find a way of transferring the loads of the addition to the outside walls. The outside walls are 26 ft. apart, which is more than standard-size single framing members can span, but the budget was too low for steel or timber. With the help of structural engineer Don Hallama, we came up with a simple, low-cost design using standard materials.

New trusses from old rafters—Our solution was to carve away part of the roof and use the remaining roof structure to make four built-up wood trusses that bear on the outside walls. We spaced the trusses at 6 ft., 3 ft. and 6 ft. o. c., allowing bathroom, stair and closet walls to bear on the top chords. New floor framing fits between and parallel to the lower chords.

Builder Alan Viitanen fit the addition to the house. He removed the roof rafters from the portion of the roof where the addition was to go. Then he built the two end trusses by spik-

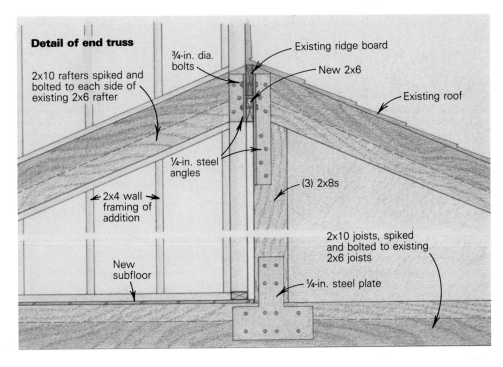

Detail of end truss

- 2x10 rafters spiked and bolted to each side of existing 2x6 rafter
- ¾-in. dia. bolts
- Existing ridge board
- New 2x6
- Existing roof
- ¼-in. steel angles
- (3) 2x8s
- 2x4 wall framing of addition
- New subfloor
- 2x10 joists, spiked and bolted to existing 2x6 joists
- ¼-in. steel plate

ing and bolting 2x10s to the 2x6 rafters and joists that remained at the edges of the opening in the roof, and added three 2x10s to the center (drawing above). Connectors are ¼-in. thick shop-fabricated steel plates and angles bolted to each side of the truss with ¾-in. dia. through bolts.

Viitanen built each of the two middle trusses from a triple layer of 2x10s, spiked and bolted together like the end trusses (photo right). He was able to snug the trusses under the remaining roof by measuring them carefully and assembling the members on the ground. To finish the floor structure, 2x10 joists were sistered to the existing 2x6 joists. A plywood subfloor was attached to the new joists, leaving the middle bay open for stair framing. □

April Tome and Peter Siegrist are architects in Greenwich, Connecticut.

Drawings: Vince Babak. Rendered from originals by Tome and Siegrist
From *Fine Homebuilding* (August 1989) 55:69

Raising a House Addition

Months of planning, weeks of prefabrication and a day of family and friends

by Allan Shope

In late 1985 my wife Julie and I began the first of 57 consecutive weekends building a house with our own hands. From excavating the foundation with two shovels to painting the trim, we found that working on the house was a tiring but ultimately rewarding labor of love. We kept the house small (about 700 sq. ft.) to match our budget, possessions and the two of us.

Two years, two dogs, and two children later, we found ourselves desperately in need of an addition. As the summer of 1988 approached, we decided to build a 900-sq. ft. addition that would add two bedrooms, one bathroom and a real kitchen (our original house had no oven because we liked to cook outdoors year-round). We spent three months designing the addition with two thoughts in mind: to keep from overpowering the original house in scale or detail and to put the addition gently on the site, without disturbing the natural grade. To accomplish both goals we pulled the addition away from the house and pinned it partially to one of the many outcroppings of rock on our steep site, connecting the two with a long enclosed corridor. This would give the little house room to breathe (photo facing page).

Despite a year's worth of working weekends on the original house, we weren't yet exhausted with building and decided to embark on an addition that would be erected as a house-raising. Although the product of a house-raising may be virtually identical to a structure built by a hired crew of carpenters, the process adds additional meaning to the structure—that of community involvement. Julie and I have always considered our house a personal object, so inviting friends and family to participate seemed ideal.

The addition went up on August 6, 1988, and it turned out to be far more than just a condensed version of framing a building the usual way. I am not an expert on house-raising, but anyone considering building a simple house this way might like to hear a few of the lessons we learned.

Planning the job—The first step should involve building a model of the building frame at a scale large enough to see the parts of the building clearly, and lettering or numbering the various parts. Post-and-beam frames are the most common structures raised, but for our addition, I thought that a 2x stick-frame would be equally accommodating to the simple design. I used a scale of ½ in. = 1 ft. and

As the sun sets, a day's work of house-raising from deck to sheathing seemed worth celebrating with dinner at a 120-ft. long picnic table.

a simple method of labeling parts that included a letter designating the elevation (such as E = East or W = West), followed by a letter designating the part type (such as D = dormer), and ending with a letter for top, bottom, left or right. It was an easy labeling system to track and to explain to other people. A model is also helpful in understanding the building three-dimensionally, and if changes need to be made they can be made quickly with the model rather than wastefully with the real building.

After completing the model, I drew full-scale details of each of the major connections of the building on sheets of plywood. These drawings were to serve as templates during both the prefabrication process and the house-raising to explain to our friends what we were building.

It was important to think about the physical act of a house-raising. I made lists of what I thought 40 people could accomplish in a day and what I thought 60 or 80 people could do. I thought about what could go wrong and how much time would be required to fix various problems. I tried to estimate the level of practical skills that people would bring to the event, and tried to account for the sincere but unskilled efforts of most. Above all I tried to keep in mind that a house-raising could work only if everyone could contribute; it was not a day for some to watch others work. The building should belong to everyone at a house-raising, and the planning of the day should reflect this condition. With these thoughts in mind I decid-

ed how much we should try to accomplish in a day and what needed to be done in advance.

My first solo construction tasks were to build a foundation of pier footings pinned directly to the rock outcropping, then to erect a level floor deck. Once the deck was on, it defined the precise dimensions of the perimeter walls and served as a work surface for prefabricating the remaining parts. I spent approximately four weeks after work and on weekends cutting and labeling the rafters, collar ties and blocking, and assembling the dormer faces and side walls, the 2x6 perimeter walls of the addition and the ridge beam. I built the 40-ft. ridge beam from doubled and staggered 2x12s.

During this last month, I hired Chris and Jason, two neighboring high-school students, to help pick up, unload, clean up and stack the cut and labeled materials and preassembled parts. We stickered the cut lumber and furring in orderly stacks so the wood wouldn't warp before being erected and so we could retrieve the pieces easily during the raising. When I had completed cutting every piece I anticipated needing, we built a 120-ft. long picnic table with benches on each side for the post-raising dinner.

Two days before the raising I felt nervous about the preparations and wasn't sure they would be adequate for the task. I had built a mountain of building parts without any guarantee that they would go together, but was hopeful and excited about the upcoming event.

The big day dawns—At 2 a. m. on August 6—raising day—the dark sky loomed over our little house, and I was wide awake with anxiety. I had rehearsed the process a hundred times in my head: would all of the pieces fit? Would I be able to direct the participants effectively? Could we keep a large group of children safe from the perils of a construction site? Would there be enough food? Would everyone come? The stars seemed to lend perspective to the problems at hand and I tried to go back to sleep.

The sun arrived at 5:30 as did the first of family and friends. After a quick breakfast of coffee and doughnuts, we embarked on the first tasks of the day, taking advantage of the relative cool of the morning. The first pieces we raised were the perimeter walls: first knee wall, then back wall, then gable walls. Although they were heavier than expected for us eight or ten early risers, they fit well and were

From *Fine Homebuilding* (Spring 1990) 59:74-77

fastened to the floor deck by 7 a. m. We used stringlines and shims to plumb and square the walls, then braced them temporarily. The temperature had reached 75° by 8 a. m. and we had close to 30 people for raising the ridge beam. Because of its length and weight, the ridge took close to 15 people to lift it into its final resting place 26 feet above the ground (top right photo, next page). We then nailed up temporary posts to keep the ridge level and straight while we set rafters.

Two groups of people worked from both gable walls toward the center of the structure to secure the rafters. Days earlier I had notched the rafters and had marked their locations on the ridge beam and top plates. Simultaneously with the rafters being set, we hoisted and fit together the preassembled sides and faces of the four large dormers (bottom photo, next page). We nailed the collar ties in place by 1 p. m. and stopped for a lunch of sandwiches that had been assembled and stacked all through the morning by ranks of sandwich specialists.

By this time, the house was taking shape, and there was a sense of excitement and comradery. A group of children had formed its own little commando group to explore the woods around the house and build small structures with scrap material. Our dogs had found happiness sitting in the ice tubs with the soda.

Despite the brutal August sun it seemed that the birth of a new building was at hand.

After lunch we set up scaffolding and began fastening 4,000 ft. of skip sheathing for a cedar-shingle roof; the shingles would go up several weeks later. We worked from both sides of the gable roof with one person per three rafters, forming an elbow-to-elbow line of people and hammers working their way toward the ridge (top left photo, next page). An equally diligent group worked on the ground, supplying lumber and nails to those above, while still another crew worked to position and secure the dormer valleys before the sheathing reached them.

I was counting on little surplus material, so

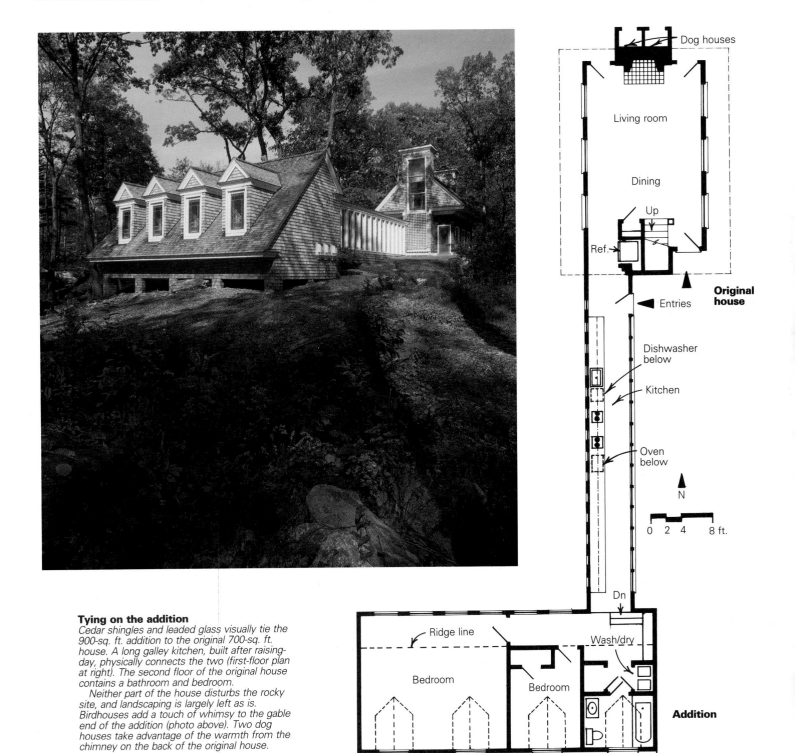

Tying on the addition
Cedar shingles and leaded glass visually tie the 900-sq. ft. addition to the original 700-sq. ft. house. A long galley kitchen, built after raising-day, physically connects the two (first-floor plan at right). The second floor of the original house contains a bathroom and bedroom.

Neither part of the house disturbs the rocky site, and landscaping is largely left as is. Birdhouses add a touch of whimsy to the gable end of the addition (photo above). Two dog houses take advantage of the warmth from the chimney on the back of the original house.

Drawing: Michael Mandarano

Raising the roof. By 8 a. m., the ridge beam is almost in place, with temporary posts bracing it until the rafters are set (photo above). Next, the day's builders fasten a precut rafter to the premarked top plate and ridge beam (photo right) to prepare for raising the dormers. The four dormer faces and their sides are hoisted up and nailed in place (photo below). These preassembled parts fit with minimal persuasion. Only the skip sheathing, dormer rafters and a miscellaneous stick needed cutting during raising-day, so the two power saws on site weren't overworked, at least not until the sheathing crew swarmed over the roof (photo left). Keeping the structure simple was meant to avoid overshadowing the original house, but it also proved a boon to the house-raising.

I had cut only the rafters we needed and stockpiled only the materials I thought we'd actually use. We had one circular saw and one worm-drive saw to use for cutting the skip sheathing and dormer rafters, and this seemed enough. Many people brought their own tool belts, so there were just enough hammers to go around (it is essential to mark tools before going to a house-raising, I might add). We fell short only once with a miscut dormer rafter, but one of the picnic benches was taken apart for replacement lumber. The picnic table and benches themselves would eventually become the structure of the enclosed corridor in the weeks following the raising. If today you peeled the drywall off the walls of the corridor, you'd see my full-scale detail drawings as well as many children's drawings on the plywood sheathing that was once the picnic-table top.

Although we had proceeded slowly in the morning with the heavier tasks, we gained speed in the afternoon and by 5:30 we came out exactly as I had hoped: the addition was entirely sheathed. We switched from soda to beer and, amid applause, secured a small pine tree to the peak of the roof. The building was far from complete, but it looked like a house. Framing and sheathing were complete in one day, a feat that seemed miraculous for a group made up largely of amateurs.

I had been under a lot of pressure to coordinate the day and couldn't relax, but heard the next day that the raising was great fun for everyone. Seven or eight contractors who've built houses for our firm arrived early and stayed late, leading small groups of inexperienced helpers on tasks such as framing the dormer roofs. I was told that after managing jobs from the office, it was a pleasure for them to swing a hammer for a day.

Our goal accomplished, work gave way to a picnic filled with self-congratulation and laughter. The day before, Julie had stockpiled steaks, mountains of bread, vegetables, drinks and pies; some generous family members and friends had brought side dishes. All afternoon one of my sisters led a brigade hauling scrap wood to the two large fire pits that Julie and I had used as a stove for the past two years. When the flames were tamed, we grilled the steaks on the open fire and dug into our dinner at the long picnic table, still in awe of our day's work together.

Afterward, the finishing—The hectic nature of a house-raising and uneven skills of the participants can lead to small oversights. I would recommend a general inspection of the

Shope spent the following year milling a huge white oak and building kitchen cabinets from its planks. To emphasize the repeating figure of the oak in doors and window casing, the oven is concealed in a floor cabinet. Glazed doors and cabinet bottoms extend the light.

house following the raising day. Our only oversight was an occasional gap in the nailing patterns, which I later filled. The completion of the house generally paralleled that of a conventional house project, at least one with considerable owner labor.

It seemed important not to lose momentum, so during the week following the raising I framed the corridor between the addition and the original house. Soon after, I had the roof of the addition shingled with cedar. A metal roof seemed the best way to finish the shallow pitch of the corridor roof framing, so I hired a roofer to instruct me in installing a gabled standing-seam copper roof over the kitchen. I hired an electrician and a plumber and got help with drywall and trim, but installed the oak T&G flooring myself. We installed double-glazed Tilt-Turn Marvin windows (Warroad, Minn. 56573) and in the spring, added leaded-glass panels made by Thomas Finsterwald, a glass artisan from Brooklyn, N. Y., who also made the windows in our original house.

One of the most challenging aspects of finishing our project was the kitchen cabinetry (photo above), which I built with the wood from a 4-ft. dia. white oak tree taken from a nearby site where another house was to be

built. The original owner of the tree was pleased that it would become more than firewood and I was grateful to have the lumber, so friend and carpenter Roy James and I cut the 20-ton tree into four enormous sections and hauled them to the house. We sliced up the sections with my portable chainsaw mill, quarter-sawing to take advantage of the beautiful figure of the oak. Milling was hard work but fascinating as we uncovered wind-stress scars from the devastating 1938 hurricane and bullet marks from century-old hunting trips.

The quality of the oak was lovely, but it would need a lot of work before becoming a cabinet. I stickered the planks until I was ready to plane and joint them for the cabinet pieces. After milling the planks into stiles, rails, panels and face frames, I stickered the pieces indoors in a kiln that we built in what would be the new bathroom. It took approximately eight weeks to bring the moisture content down to 8%.

Seeing it through—The detailing of our house was an important part of the design. I believe that most good architecture has a simple concept that is supported by its details. Elements such as simple shapes, leaded glass, oak cabinetry and birdhouses on one gable end created a consistent, but not exact, architectural link between the addition and the original house, which has similar materials and details.

A building is the product of thought, craftsmanship, and materials. It derives aesthetic quality from its design and physical quality from its craftsmanship and materials. Both are essential, but buildings today too often fail to balance these two qualities. If you care enough about the process of building to go forward with a house-raising, you should also make the effort to care about the aesthetic and physical quality of the building you make.

Our house-raising wasn't really a time-saver considering the months of planning it took. But the intangible benefits of the raising made it priceless. During the difficult times of completing the addition over the next year, I was often encouraged to carry on by the memories of the raising. Each piece of the building has a friend or family member associated with it, and they in turn have become part of the building. It is a home that will always enrich our lives because of the time we were able to share with those who cared to help. □

Allan Shope is a principal in the architecture firm Shope Reno Wharton in Greenwich, Conn.

Rock-Bottom Remodel

How an architect turned an old garage into his house and office

by Ira Kurlander

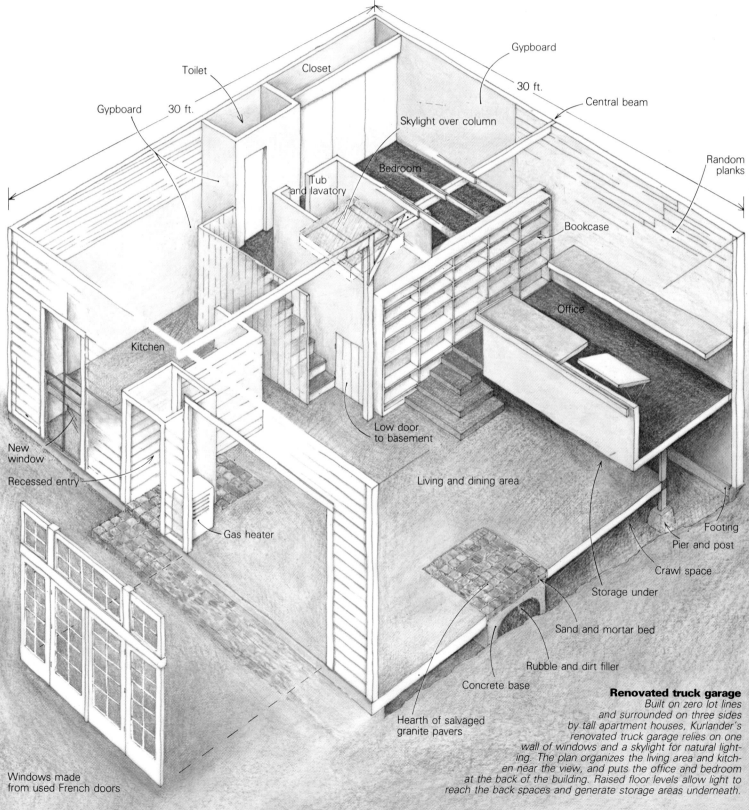

Toilet

Closet

Gypboard

30 ft.

Central beam

Gypboard

30 ft.

Skylight over column

Bedroom

Random planks

Tub and lavatory

Bookcase

Office

Kitchen

Low door to basement

New window

Recessed entry

Living and dining area

Gas heater

Footing

Pier and post

Crawl space

Storage under

Sand and mortar bed

Rubble and dirt filler

Concrete base

Hearth of salvaged granite pavers

Windows made from used French doors

Renovated truck garage
Built on zero lot lines and surrounded on three sides by tall apartment houses, Kurlander's renovated truck garage relies on one wall of windows and a skylight for natural lighting. The plan organizes the living area and kitchen near the view, and puts the office and bedroom at the back of the building. Raised floor levels allow light to reach the back spaces and generate storage areas underneath.

From *Fine Homebuilding* (December 1982) 12:42-45

Sometimes the most challenging design problems an architect gets are those with the most limitations. I'd purchased a piece of inner-city property with a 900-sq. ft. outbuilding at the back of the lot, and wanted to convert it into my office and residence, so that I could rent out the main house to help pay the mortgage. But this old truck garage, built in the 1920s, had an uncommon set of restrictions that I'd have to design around.

Three of the four 30-ft. long walls of the building were located on property lines, and the law required them to remain windowless. Inside, the 13-ft. ceiling was too low to allow a second floor, and a column occupied the exact center of the building. To make matters worse, the garage had already been converted into a dingy, poorly organized dwelling. Last, local codes and my $7,000 budget meant that I wouldn't be able to increase the size of the building. My only alternative was to rearrange the interior spaces.

A multi-level floor plan—I gutted the building, and while I sorted and stacked the reusable materials, I pondered my options. Given a choice, people will move toward the part of a room that offers natural light and an outdoor view. I could put windows only on the south wall, so I located the living and dining area and the kitchen in that sunny part of the building (drawing, facing page).

Taking advantage of the fact that the low-pitch shed roof was highest to the north, I arranged the interior like a theater, with rooms far from the windows lifted above the main floor to get an unobstructed view and more light. The office is 30 in. higher than the living area, separated from it by a low wall that defines the space and provides a needed measure of privacy. In plan, the office may seem isolated, but the view of the garden from the drafting table makes this workspace seem larger, and more a part of the rest of the house.

I placed the bedroom in the darkest corner at the highest possible level (60 in. above the main floor). For convenience, I located the bathroom on the same level. I built some badly needed storage space into the area between the slab and the bedroom floor, reducing the number of head-bumping joists by spanning the widely spaced 4x6 beams with extra-strong 2½-in. tongue-and-groove decking. Someday, the washer and drier will be located in this generous storage area. If I could get a window into it, I would be tempted to convert it to a second bedroom.

The only walls in the house that actually

Three pairs of recycled French doors fit together to fill the original garage-door opening. Waxed hardboard floors in the living and dining area, above right, are inexpensive and easy to clean; they give a pleasant earth-tone background to the area rugs and cobblestone hearth.

A broad cobblestone step, right, sweeps across the courtyard and links the garden to the doorway. The recessed entry offers shelter, and makes the interior of the small house seem spacious by contrast.

Illustration: Christopher Clapp

reach the ceiling enclose the toilet. The other rooms are open, and share light and ventilation, yet they remain clearly separate from one another. From the living area, it is impossible to see the mess in any of the other rooms, and the whole house can be tidied up quickly for clients or guests.

Because the local zoning code prohibits outside additions, I wasn't able to extend a typical roof projection over the front porch. Instead, I recessed an entry into the building, creating a sheltered area where I could fumble for my key while holding a bag of groceries. Because of the entry's small size (3 ft. square and 6 ft. 10 in. high), the interior of the house seems generous and expansive when you open the door. In fact, the space inside is larger than the courtyard, and the bottleneck entry makes the contrast still greater.

Windows for the south wall—The old double-door garage opening was about 12 ft. wide by 10 ft. high. I wanted to fill this space entirely with windows. Since a two-story building was located only 22 ft. to the south, the more height the windows had, the more sunlight they would let in. My first thought was to install a gas-station garage door with glass panels, but it was impossible to find one—at least one I could afford.

Instead, I decided to use French doors that I had collected from various remodelings. I combined three pairs, all of different widths, to create a low-budget window wall. The final arrangement (top photo, previous page) has a Palladian formality.

The framing for the new window was simple—4x4 posts from subfloor to header, with the two widest doors hung in the middle. I fixed the midsized pair in place on either side of the operable doors and ran the narrowest pair across the top. One full door was mounted sideways over the two center doors, and the last door was cut in half to fill the remaining gaps. For the time needed to replace a few broken panes plus the cost of the posts and trim, I had 120 sq. ft. of glass.

I needed an operable window with maximum ventilation for the kitchen. I took the easy way out and had a new aluminum casement made. It's the same height as the living-room window and runs all the way to the floor (photo facing page), thus opening the small kitchen to the garden outside.

The skylight—The lack of windows in the house tempted me to pepper the roof with skylights. But it's been my experience that lots of skylights with just a few windows is not a good combination; the skylights emphasize the lack of a view and suggest the feeling of being at the bottom of a well.

I decided to get by with a single skylight, placed right over the center column. Its location in the center of the house anchors the rambling collection of levels around the post, and transforms this obstacle into a unifying element. The skylight also helps to balance the light that comes in from the one window wall. One-quarter of the skylight is directly over the bathtub, giving this interior room a glimpse of the sky and the tall trees in the courtyard.

The 2-ft. o.c. roof joists favored a dome skylight either 4-ft. or 8-ft. square. I chose an economical 4-ft. square double-dome, and during noisy rainstorms and in cold weather, I am glad to have less skylight and more solid roof. Only one problem remains—the neighborhood raccoons have discovered that the skylight is a warm place to congregate.

Interior finishes—The original roof beam and joists are barely adequate for their spans, and 50 years had resulted in visible deflection. I chose to leave these members exposed, since covering them would have added considerable weight to the structure and cost a lot of money to boot. To strengthen and match the existing framing, I added roughsawn knee braces at the central post. Two of the interior walls were then partially sheathed with random-size planks salvaged from neighborhood debris bins. Fitting the various lengths and widths was time-consuming, and the many small cracks had to be caulked. But the only costs were for nails, caulk and the frequent saw sharpenings necessitated by cutting nail-embedded boards. These boards looked shabby at first, but when they were painted white, things came together. Work like this is best done by an amateur—I think it would drive a good carpenter crazy.

As an inexpensive substitute for a hardwood floor, I glued 4x8 sheets of $\frac{1}{4}$-in. tempered hardboard to the $\frac{3}{4}$-in. plywood underlayment. When it is machine waxed, this material's dark brown color acquires a depth and sheen that make a pleasing background for furniture and rugs. Unfortunately, the floor's location just off the courtyard garden means that lots of outdoor grit gets ground into the finish, and the hardboard needs power waxing and polishing three times a year to maintain its looks. Next time, I'll try a urethane-type coating as a sealant before waxing, for greater protection against moisture and scuffing.

The entry area and the hearth required a sturdier floor. Luckily (for me), streets in San Francisco's old produce market were being torn up, and the original granite cobblestone pavers were free to those who'd haul them away. I laid them on their sides in a bed of dry sand mixed with cement, so that they could be pushed around and leveled as needed. When the arrangement was satisfactory and the dry mortar joints were at an even height (about 1 in. below the top of the pavers), I topped off the mortar joints with sand and poured water over the surface. The sand kept the mortar mix from splashing, and retained moisture while the grout joints cured. After a week, I swept off the stones and vacuumed the loose sand out. Surprisingly, installing the pavers was the easiest part of the remodel. Later I added more pavers to the courtyard, making a broad step across the front of the house that includes both the French doors and the entry (bottom photo, previous page). Big design gestures like this make a small place feel larger.

A top-loading cast-iron stove from the 1890s helps heat the house and brightens up a windowless wall. Steps beside the bookcase-wall lead to the office, which has been left open to take advantage of the view, natural light and ventilation.

As seen from the top of the bedroom stairs, a custom casement window opens the kitchen to the garden and lets in fresh air. Second-hand cabinets and appliances behind the kitchen wall are in keeping with the white-washed paneling and sideboard, both made from salvaged planks.

The heating system—Since so few of the walls in the whole place reach the ceiling, an old freestanding gas heater is adequate for heating most of the house. An 1890s cast-iron stove (photo facing page) is the one thing I splurged on. Its Victorian decoration has great style, and although it's not airtight, it's still quite efficient. Its top-loading door, originally meant for coal, is handy for loading short lengths of wood and is neater than side-door designs that drop ashes on the hearth. And its mica windows let the firelight shine through.

Electrical—The entire electrical system was redone from scratch by a licensed electrician. To save his time (and my money), I had him run the wiring in exposed conduit and boxes along baseboards and beams. Later on I added a plug-in light track to the living-area ceiling for more lighting flexibility.

I like this exposed system, but if I'd had more time and money, I would have made custom metal cover plates to hide the punch-out sides of the electrical boxes. The present combination of plastic cover plates on metal switch boxes is unappealing.

Summing up—My only real regret is that I didn't install enough insulation. Next time I re-roof, I'll add a couple of inches of rigid foam on top of the 1-in. rigid fiberglass already installed, and when the time comes to renew the exterior siding, the walls will get a full 3½ in. of fiberglass batts.

The two most important lessons I learned from remodeling the garage were about economy and planning. Rather than diminishing the finished product, the strict budget made me search out alternative materials, which in turn set the style of the house. Having a flexible approach, I was able to switch from high-tech gas-station doors to traditional French doors. Instead of buying a sideboard for the dining area, I built one out of the same salvaged planks I used on the walls.

Hiding the kitchen behind a storage wall let me use an odd assortment of castoff kitchen cabinets. Likewise, the exposed roof joists and the view through the skylight make the old pedestal sink in the bath seem less obtrusive. I also avoided getting bogged down in hiding vents and flues. As long as the space is open and interesting, used materials and simple solutions to mechanical problems aren't distracting.

The open plan has indeed become a cliche of contemporary architecture, but sometimes it does make sense. This house has the same square footage as a four-room Victorian cottage that I used to live in. But even though the cottage had lots of windows and a good view, its hallways and boxy plan made it a tight maze compared to my transformed garage.

Trying for maximum light and openness within such demanding restrictions created pleasant, livable spaces, which I think is the ultimate goal of good architecture. ☐

Architect Ira Kurlander practices in San Francisco, Calif.

Interior photos: Michael Nichelson

Converting a Garage into Living Space

A new facade, a restructured ceiling and an insulated floor turn a garage into a library

Ready for a remake. **After building a freestanding garage in the back of his property, the author was ready to convert his one-car garage (shown here) to a library/study.**

Blending in a bay. **A bay window replaces the garage door and adds visual interest to the facade. To avoid the garage-conversion look, the author dug up the old driveway and landscaped the yard.**

by Neil Hartzler

When my wife and I postponed the building of a custom home for ourselves, it was on condition that we would instead add two major features into our present residence: a library/study and a large two-car garage with workspace for my tools. Located in Colorado Springs, Colorado, our neighborhood does not provide the outdoor space we wished for in a new house, but it has been a pleasant place to live.

By working weekends and evenings we built the freestanding garage behind the house, al-lowing access to an adjacent alley. Then, over five months, my wife and I turned the attached single-car garage (top photo above) into a library and study (floor plan, p. 34). Being a cabinet-maker, I looked forward to making the trim and casework. But first we had to solve three problems typical of a garage conversion: (1) How do you keep the facade from looking like a converted garage? (2) What do you do about the built-up beam that supports the ceiling joists? (3) How do you deal with the slab floor?

First, a face-lift—We were concerned with the exterior appearance of the house following the conversion. Many times I've seen a garage conversion accomplished by the installation of a sliding patio door in the space formerly occupied by an overhead garage door. This approach reinforces the converted-garage appearance, especially if the old driveway is not removed. To avoid this problem we decided to build a floor-to-ceiling bay, where the garage doors had been, and to continue the existing brick

Top photo: Neil Hartzler

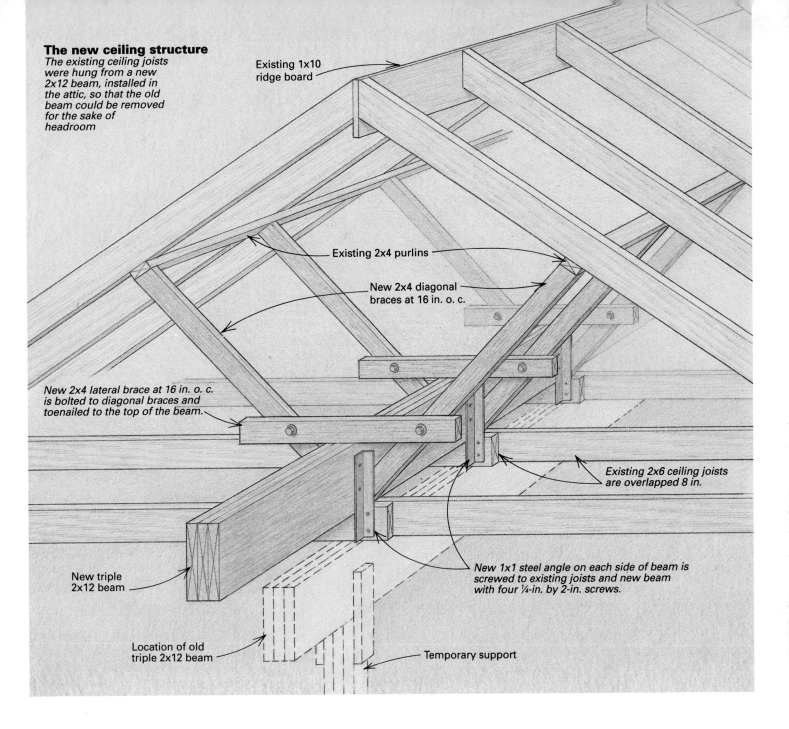

The new ceiling structure
The existing ceiling joists were hung from a new 2x12 beam, installed in the attic, so that the old beam could be removed for the sake of headroom

Existing 1x10 ridge board

Existing 2x4 purlins

New 2x4 diagonal braces at 16 in. o. c.

New 2x4 lateral brace at 16 in. o. c. is bolted to diagonal braces and toenailed to the top of the beam.

Existing 2x6 ceiling joists are overlapped 8 in.

New triple 2x12 beam

New 1x1 steel angle on each side of beam is screwed to existing joists and new beam with four ¼-in. by 2-in. screws.

Location of old triple 2x12 beam

Temporary support

facade around the bay capped by a hip roof (bottom photo, facing page).

Leaving eave design and soffit and header heights consistent with existing roof and windows provided continuity, yet the angled bay walls helped break up the straight facade. The angle bay also provided the additional floor space we needed for a desk and a chair. Once we took out the driveway and landscaped the space where it had been, all evidence of the original garage was eliminated.

Second, a structural overhaul—The ceiling of the existing garage was composed of 2x6 joists that were lapped over a triple 2x12 beam exposed below the ceiling line. The existing beam would be too low once we framed a new floor over the old garage floor, and it would interfere with the space we would need for a header over the new French doors into the house. To eliminate the beam we had to find another method of supporting the joists.

We solved this problem by building another beam above the joists and hanging the joists from it (drawing above). This beam had to be built in place because there was no way to get a completed beam into its space without cutting a hole in the end of the house; we considered this method only as a last resort.

The ends of the original beam rested on cripple studs, directly above where we wanted the French doors and the fireplace to go. We would not be able to install the new beam until the headers for these openings were in place. And we couldn't install the new headers with the old beam in our way.

To get around this problem we decided to support the old beam temporarily on posts so that we could cut off the ends and insert the new headers. We placed tripled 2x4s under the existing beam and braced them to the existing frame. We prevented the bottom of each built-up post from moving by bracing it to the existing bottom plates of the garage walls. Then the ends of the

old tripled 2x12 beam were cut off and removed. This allowed for new framing over the new doorway and fireplace openings.

In the existing wall between the garage and the house, there wasn't enough maneuvering room to install a conventional header built with 2x8s and a ½-in. spacer. Instead, we built a header out of plywood, in effect making our own laminated beam in place. We glued five layers of fir plywood together and, after the glue had set and the clamps were removed, nailed the laminated beam from both sides with three rows of 16d nails, 8-in. o. c. I've found the best glue for such applications is a waterproof product manufactured by the National Casein Co. (601 W. 80th St., Chicago, Ill. 60620; 312-846-7300) called Cross-Link Adhesive, which employs both a liquid catalyst and a liquid resin.

The door header spanned 52 in. The header over the fireplace, which we built the same way, spanned 44 in. We installed the door header tightly against the underside of the existing wall's

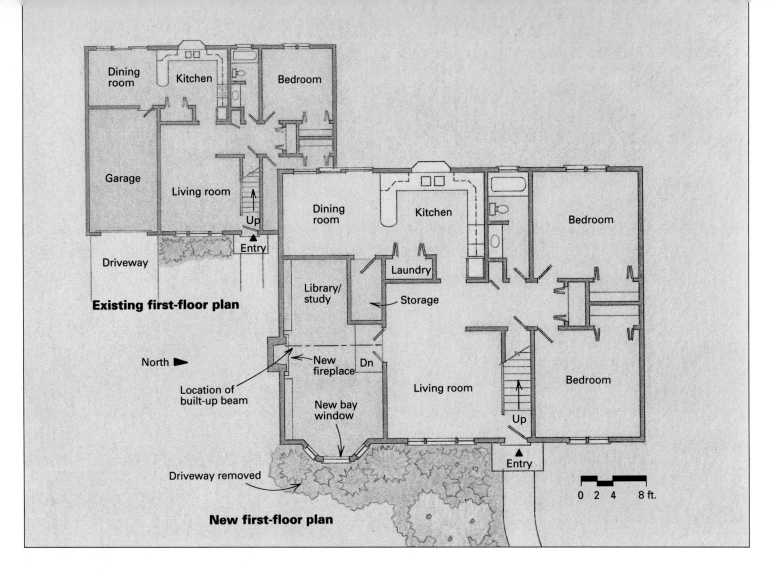

Existing first-floor plan

Dining room · Kitchen · Bedroom · Garage · Living room · Up · Entry · Driveway

North ▶

New first-floor plan

Dining room · Kitchen · Bedroom · Laundry · Library/ study · Storage · New fireplace · Dn · Location of built-up beam · New bay window · Living room · Up · Bedroom · Entry · Driveway removed

0 2 4   8 ft.

top plates. We installed the fireplace header just above the zero-clearance firebox. Then we nailed cripple studs between the plywood header and the existing top plate, with triple studs beneath the bearing point of the new beam.

Using three new 2x12s, we assembled the new beam in the attic over the new room and installed it over the existing top plates, directly over the location of the old beam. We used steel angle and lag screws to fasten the old joists to the new beam (drawing previous page); we toenailed diagonal braces to the roof purlins and the new beam. To prevent further twisting or movement of the beam, we bolted horizontal 2x4 braces to the 2x4 diagonal braces (perpendicular to the new beam) and toenailed the braces to the top of the new beam. Finally, we removed the old beam and all temporary bracing.

An insulated floor—Before dealing with the floor over the slab, we built a 4-ft. by 7-ft. closet in the corner of the garage for a freezer and gave the space a door to the existing dining room. We insulated the closet walls, as well as the existing wall between the dining room and the new library/study.

The garage slab sloped toward the driveway, and we could have built a level floor by putting down tapered sleepers with plywood over them. But we wanted plenty of insulation underfoot, so we suspended a conventional floor frame, with 2x6 joists, over the slab. We lag screwed 2x6 rim joists to the existing walls around the perime-

ter of the room. The difference in floor level between the living room and the garage was 12 in., so the top of the rim joists were still below the level of the existing living-room floor. A 6-in. landing at the French doors made up the difference, allowing a greater ceiling height in the library.

We framed the floor with 2x6 joists hung on joist hangers that were fastened to the rim joists. The total span was 12 ft., so we wedged metal shims between the floor joists and the existing concrete floor in the center of the span to prevent deflection. These 2-in. wide by 3-in. long pieces of metal—we call then framing shims around here—are used wherever there's a gap between framing members. Our inspectors routinely call for them, particularly where bearing surfaces do not meet exactly.

After floor joists were in place, we ran electrical feeds in the floor and the walls. We ran a gas line under the main house and later hooked it up to a gas-log unit in the fireplace.

I considered placing a vapor barrier over the concrete but decided against it because we never had moisture problems in the garage. Besides, the air here in Colorado is pretty dry. If you live in a more-humid part of the country, a vapor barrier would be a good idea. We stapled 6-in. fiberglass batts between the joists, then installed the subfloor. We installed 3/4 T&G waferboard subflooring using 8d ring-shank nails and panel adhesive.

Textured walls—Before hanging drywall, we added 3½-in. fiberglass batt insulation to the new

walls, including interior walls, which would soundproof our study somewhat. We had to use ⅝-in. drywall to patch the ceiling where we had removed the old beam. And we had to patch existing walls to match the existing ⅝-in. fire-rated drywall. On new walls, we used ½-in. drywall.

Once the drywall was hung, taped and sanded, we textured the ceiling and all walls that would be exposed and painted. Areas to be papered were sanded smooth. We used two different textures in the library; both were applied with a damp sponge, using a slightly thinned mixture of joint compound. To texture the ceiling we dipped the sponge in the mixture, then applied it to the ceiling in a sweeping motion. This technique left a series of thin raised lines that look much like heavy, random brush marks.

When we applied the texture to the walls, we again used a sponge, but this time the thinned compound was daubed on the wall. To add variety we occasionally gave the sponge a twist, then pulled it away.

Adding a fireplace—Our home had no fireplace prior to this addition. Although a fireplace is a feature much sought after in the Rockies, there is also a great deal of concern about air pollution here. With the possibility of restrictions on wood-burning fireplaces and stoves on the horizon, we installed a gas-log fireplace.

For the fireplace box, we chose the Majestic MBUC 36 brick-lined wood-burning unit (The Majestic Co., 1000 East Market St., Huntington,

Ind. 46750; 219-356-8000). To accommodate burning wood we installed a triple-wall flue system. We had a sheet-metal cover made to fit the top of the flue chase and then used a standard storm collar and flue cap on the flue end.

We purchased the gas-log unit for $240 from a local dealer (Real-Fyre Gas Log Set; manufactured by Robert H. Peterson Co., 530 Baldwin Park Blvd., City of Industry, Calif. 91746; 818-369-5085). The unit includes ceramic logs, a fire grate, a gas burner, a valve and pilot unit, and a length of brass fuel line to be attached to lead pipe fittings. Installation of these units is not cheap—$300 in our case. At this point the cost of this fireplace, without the framing or finish materials included, was $1,300. It was a costly part of the project, but we enjoy the fireplace, and it has certainly added to the value of our home.

Cherry casework—I chose cherry for all the casework and trim in this room (photo right). Cherry is my favorite domestic wood because of its color and figure, but it is not easy to work with. Cherry is of medium hardness, the grain can be very difficult to read and it tears easily if planed in the wrong direction. This tendency to tear is aggravated by humidity changes, even if the cherry is properly dried. Cherry also is a relatively expensive domestic hardwood. If I had built the casework out of oak, my lumber cost would have been about 60% lower.

I built and installed a cherry fireplace surround, with tile recessed 2 in. from its face. To make the mantel I stacked shaped pieces of cherry to create the effect of a crown molding (drawing right) and returned each piece to the wall. The top of the mantel was attached with glue and concealed screws to the top of this built-up molding. I made all parts with a table saw and a router. Many interesting and diverse moldings can be created by building up different profiles made with just these two tools.

I constructed the bookcases with 4-in. wide fluted stiles. Where necessary, I made double case sides so that the stiles overlapped the case sides by only ⅛ in.; no books are hidden behind stiles. The adjustable shelves are supported by metal shelf standards mortised into the case sides. The crown molding around the top of the bookcases matches that on the mantelpiece.

Prior to installation I finished the casework with a cinnamon stain and a sprayed catalytic finish called Fullerplast (Fuller O'Brien Paints, 450 E. Grand Ave., South San Francisco, Calif. 94080; 415-761-2300). It depends on a chemical reaction for curing and is more water-resistant than is a conventional lacquer finish. It's a durable finish, but drying and recoating times are longer, and it's fairly expensive. I could have cut my finishing costs by using a conventional lacquer. In the future I'll restrict my use of the material to applications where there will be water or moisture, such as on wooden bar tops or bath cabinets. After doors, casework and trim were in place, carpet was installed, completing the room. □

Neil Hartzler is a cabinetmaker in Colorado Springs, Colo. Photos by Michael Fulks except where noted.

Cozier than a car park. **The author's site-made, built-up cherry casework completes the garage conversion. A new gas-log fireplace adds both heat and ambience to the library/study without the possible pollution of a wood fire.**

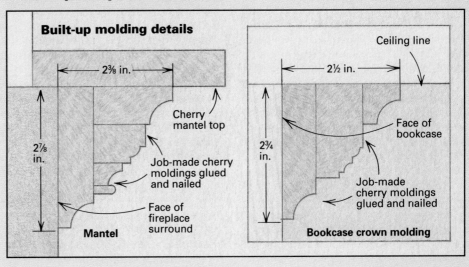

Built-up molding details

2⅜ in.

2⅞ in.

Cherry mantel top

Job-made cherry moldings glued and nailed

Face of fireplace surround

Mantel

Ceiling line

2½ in.

2¾ in.

Face of bookcase

Job-made cherry moldings glued and nailed

Bookcase crown molding

Make Room for Trudy

Adding an in-law apartment above the garage

by Don Price

During one of our planning sessions I made the mistake of asking Trudy Estes if she was up for the strain of construction. She replied that in her 88 years she had managed a successful business, buried two husbands and educated her son. Would any of these, she wanted to know, have prepared her adequately? I conceded that she'd probably do just fine.

This was the first time I'd signed a building contract with three clients' names on the document—the house's owners, Charles and Marilyn Shipman, and Charles' mother, Trudy. The project entailed the construction of a separate, one-bedroom apartment for Trudy over the existing 24-ft. by 26-ft. garage (drawing facing page). Building the apartment over the garage ensured that assistance would be close by in case it was needed, yet still maintained privacy by keeping the house and apartment separate. In addition, by not changing the footprint of the building we could avoid dealing with setback issues, thereby minimizing the probability of permit snags. The lake on which the house is situated is not overbuilt, and the local government wants to keep it that way.

Obtaining a permit wasn't all smooth sailing, however. The county was unable to locate any records for the existing septic field so a new field was called for, the dimensions of which seemed adequate for a small hotel. Once we had the new field dug, we were able to get our permit.

Compromise solutions—At the outset of our planning discussions, Charles mentioned his admiration for cedar kit homes. Trudy, on the other hand, spoke fondly of her previous home in California, with its white walls and ceilings. I mentioned that an all-white interior in the Midwest can be too intense in the winter; it's usually best to keep the outdoors out.

An open plan with a vaulted ceiling appealed to all parties, however, as did the use of structural foam-core panels. The possibility of a timber frame was mentioned, but we decided instead to wrap doubled fir rafters in cedar, simulating the timber-frame look but at a fraction of the cost. The foam-core panels would go above. The panels were faced on the interior with T&G cedar and on the exterior with ½-in. sheathing-grade plywood. The cedar ceiling and white wall combination (photo above) appealed to everyone, and the cedar later suggested a choice for the interior trim.

Storage dilemmas resolved—The need for lots of storage space became apparent during the planning stage. Charles indicated that with the usable space in the garage diminished by the stairs and the mechanicals serving the apartment above, some tool storage would be in order. Trudy mentioned the need for plenty of storage as well, because she would be moving from a seven-room house into a one-bedroom apartment.

We could address Charles' need for tool storage by extending the framing for the bay window at the east end of the house to the ground, creating a walk-in tool shed for his displaced yard tools. Glass shelving in the bay would give Trudy a place to display her prized collection of glass goblets and vases. An ample pantrylike storage unit in the kitchen would provide space for most housewares (drawing facing page). More storage was needed, so I suggested a 4-ft. high built-in cabinet running under the windows along the south wall through the living room and on into the bedroom. Trudy and the Shipmans approved, but with Trudy stipulating that we move the bedroom closet onto the living-room side to provide more space in the bedroom.

With the addition of two decks, one to the north, one facing southwest, our rough plans were complete. It was time to commit them to paper and hone them a bit. We approached Marc Rueter, an Ann Arbor architect with whom I had worked before, and asked him to prepare working drawings.

Off with the roof—We began the construction phase by stripping the existing garage roof to the framing. We then built a long, straight run of stairs along the garage's north wall, with a landing situated at the halfway point. In addition to being a place to rest, the landing afforded an opportunity for a window with a lake view.

With the stair in place, we could easily reach the intersection of the framing for the addition and the gable end of the existing house. We cut the existing roof sheathing back, moved the gable-end rafter in 3½ in. and doubled it. This made room for a new second-floor wall, which we framed on the now-exposed top plate.

Faux frame—After putting down a ¾-in. plywood subfloor and framing the walls, we turned

A bright kitchen. The cedar ceiling and beams visually warm the apartment, while the crispness of the white walls and cabinets keeps a small space from feeling cramped.

our attention to the roof structure. We set doubled 2x10 rafters on 4-ft. 6-in. centers over built-up posts. The posts also serve as trimmers for the ribbon windows running along the north and south walls. The rafters terminate at a structural ridge beam consisting of a pair of glulams that we spiked together on the ground, then hoisted into place with a crane. After Charles and Marilyn had prefinished the cedar side of the foam-core roof panels on the ground, we used the crane to set them—some were as long as 18 ft.

Details inside and out—We routed the panels along the eaves and rakes for 2x4 nailers, to which we attached redwood fascia boards. We matched the existing 1x10 redwood clapboard on the garage, mitered the corners and capped them with aluminum covers, in keeping with the original finish detail. Old and new alike were painted an earthy green to contrast with the brick-veneer finish on the house.

We wanted a clean, uncluttered look for the kitchen and bath at a reasonable cost. We used stock, laminate-faced cabinets with wood

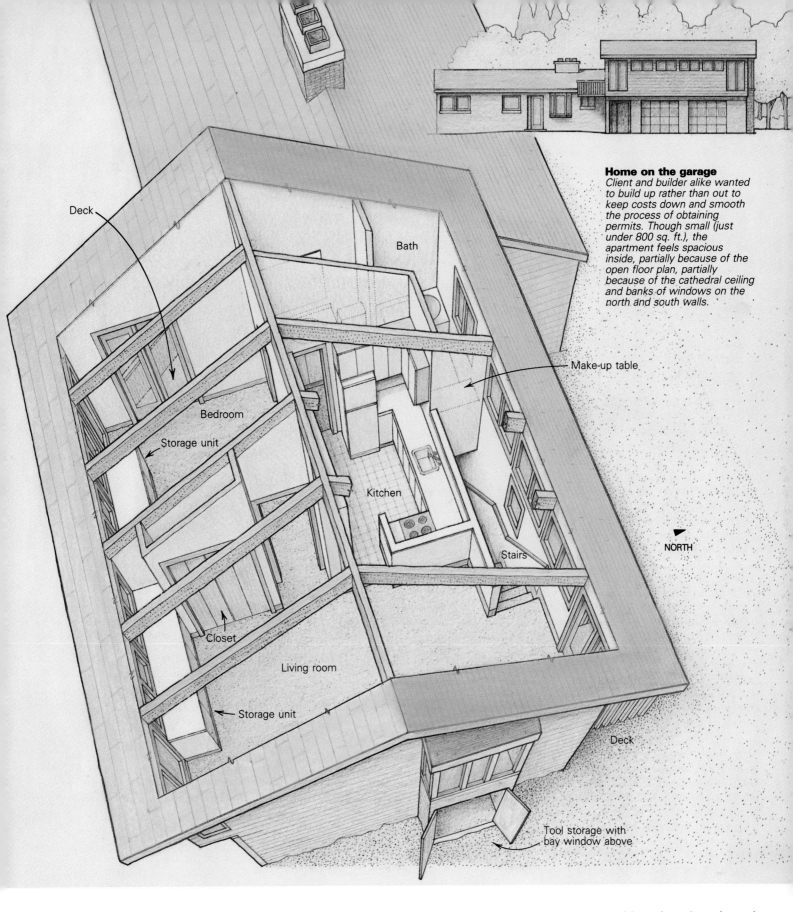

Deck

Bath

Home on the garage
Client and builder alike wanted to build up rather than out to keep costs down and smooth the process of obtaining permits. Though small (just under 800 sq. ft.), the apartment feels spacious inside, partially because of the open floor plan, partially because of the cathedral ceiling and banks of windows on the north and south walls.

Make-up table

Bedroom

Storage unit

Kitchen

NORTH

Stairs

Closet

Living room

Storage unit

Deck

Tool storage with bay window above

trim and matching white laminate countertops. The cabinets are relatively inexpensive and easy to clean. The white sink and faucets are simple yet elegant. We used a built-in stove and an apartment-sized refrigerator because they conserve space and are sufficient for Trudy's needs. These elements, combined with the skylight and the row of windows facing the lake, make the kitchen a nice space in which to work.

Safe but not sterile—Our aim was to create a safe bathroom without stainless-steel finishes and an institutional feel. To that end, we used a Kohler tub (Kohler Co., 444 Highland Dr., Kohler, Wisc. 53044; 414-457-4441) with built-in yet unobtrusive handles, and installed a white Corian shower kit (E. I. Du Pont de Nemours & Co., Inc., Corian Bldg. Products, Room G52064, Wilmington, Del. 19898; 800-426-7426) above the tub. We also built in a cedar make-up table and put in cedar grab bars next to the Kohler special-needs toilet. We chose their Highline model, even though Trudy is fully mobile, because of its added height. The cedar details lend warmth without sacrificing safety and reinforce the motif established by the "beams" and ceiling. □

Don Price is a builder in Ann Arbor, Michigan. Photo by Fred Golden.

A Family at Home
Making room for an elderly parent

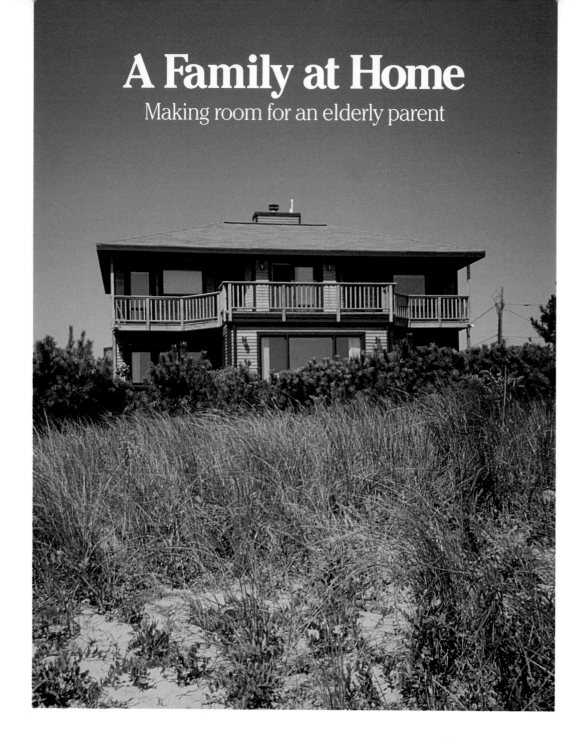

by Stuart Baker

We were hired by Karen and Frank Carroll in August 1988 to remodel the bath and rework the hallway of their beachfront summer cottage. The 50's-era cottage, facing Cape Cod's Nantucket Sound, was quite modest so we expected to complete the job and move on. Karen was excited as she watched our progress on the bathroom, though, and mentioned that she planned eventually to remodel the entire house and add a second floor. She finally showed me a blueprint of the project planned the year before and asked for an estimate; after adapting the plans to the family's current needs, we got a contract to remodel the entire house. Though the existing building had its share of failings—it ignored the prevailing breezes, the kitchen didn't have any drawers and the electrical system frequently blew fuses—the real purpose of the remodeling was to provide space for Karen's elderly and increasingly frail mother while expanding the whole house.

Until this project, I had never been quite so immersed in looking at the use of rooms, their proximity to each other and at the internal traffic flow in relation to the lifestyle of the family. I have since become very conscious of barrier-free planning, particularly as it regards the elderly and the provision of multiple-use, flexible rooms.

Suite silence—Because Karen's mom was legally blind and had limited mobility, full accessibility and privacy (both for her and for the rest of the family) were high on our list of requirements. The resulting floor plan (drawing, p. 40) is very open, and allows easy access to all the common areas of the main floor. The key ingredient, however, is a separate suite that can be opened to the rest of the house or closed off as needed. The suite has its own outside entrance, with a gently sloped, 42-in. wide ramp leading up to it.

Ten feet of folding doors separate a small sitting room and kitchen from the rest of the house (photos facing page). Mrs. Rohdin can close these doors for privacy; otherwise her sitting room is an extension of the family room. Even when the doors are closed, however, the sitting room feels far from confined because a sliding-glass patio door opens it to the deck, as well as to the ocean beyond.

The sitting room is separated from the bedroom by an airlock of sorts; a standard door

From *Fine Homebuilding* (February 1991) 65:76-79

on the bedroom side and French doors on the sitting-room side help to isolate the bedroom from any noise in the rest of the house. To further isolate the bedroom acoustically, soundboard and high-density fiberglass insulation have been placed in the walls, and there's a layer of insulating sheathing under the drywall ceiling for the same reason. This may seem like overkill, but it really isn't; though her sight isn't what it used to be, Mrs. Rohdin's hearing is very good, and Karen didn't want her mom's privacy to be invaded by sounds filtering in from the rest of the house.

An accessible bathroom—The bathroom features a "drive-in shower" that allows a wheelchair to be rolled in without obstruction (bottom photo, p. 41). The shower is approximately 5 ft. by 3 ft. and has grab bars placed in strategic locations; a hand-held sprayer makes it easy to control water direction, whether standing or seated. There is no real lip on the tile floor at the shower door. Rather, the subfloor was built up so that the shower floor pitches to the drain. A simple rubber sweep was put on the bottom of the shower door, and has proven so far to seal very well. The tile floor has a non-skid finish.

Other features in the bathroom include a toilet that's higher than normal, easily turned handles on the faucets and enough floor space to accommodate a wheelchair or walker.

Details for livability—It's one thing—an essential one at that—to design the spaces to accommodate someone who has limited mobility. But the design shouldn't stop until all the little details have been thought about and resolved. For example, all of the door openings in the downstairs portion of the house (including the door to the shower and the pocket door into the bathroom) are 3 ft. wide and situated to allow for easy wheelchair access (or stretcher access in an emergency).

Another detail that makes everyone feel better is the call system. At various locations in Mrs. Rohdin's suite, we installed pull chains linked to a buzzer that would sound throughout the rest of the house. There's one above the bed's headboard (top photo, p. 41), one near the toilet, one near the shower, and one in the sitting room. Mrs. Rohdin can buzz if she needs help; doorbell chimes linked to the system are located both upstairs and downstairs to make sure her call can be heard. There's also a separate telephone line into the suite so calls intended for that location needn't involve the rest of the family.

An open floor plan for everyone—The Carrolls are active, social people, and the openness of the floor plan outside Mrs. Rohdin's suite reflects that. The kitchen (photo next page) is separated from the dining area by a breakfast bar, and the dining area is totally open to the family room. The family decided on modest-size bedrooms upstairs to allow space for a second family room; this would provide a private place for the children and their

The extra suite can be opened to the rest of the house (photo above), or closed off (photo below), depending on the needs for privacy. It includes a separate entrance and kitchen, separate telephone line, and is insulated to prevent noise from filtering in.

friends. All rooms in the house have some view of the ocean, and in the large open areas one can look through to an ocean panorama and feel that the outdoors is very close.

Winnowing windows—Frank Carroll is extremely affable, and agreed readily to his wife's dream of a house for the whole family. I figured he was a nice, mild guy. Then one day he leveled a stare at me, aimed a finger at my head and said, "I have one requirement; no Andersen windows!" As I later found out, he once had problems with rusted hardware in an old set of Andersen casements. But his demand sent me back to window school because we have used Andersens more than any other window and have found the quality to be very good. These days they offer stainless-steel hardware, too. But I've learned that when a client says "no" like Frank said it, it's time to look for alternatives. It was clear that the choice of windows and doors was extremely important to Karen as well, because she went with me to several different suppliers to examine Pella, Hurd and Malta windows.

We ended up with an eclectic combination of sliders, double-hungs, casements, awnings and fixed windows, all chosen either to maximize the view, respond to specific energy needs or simply to fit into the different rooms.

Karen wanted the house to keep a traditional look with double-hungs. But on the south side we chose tall casements to give a generous vertical view of the ocean. Between upper and lower kitchen cabinets, we used awning windows. The double-hungs had to be tilt-

sash for ease of cleaning, and we eventually decided upon Hurd Heat Mirror units (Hurd Millwork Co, 575 S. Whalen Ave., P. O. Box 319, Medford, Wis. 54451; 715-748-2011.

The Heat Mirror windows deflect much of the summer sun from the interior of the house. At the same time, the windows have an R-4 rating to slow the escape of conditioned air.

We chose Pella (The Rolscreen Co., 102 Main St., Pella, Iowa 50219; 515-628-1000) for the casements because they pivot to allow for easy-reach cleaning, and they operate smoothly. Pella sliding doors were chosen because they have a spring-mounted screen door that returns automatically to the closed position. Karen said that this was a must with her active children.

When all the windows were installed, Karen was bothered by the width of the double-hung window sash in the main family room, where the view to the ocean is especially dramatic.

She felt the sash joint obstructed the view too much. Our Hurd supplier eventually worked out a deal where Marvin Windows (P. O. Box 100, Warroad, Minn. 56763; 800-346-5128) made up fixed-glass replacement sashes to slip into the Hurd frames, thereby keeping the view free of horizontal obstructions.

Heating and cooling—The house would be lived in especially during the summers, so the house needed more cooling than heating capacity. A split system of one small gas hot-air furnace downstairs and one upstairs covered the heating needs, while a pair of air-conditioning units handled the cooling. The furnaces are designed for such efficient heat extraction that combustion gases can be exhausted through a PVC pipe—there is no need for masonry. The system is quiet and very responsive.

Out with the new—This project was memorable for its thoughtful approach to bringing an extended family together. But much as we'll remember working closely with the clients, we'll remember more how the construction side of the project sorted out. I think it's safe to say that most remodeling contractors have never demolished a client's house after remodeling their bathroom. That is, however, what happened here.

The kitchen for the rest of the family features an open plan, and windows of various sizes to add visual interest and plenty of sunlight.

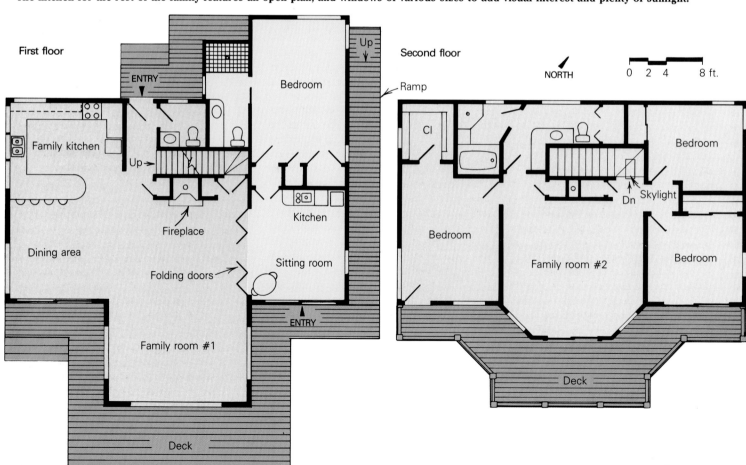

Two months after we completed the remodeling of the Carrolls' bathroom, we started work on the rest of the house. The original house was like a large bungalow with a single-plane pitched roof (photo, p. 38). Our construction strategy called for girdling the house with a level cut line, cutting off the roof, then setting in new top plates and building up from there. We also planned to knock down the brick chimney, install an insert fireplace with metal flue on the first floor and gain closets on both floors where the chimney had been.

As demolition progressed it became apparent that the changes of windows and doors would be so extensive in the old blocked and braced walls that life would be much simpler if we just knocked the walls down and started with fresh 2x6s all around. The local building inspector agreed that new 2x6 walls would make a better and safer house, so he went along with us. Comically, we almost did save the bathroom we had remodeled just two months earlier, until working around it finally drove us nuts and we leveled it, too.

Once the house was down, the reconstruction was fairly straightforward. The walls have 2x6 studs sheathed with ½-in. CDX plywood, with Tyvek to seal the house from drafts. In deference to the weather and salt spray, we used stainless-steel siding nails and red cedar A-and-better clapboard. As is common here, we ran the clapboard 4 in. to the weather. To keep the heat in, there's R-19 insulation under the first floor, paired with R-38 attic insulation and R-30 in the cathedral ceiling.

The house faces the ocean, so it's subject to driving Cape Cod storms. We roofed with asphalt shingles and gave them a scant 4½-in. exposure. We also placed "Ice and Water" barrier at the bottom of the roof to guard against ice damage and driven rain (Bird Roofing Products, Inc., 1077 Pleasant St., Norwood, Mass. 02062; 800-247-3462).

One section of the house—the flat roof deck over the family room—lies over conditioned space, so we used our tried and true Sarnafil membrane, which we've used several times before (Sarnafil Inc., 100 Dan Rd., Canton, Mass. 02021; 800-451-2504). Our roofing contractor, Clayton Merrick, has always guaranteed this product, a reinforced thermoplastic membrane, under almost any conditions. We placed a pressure-treated duckboard deck over the roof and cemented strips of the Sarnafil to the bottoms of the deck sleepers for protection. The Sarnafil is cemented and "heat welded" over AC plywood. Heavy-duty coated metal drip edge and wall flashing are used with the product. Sarnafil doesn't move and flex like rubber, so it's better rated to hold its seal.

The deck on the original house had been built smack against the house and had little in the way of flashing. That wasn't what we wanted, so we installed a pressure-treated band joist all around and spaced it away from the house with pressure-treated 5/4x6 blocks.

Essential ingredients—Part of what makes a project like this successful is the commit-

Helpful details. Pull chains connected to a buzzer system are located at strategic locations around the house (top photo). A quick pull will bring help from the rest of the family. The bathroom (photo above) features a very accessible shower area with room enough to accommodate a wheelchair. The shower pan was sloped to a drain, so there's no lip between shower and the rest of the bathroom floor to interfere with wheelchair movement.

ment of clients who care about the details. From the outset Karen was very involved in the project, paying close attention to detail and having the capacity to envision the finished product, as well as having a good sense of what would work for the family. I found out just how detail-conscious Karen was after she made several 3 a. m. phone calls to our office answering machine so she would be sure to pass on ideas as they came to her. Her sincerity about making the house as functional as possible for the whole family was marvelous.

As I said at the outset, this project taught us to pay more attention to the opportunities in barrier-free design. We now encourage customers to look into the future, to the time when they might have elderly parents living with them. As more and more families find different generations living together under one roof, good planning for meeting the needs of different ages doesn't have to be expensive, and it's wonderfully practical. □

Stuart Baker is a custom-building and remodeling contractor in Falmouth, Massachusetts. Photos by Mark Feirer.

Rejoining the family

Psychologically and economically, the family has been a great strength of our nation. But the mobility of our modern society has placed undue stress on the extended family, with the result that aunts, uncles and grandparents aren't readily available to babysit or be of emotional support, or to be supported. Professional home care for our aging population seems too costly for all but the wealthy. That's why I think a well-designed, functional home that can accommodate all ages is a necessity. It not only makes life fun, but can reduce or eliminate the need for day care for children or senior citizens and may avoid many premature nursing-home placements.

Because of my strong feelings, we first attempted to have my mother, legally blind and with limited mobility, come to live with us about ten years ago. It did not work. Noise, lack of privacy and the needs of children versus the traditions of age made it impossible. But five years later we succeeded with the same people. What was different? We added on to our home to give each family member an individual space, and provided multi-functional common areas. We also added excellent soundproofing. Living together gave us more space, better relationships, a stronger economic base and more free time.

To accomplish this we needed imagination, cooperation, goodwill and time. A project of this magnitude could not be rushed. For us it took three years of planning and one year of construction. The original home had been designed and built in the early 1950s. It featured panoramic views of Nantucket Sound and had provided years of happiness. But among other failings, the layout allowed no room for my mother. To accommodate her changing medical needs and the necessity for a wheelchair, we paid close attention to the traffic flow in the house to ensure ready access by wheelchair, and we avoided difficult angles on the approach to her bedroom just in case a stretcher would ever be necessary. The wall between her kitchenette/sitting room and our family room was opened up, making her feel more a part of our lives, but bi-fold doors were included to allow privacy when she needs it.

The bathroom has non-skid tile, a high toilet, handicap levers on the sink and an extra-large shower with no lip to allow easy access for a wheelchair or walker. There are pull-chain buzzers near her bed, shower and toilet areas, similar to those in a hospital.

But the most important feature for her is that she does not have one single step or steep incline from the driveway to the deck to any part of her suite or our entire first floor. The feature gives her complete access to all social activities in our family room, dining room, kitchen or on the expansive deck facing the ocean. It also gives her independence and a feeling of belonging, while we can all retain our privacy. *—Karen Carroll*

A Greek Revival Addition

Joining stock and custom-milled trim to make a formal entryway

by Joseph Beals

A modern and unremarkable Cape Cod cottage needed a new gable-end door and entry. The existing frame was falling apart, the laminated oak sill had delaminated, the brick stoop was crumbling and the apron under the door was rotting, along with the sidewall shingles that the stoop abutted. Because the entry had failed in so many ways, the owner took advantage of circumstance and asked us for a new entry. We chose to use two doors with an airlock to make an enclosed entrance.

Greek Revival architecture was the style of choice; not only is it common in this part of New England, but it also lends itself to full expression even on a small scale. The entryway had to be big enough to include the many formal elements that make up the Greek Revival style, but not so big as to overpower the gable end of the house.

In the transition from the marble buildings of ancient Greece to the woodwork of the early United States, Greek Revival architecture has retained the elements of form, yet has allowed a freedom of ornamentation ranging from the austere to the exquisitely ornate. A gable wall rather than a sidewall most often serves as the front of a Greek Revival house and is the focus of the design. An entablature surmounts the sidewalls under the roof and continues horizontally across the gable, forming a pediment above. Where it appears on the sidewalls, the entablature is typically surmounted by a crown molding, which is mitered to raking crown moldings that meet at the peak of the gable. The face of the pediment is recessed behind the rake trim and entabulature, creating a strong play of light and shadow. In Greek architecture, the gable-end entablature is supported by columns around the entire building, but in many Greek Revival buildings, the columns are replaced by pilasters and detailed corner trim, which echo the effect of columns without the function.

Designing the entryway—The width of the entryway was critical because of tight space. The owner requested a 36-in. outside door flanked by sidelights that he had salvaged some years before. I drew a front elevation incorporating a pair of fluted pilasters outboard of the sidelights on the front corners, and another pair between the sidelights and the door. I sketched the details of the entablature above the door so that I could derive the height of the sidewall

and figure the length of rafters and location of cuts. The entryway depth was less critical, but it was important not to make it protrude too far. An interior depth of 4 ft. would allow a comfortable margin for opening the outside door, and would also mean that a single sheet of drywall could finish each interior sidewall. An invaluable resource for me during design was *New England Doorways* by Samuel Chamberlain (Hastings House Publishers, N. Y., 1939; out of print).

The entryway would have a 12:12 pitch roof—steeper than a traditional Greek Revival roof, but identical to the pitch of the main roof. This ensured that the entryway would look like part of

the house rather than like a contrived addition. The steep gable makes an unusually tall pediment, so to soften the height we added a half-round window above the cornice. This solution was more luck than genius: the window was the top of an old door that had arrived in a pile of junk from another job, and it begged to be saved. A few days in the shop was enough time for me to saw it free, then fabricate the curved casings and add a sill.

Foundation and steps—After the existing brick stair and landing were broken up and removed, we found that rot in the wall was more

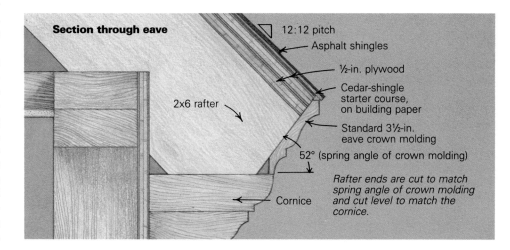

Section through eave

- 12:12 pitch
- Asphalt shingles
- ½-in. plywood
- Cedar-shingle starter course, on building paper
- Standard 3½-in. eave crown molding
- 52° (spring angle of crown molding)
- 2x6 rafter
- Cornice

Rafter ends are cut to match spring angle of crown molding and cut level to match the cornice.

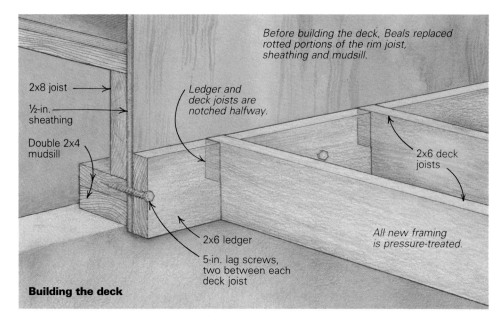

Before building the deck, Beals replaced rotted portions of the rim joist, sheathing and mudsill.

- 2x8 joist
- ½-in. sheathing
- Double 2x4 mudsill
- 2x6 ledger
- 5-in. lag screws, two between each deck joist
- *Ledger and deck joists are notched halfway.*
- 2x6 deck joists
- *All new framing is pressure-treated.*

Building the deck

extensive than we had expected. Not only were the sill and rim joist compromised by water damage, they were also full of carpenter ants. Because a gable-end wall doesn't carry much load, replacing the rotten portions of the rim joist and sill and patching in new sheathing took only half a day.

The existing entry would remain in use during construction, so I built a foundation deck at once. To achieve the width we needed for door, pilasters and sidelights, the deck would be too wide to center on the existing door, as its left corner would lie over the water supply line. I moved the deck 2 ft. to the right to clear the water line, and later framed for a new door. Moving the door over solved a minor problem inside the house, where the entrance had been too close to the corner of the room to allow for usable space against the wall.

I lag-screwed a ledger to the new sill and fit notched pressure-treated 2x6 joists into notches cut in the ledger (bottom drawing, facing page). The 4x4 outer posts of the deck bear on cast-in-place concrete piers. The surface of the deck is 6½ in. below the floor of the house. The two lower steps have 12-in. treads, while the top step is 30 in. deep and serves as a landing (photo right). It also makes a graceful transition from the narrower steps to the door. In a traditional entry, the landing would be stone or brick and have an iron boot scraper fitted at one end, but those are costly details this project had to do without.

The cornice and pediment—The entry framing is conventional, but the roof required careful planning to accommodate the entablature. I cut the rafter tails to match the spring angle of the crown molding (the spring angle describes the cant of the molding in relation to the horizontal) and cut the bottoms level to provide support for the cornice (top drawing, facing page). To provide a solid backing for the crown molding at both rake and eave, I sheathed the roof deck with two layers of ½-in. plywood. At the gable face, I ripped the cantilevered ends of the plywood slightly to match the spring angle of the raking moldings.

The trim for the entryway was built up from standard lumberyard moldings and from moldings that I milled from 1x or 2x pine stock. The first trim I installed, after sheathing the entryway walls with plywood, was the top piece of the cornice, which I milled from 2x6 stock. I nailed it to the rafter bottoms on the sidewalls and toenailed it into the studs along the gable end. Along the gable end, where the top of the cornice is exposed to the weather, I planed its top to a 3° slope to allow for water runoff (drawing next page).

The pediment had to be finished next. In a small structure like this, the recessed face of the pediment is traditionally a monolithic surface—shingles or clapboards would destroy the purity of appearance. I built this one by edge-gluing lengths of clear pine with resorcinol adhesive, and sealed the joints with orange shellac to prevent glue lines from show-

ing through the paint. Then I primed both sides with oil-base paint.

To attach the pediment, I worked lead flashing into the corner between the top of the cornice and the gable sheathing, then fastened the pediment to the studs with a few finish nails. I built up the rake trim—all but the crown molding—fitting it tight to the cornice at its lower ends, and mitered each piece at the peak (top drawing facing page).

The next step was to fit the eave and raking crown moldings that are such a strong feature of Greek Revival architecture.

Matching raking to eave molding—On the Greek Revival houses of New England, eave crown moldings mitered to raking crown moldings are such a common sight that I was not prepared for the complexity of the joint between the two. A raking molding, which

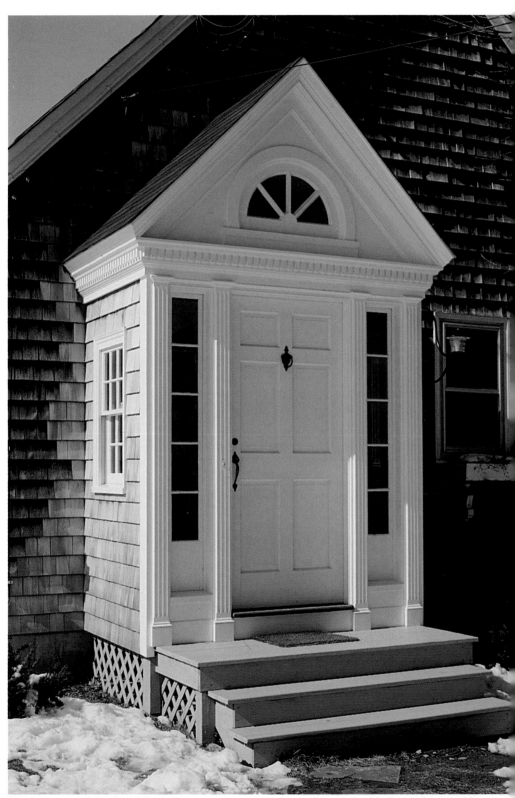

The influence of the Greek Revival style is apparent in the pedimented gable facing front and in the strong lines of the entablature of this entryway addition. The most challenging task to building a pedimented gable is mitering eave and raking crown moldings. Here, the author milled and hand-planed his own raking molding to a modified profile of the eave molding.

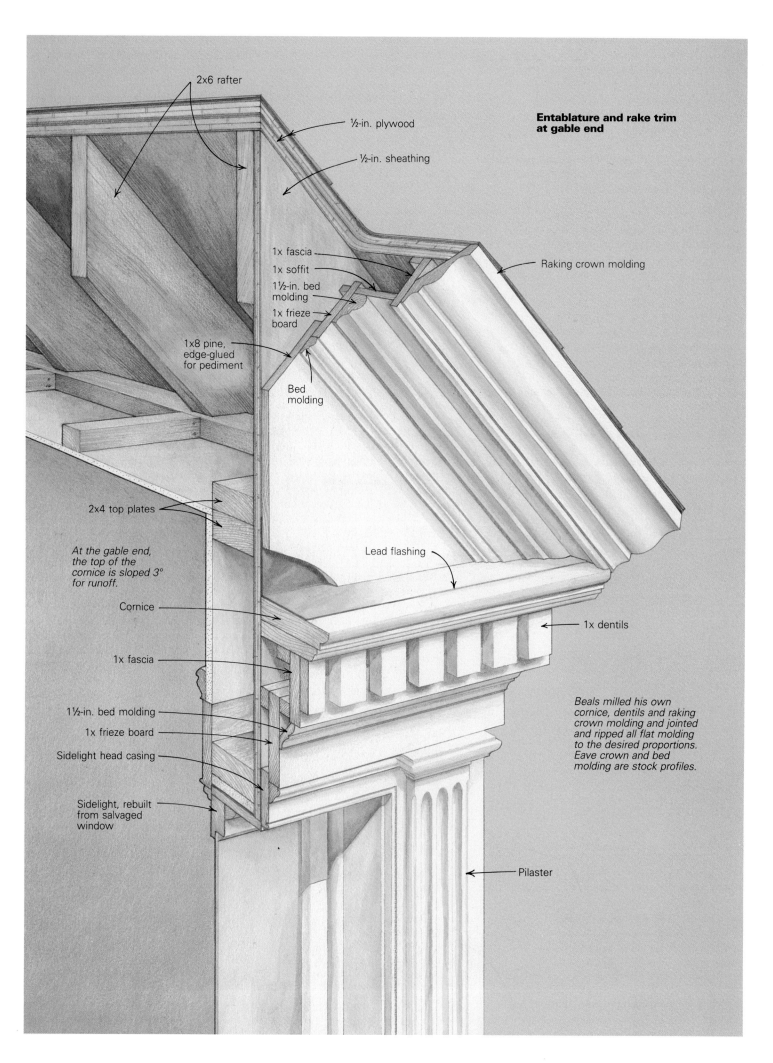

Entablature and rake trim at gable end

2x6 rafter

½-in. plywood

½-in. sheathing

Raking crown molding

1x fascia

1x soffit

1½-in. bed molding

1x frieze board

1x8 pine, edge-glued for pediment

Bed molding

2x4 top plates

At the gable end, the top of the cornice is sloped 3° for runoff.

Lead flashing

Cornice

1x fascia

1x dentils

1½-in. bed molding

1x frieze board

Sidelight head casing

Sidelight, rebuilt from salvaged window

Beals milled his own cornice, dentils and raking crown molding and jointed and ripped all flat molding to the desired proportions. Eave crown and bed molding are stock profiles.

Pilaster

slopes downward and outward, can only meet an eave molding if its profile is milled wider than and in a precise distortion of the profile of the eave molding. The profile of the raking molding is a function of roof pitch, reaching a maximum elongation when the roof pitch is 1:1. A hundred years ago, it was doubtless common practice for lumberyards to stock suitable complements of eave and raking moldings. But those days are long past. Now we improvise.

I used standard lumberyard crown molding on the eave walls and mitered their outboard ends in the usual way, as if they were to intersect horizontally with another eave molding (drawing below). Then I held a 1x6 in place on the rake fascia in contact with the mitered end of the eave molding, and traced the eave profile onto the 1x6. To achieve the approximate profile of the raking molding, I gave a 1x6 a number of passes with different knives on the molding head of my table saw. I used molding planes and sandpaper to true the profile.

I marked the bottom miters of each length of raking molding with both a square and a bevel gauge, then cut proud of the line with a handsaw and trimmed with a block plane until the joint came up tight. This seems straightforward, but was really a devilish exercise. Intuition is no help: the miters of the raking moldings look improperly cut until the moment when the piece slips into position and the puzzle comes together (see *FHB* #41, pp. 64-65 for more on raking molding). My reference for this art of the past, as well as for other joinery techniques, is *Modern Carpentry* by Fred Hodgson, published in 1917. It's out of print, but a similar reference is George Ellis's *Modern Practical Joinery*,

published in 1908 and reprinted by Linden Publishing Co. (3845 N. Blackstone, Fresno, Calif. 93726).

Completing the entablature—Before beginning work on the entablature, I closed the entryway to weather. I shingled the roof with asphalt shingles, beginning with a cedar-shingle starter course along each eave to keep a traditional appearance. (We did not consider the use of an aluminum drip edge, which is out of place in restoration or reproduction carpentry.) I replaced the wall shingles that I had stripped to accommodate the new entryway, except for a small space at the top of each sidewall where the entablature would butt against the house. I scribed and fitted those shingles after finishing the entablature. I nailed 5-in. corner boards to the sheathing, then built and installed sidewall windows and shingled the walls.

Making the components of the frieze was my next task. A number of visitors have looked in wonder at the dentil molding and remarked on the skill and patience required to fit each dentil in place. The technique they are imagining certainly would demand patience and a talent closer to madness than skill. They would be surprised to find that making the dentils took me 20 minutes.

To make the dentil moldings, I began with three lengths each of 1x3 and 1x4 stock (for the three lengths of the entablature). I have no respect for the edges you get on lumberyard stock, so it's my habit to joint such stock, rip it to width and joint the other side. I ripped the 1x3s to 2¼ in. and the 1x4s to 3 in., then glued the narrower stock (for the dentils) to the wider stock (the frieze board), aligning the top edges. Then I cut between

the dentils with a dado blade in a radial-arm saw, using a gauge block screwed to the fence to keep the spacing accurate.

I primed and topcoated all moldings in the shop, brought them to the site and nailed them in place. The frieze is blocked out to allow sidewall shingles to be tucked underneath, and it runs over the corner boards. A bed molding under the dentil molding returned the fascia to the frieze below, and the entablature was complete.

Salvaged sidelights—The owner had salvaged the sidelights long ago from a two-hundred-year-old house. Little about their overall appearance suggests their age, but some anonymous artisan had sawed his stock and planed the parts in the quiet of a colonial New England village. He chiseled the joints and secured them with wood pegs, and two centuries later his sash was returned to use with a few repairs, new glazing and new paint. It was a particular pleasure to give new life to the work of an earlier century.

The sidelights were 8 in. shorter than the stock door, which caused a problem. To line up the heads, I built the sidelight frames with a filler panel below the sill. The sidelight frames and the stock door jambs are finished with beaded casings, or architraves. An apron runs the width of the entryway between the corner boards, and is raised a fraction above the landing to prevent moisture from being trapped underneath.

I made the fluting for the pilasters with a molding knife on the table saw. Each pilaster is fitted with a plinth block and a capital. The plinth is no more than a block with a standard base cap mitered around the top. The capital ends under the frieze, as would the top of a column supporting the entablature of a portico. Strict attention to form would require that the capitals be an independent part of each pilaster, but a more graceful appearance was achieved by running the upper capital molding across the tops of the sidelights and door (photo, p. 43).

We used solid oak sills in the new entryway for both the outer door and the new inside door. Although they are more expensive, I prefer solid oak to laminated oak sills because laminated sills will eventually come apart.

Assessing the entryway—One question still concerned me, even when the entryway was finished: How will a formal Greek Revival entry look on a Cape Cod cottage? I had made detail drawings and perspectives a dozen times over, but nothing tells the truth better than a casual view from a distance. And coming down the long driveway in the last days of a New England summer, the entryway does just what the owner had in mind. It is neither obtrusive nor frivolous, but looks if it has belonged to New England for years. □

Joseph Beals is a designer and builder who lives in Marshfield, Massachusetts.

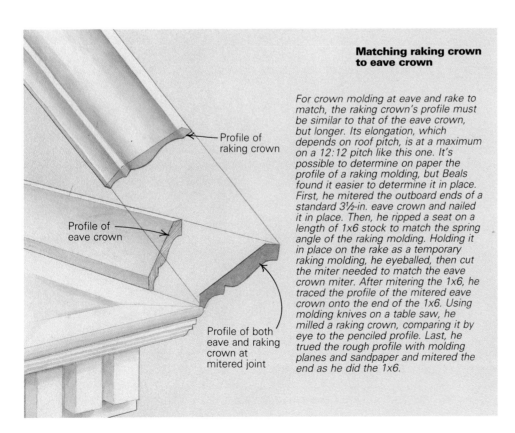

Matching raking crown to eave crown

Profile of raking crown

Profile of eave crown

Profile of both eave and raking crown at mitered joint

For crown molding at eave and rake to match, the raking crown's profile must be similar to that of the eave crown, but longer. Its elongation, which depends on roof pitch, is at a maximum on a 12:12 pitch like this one. It's possible to determine on paper the profile of a raking molding, but Beals found it easier to determine it in place. First, he mitered the outboard ends of a standard 3½-in. eave crown and nailed it in place. Then, he ripped a seat on a length of 1x6 stock to match the spring angle of the raking molding. Holding it in place on the rake as a temporary raking molding, he eyeballed, then cut the miter needed to match the eave crown miter. After mitering the 1x6, he traced the profile of the mitered eave crown onto the end of the 1x6. Using molding knives on a table saw, he milled a raking crown, comparing it by eye to the penciled profile. Last, he trued the rough profile with molding planes and sandpaper and mitered the end as he did the 1x6.

Attic Art Studio

Dropping the garage ceiling to create a studio/office

by Kevin Ireton

Several years ago, Marcia Hartman hired Bob Eggert to remove a large casement window in her family room and replace it with a bay window. Being the thrifty sort, Eggert carried the old casement down to Marcia's basement and told her to save it. She couldn't imagine ever needing the window, however, and wanted to set it out with the garbage cans so the trash collectors would haul it away.

But Eggert wasn't just Marcia's contractor, he was her next-door neighbor and her friend. If she set the window out with the trash, Eggert would see it when he left for work in the morning and give her a hard time. So Marcia decided to wait until the one week in the summer when Eggert went on vacation; then she could throw out the window. But year after year she always forgot.

When the time came to remodel the attic over the garage and turn it into a studio for Marcia, Eggert carried the old casement up

from the basement, installed it in the gable (photo above) and saved Marcia more than $400. Now she sits at her drawing table and looks out that window every day. If she cranes her neck, she can even see the end of the driveway where the trash cans sit.

Saving $15,000—A general contractor in Cleveland, Ohio, Eggert built the Hartmans' four-bedroom ranch house for the original owner in 1963. It's part of a community of 50 or so homes on wooded lots, which he developed and eventually moved into. Typical of the 1960s, the Hartman house features tiny bedrooms and a small, uninspired kitchen. The living room and family room are long, narrow and dark. All this, along with a two-car garage, is sheltered by a simple 5-in-12 gable roof.

A former art teacher, Marcia is a watercolor painter and an art consultant. As her business grew, she needed more room—a studio for her-

self and storage space for 500 or so paintings by artists she represents. So Marcia approached Eggert about building an addition.

Eggert suggested instead that she could perhaps save $15,000 over the cost of an addition by converting the unused attic space over the garage. Although the house is one story, it was built on a gently sloping lot, which resulted in the garage floor being 4½ ft. lower than the main floor (photo facing page). To simplify the original construction, though, the tops of the exterior walls were built level all the way around the house—they don't step down at the garage like the floor does. This meant that the ceiling in the garage was 12½ ft. high and could be dropped considerably to provide more headroom in the attic above.

Eggert drew up plans for a studio that included just over 400 sq. ft. of floor space. With a cathedral ceiling and four large skylights, there would be plenty of natural light. Built-in

From *Fine Homebuilding* (December 1990) 64:84-87

storage for paintings would extend the full 20-ft. length of the north wall. And a sink to service the needs of Marcia's watercolors would anchor the end of a counter built to provide headroom for the garage stairs below. The entrance to the room would be at the west end of the house between the living room and the kitchen, where an open stairway would rise seven steps up from the main floor. The plans delighted Marcia every bit as much as the notion of saving $15,000, so she approved them and Eggert called in his crew.

Dropping the ceiling—Emil Novatney, the lead carpenter on the project, began the demolition work by snapping a chalkline on the garage walls about 4 ft. below the existing ceiling. With circular saws set to the depth of the plaster and rock lath, Novatney and his helper then cut on the line all the way around the garage and removed the plaster on the walls and ceiling above the cut. Because of concern about roof loads spreading the exterior walls, the new joists had to be installed before the old ones could come out.

Even with the addition of a built-up beam along the south side of the garage, the joists had to span nearly 20 ft. That called for 2x12s, 12 in. o. c., and just to be safe, Novatney doubled every third joist. To support the joists, he notched the stud walls along both sides of the garage with a circular saw and let in a 1x6 ribbon (drawing above right). This is the typical way of supporting a floor in balloon framing.

The joists rest on the ribbon and were nailed to the studs wherever their 12-in o. c. spacing coincided with the 16-in. o. c. stud spacing. Novatney also nailed solid blocking between the joists along both sides of the garage. Muscling 26 2x12s (each more than 20-ft. long) into place, then having to nail blocking while folded into the narrow space between the new and the old joists, proved to be the toughest part of the job.

Further complicating the floor framing, two existing windows in the garage extended above the line of the new ceiling. Replacing them with smaller units would have been expensive, meant patching siding around them and destroyed the symmetry across the front of the house. Instead, Eggert decided to leave the windows alone and build what amounted to inverted window wells in the garage ceiling (drawing above).

Two feet inside the windows, Novatney installed a doubled-up 2x12 header between the joists on either side of the windows. He hung the header from joist supports, which he also used for the cripple joists that die into the header. The inside of this well was finished with drywall like the rest of the ceiling. Upstairs in the studio, these wells are visible as a pair of raised platforms in the floor of the painting storage area (photo next page). Fortunately paintings come in a variety of sizes, so these shortened spaces prove just as useful as any of the others.

With the new joists in place to tie the exterior walls together, the old joists were cut off flush with the wall of the adjacent laundry

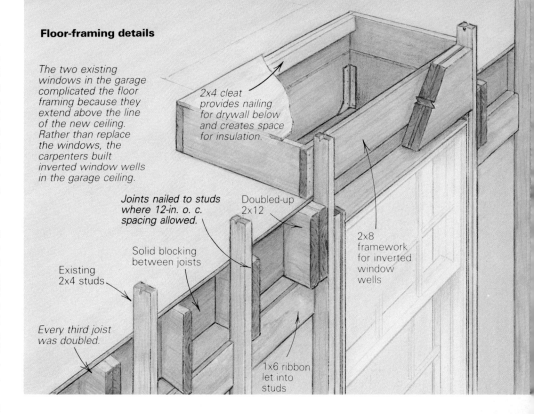

Floor-framing details

The two existing windows in the garage complicated the floor framing because they extend above the line of the new ceiling. Rather than replace the windows, the carpenters built inverted window wells in the garage ceiling.

2x4 cleat provides nailing for drywall below and creates space for insulation.

Joints nailed to studs where 12-in. o. c. spacing allowed.

Doubled-up 2x12

Solid blocking between joists

Existing 2x4 studs

2x8 framework for inverted window wells

Every third joist was doubled.

1x6 ribbon let into studs

Because the lot sloped gently, the floor of the garage is 4½ ft. lower than the house. This quirk allowed the builders to drop the ceiling in the garage and create the studio above it. The windows on the front of the house posed a problem whose solution is shown in the drawing above.

room—where some of them still serve as a ceiling—and removed. Next, cross bridging went in, and ¾-in. T&G plywood went down.

Hanging the landing—Three steps up from the main floor, the stairs to the studio take a 90° turn at a landing (large photo, p. 49). Rather than support the landing from below and encroach upon the storage space for lawnmowers and snowblowers in the garage, Novatney hung the landing from a doubled-up joist.

The landing itself was framed with 2x6s, and one side was supported by a short studwall between the house and garage. The outboard side of the landing was hung from the two corners by ½-in. threaded rod bolted to

the landing and to a doubled-up 2x12 joist with ½-in. plywood sandwiched in between (drawing, next page).

Eliminating the collar ties—The original roof structure included 2x6 collar ties on every fourth rafter, but these were removed as they would have required some awkward head ducking in the finished studio. Removing them resurrected the issue of roof loads spreading the exterior walls. Theoretically, the floor framing prevented this, but it's the sort of issue builders lose sleep over, and the sort that spawns better-safe-than-sorry measures.

In order for the walls to spread, the connection between the rafters and the ridge would

Across the 20-ft. length of the studio's north wall, vertical bins provide storage for paintings by artists whom the owner represents in her consulting business. Half-inch melamine panels with closet-pole nosing divide the bins. The floor covering is a no-wax vinyl.

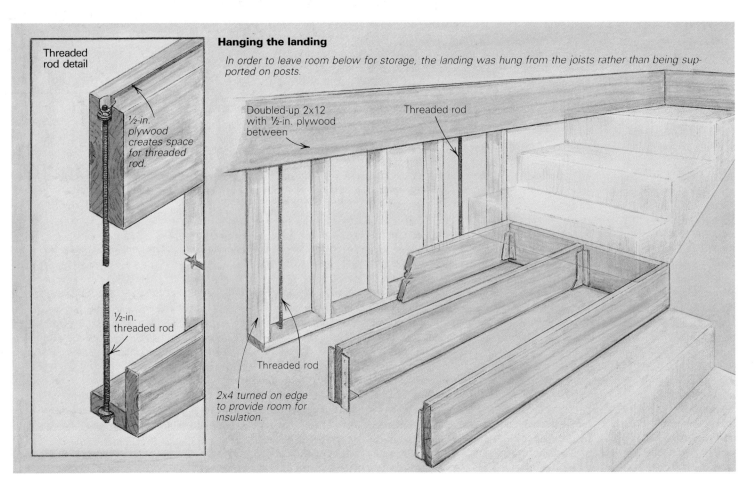

Threaded rod detail

½-in. plywood creates space for threaded rod.

½-in. threaded rod

Hanging the landing

In order to leave room below for storage, the landing was hung from the joists rather than being supported on posts.

Doubled-up 2x12 with ½-in. plywood between

Threaded rod

Threaded rod

2x4 turned on edge to provide room for insulation.

The owner needed an easy way to prop up artwork to show clients, so she asked for a "chalk rail," like the ones below a blackboard. The carpenters simply attached a lip on the front of a 1x2 and screwed it to the wall.

have to fail. So Novatney and crew cut 24-in. long pieces of heavy steel strapping, bent them over the ridge and nailed them into adjoining rafter pairs with joist-hanger nails. Directly under the ridge, they nailed short lengths of 2x4 across the rafters, like miniature collar ties.

A 6½-ft. kneewall runs the length of the studio on the south side, supporting the rafters at midspan and reducing the outward force on the exterior wall. And while the kneewall on the opposite side of the room is perforated with slots to store paintings, there is solid support under the doubled rafters on each side of the skylights.

Finishing the job—The remainder of the rough work was pretty conventional. Six inches of fiberglass was run in the ceiling between 2x8 rafters, leaving 1½ in. of ventilation space. The new sink went in almost directly above the old laundry room, so routing supply and drain lines wasn't too much trouble. A trunk line from the existing forced-air furnace feeds a pair of registers on the gable-end wall.

The drywall was painted white, as were the casings and baseboards. The skylight openings were finished without trim, keeping the lines clean. The only stained wood in the studio is the birch handrail and the oak nosings on the stair treads.

Because she sometimes paints on the floor, Marcia needed a serviceable flooring material. She picked a no-wax vinyl from Mannington (Mannington Resilient Flooring, P. O. Box 30, Salem, N. J. 08079; 609-935-3000), and while she says it scars and scuffs easily, the checkerboard pattern certainly jazzes up the studio.

The same vinyl was used in the floor of the painting storage area. Here, Novatney created vertical bins using removable ½-in. melamine dividers. At the back, the dividers fit between two pieces of 1x2 screwed to the wall. At the front, the dividers are held by wood nosing

Like the light at the end of the tunnel, the studio looms invitingly at the end of the living room and kitchen. Rather than being supported from below, the landing on the stairs is hung from the joists. With its traditional handrail and newels framing a contemporary infill of horizontals and verticals, the balustrade works as a transition from the old part of the house to the new.

made from routed closet poles. Each piece of nosing has a nail in the bottom end and a small dowel in the top. The nail, whose head is cut off, fits into a small hole drilled in the floor. The dowel slips into a screw eye.

A row of three built-in bookshelves behind Marcia's drafting table keeps oft-used volumes within reach. The shelves are plywood boxes, painted white and screwed to the wall studs. The outside corners around the sides and top are finished with drywall corner bead. A piece of beaded screen stock noses the bottom.

Marcia wanted what she calls a "chalk rail"— like the ledge beneath a blackboard—in several locations so she could display paintings for clients. Novatney simply added a lip to a piece of 1x2 and screwed it to the wall (top left

photo). The chalk rail works fine, but accumulating furniture has begun to block access to it.

The studio was finished in 1987 at a cost of about $26,000, or just under $65 per. sq. ft., which isn't too bad for the Cleveland suburbs. Marcia's only complaint was that the sun and shadows entering through the skylights made her drawing table difficult to use. Eggert solved the problem by installing Slimshades made by Pella (Rollscreen Co., 102 Main St., Pella, Iowa 50219; 515-628-1000), who also made the skylights. The shades are essentially venetian blinds that ride on tension wires mounted to the head and base of the skylights. □

Kevin Ireton is managing editor of Fine Homebuilding.

Bed Alcove

Convert wasted attic space into a bed that has drawers, bookshelves and a vanity

By Tony Simmonds

When the middle one of my three daughters grew too old for the loft bed I built for her, the youngest, Genevieve, was happy to inherit it. The loft is in a small bedroom on the second floor of our house in Vancouver, B. C., Canada. Like many second floors of old houses, this one is really a half story, with sloped ceilings where the rafters cut across the intersection of wall and roof. The bedroom has only about 80 sq. ft., so its bed had to be on a raised platform to leave space for a dresser and a desk below.

Soon after she moved into the loft, however, Genevieve started bumping her head on the ceiling over the bed. When she eventually moved the mattress to the floor, I knew it was time for the old bed to go and for a new one to take its place. The bed alcove shown in the photo on the facing page was the result.

Will it fit?—The kneewalls that defined the sides of the room had originally been a little over 6 ft. high, leaving a great deal of wasted space behind them. I proposed to recover this space by moving the kneewall over 4 ft. to accommodate a 3-ft. wide mattress and a bedside shelf beyond that. Given the 12-in-12 pitch of the roof, this would bring the ceiling down below 3 ft. at the new kneewall. Would this be claustrophobic? To answer the question, I mocked up the space with packing crates and plywood to make sure there would be room to sit up in bed. A high ceiling is not a necessity over a bed—within reason, the reverse is true: A lower ceiling increases the sense of shelter and enhances the cavelike quality humans have always favored. Furthermore, a bed in an alcove that can be closed off from the rest of the room has qualities of privacy and quiet that are difficult to achieve in any other way. To get that extra layer of privacy, Genevieve and I decided that her bed alcove should have four sliding shoji screens.

The 9-ft. length of the space would provide room for a dresser and a vanity of some sort, as well as the bed. Drawers underneath the platform would triple the existing storage space. Light and ventilation would come from an operable skylight over the bed.

I had some misgivings about the location of this skylight in spite of the obvious benefits it would confer in terms of light and space. Having never slept directly under one myself, I didn't know whether a skylight so close to a bed would make sleep difficult. But in the end I was seduced by three arguments. First, the skylight

would face north and therefore would not be subject to heat-gain problems; second, it would illuminate the shoji from behind; and third, there was the emotional pressure from my client—some drivel about the stars and the treetops and falling asleep to the sound of rain on the glass.

Tight layout—Juggling existing conditions is the challenge of remodeling. None can be considered in isolation. For example, I had to decide whether or not to keep the existing 7-in. high baseboard. I could have moved it, but I wanted to leave it in place, partly for continuity and partly to avoid as much refinishing as possible. Starting the drawers above the baseboard also meant that the baseboard heater already on the adjoining wall wouldn't have to be moved to provide clearance for the end drawer.

Four drawers fit into the space between the baseboard and the mattress platform. The drawers are 7 in. deep (6½ in. inside), which is ample for all but the bulkiest items. This brings the mattress platform to a height of about 18 in. With a 4-in. thick mattress on top of it, the bed still ends up at a comfortable sitting height.

In plan, the mattress takes up almost exactly three-quarters of the 9-ft. long space. The leftover corner accommodates a makeup table with mirror above and more drawers below. I imagined that the shojis would draw a discreet curtain over the wreckage of eyeliners, lipsticks, mousse and everything else that was supposed to go in the drawers but never would.

I knew that this vanity area, and especially the mirror, would need to be lit, but beyond making sure there was a wire up there somewhere, I didn't work out the details during the preliminary planning. I was in my fast-track frame of mind at this stage of the project.

Site-built cabinet—The underframe of the bed is a large, deep drawer cabinet. You could have it built by a custom shop while you get on with framing, wiring and drywalling. Custom cabinets are expensive, though, and after nearly 10 years in the business of building them, I appreciate the virtues of their old-fashioned predecessor, the model A, site-built version. It's economical in terms of material and expense, and you can usually get a closer fit to the available space.

The partitions supporting my daughter's bed are made from ⅜-in. plywood sheathing left over from a framing job (the rewards of parsimony). Each partition is made from three layers of sheathing (drawing below). The center layer runs the full height of the partition, but the outer ones are cut in two, with the drawer guide sandwiched between the top and bottom pieces. The guide is simply a piece of smooth, fairly hard wood, ¾ in. thick and wide enough so that it projects ⅜ in. into the drawer space.

Unless circumstances demand the use of mechanical drawer slides, I prefer to hang drawers on wooden guides. I have provoked derision from cabinetmakers because I use wooden guides in kitchens, but when it comes to bedrooms I am almost inflexible. Even large drawers like these will run smoothly year after year if they are properly fitted and if the guides are securely mounted. And for me there is a subtle but important difference between the sound and the feel of wood on wood vs. even the finest ball bearings.

I attach the guides with screws rather than with glue and nails so that they can be removed, planed and even replaced without difficulty should the need arise. A groove in the partition to house them is not necessary, but it's a way of ensuring that they all end up straight and exactly where you want them.

For this job, the pairs of guides on the three middle partitions had to be screwed to one another, right through the core plywood. I drilled and counterbored all the screws and clamped the partition to my workbench to make sure everything stayed tight while I drove the screws. Then, with the partition still on the bench and after inspecting every screw head carefully for depth below the surface, I set the power plane for the lightest possible cut and made three passes over each guide: first over the back third only, then over the back two-thirds and, finally, over the whole length of the guide. Tapering the guides so that they are a fraction farther apart in

Partition detail

Three layers of ⅜-in. ply

Drawer guide

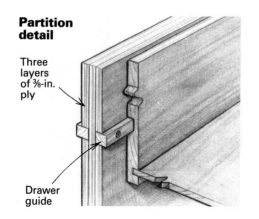

Drawings: Bob La Pointe

Tight fit. Into this 9-ft. long space, the author squeezed a single bed, a row of 30-in. deep drawers, a bookshelf and a vanity. A recessed fluorescent fixture illuminates the mirror from above while the vanity table is lit by a lamp behind the mirror. The baseboard reveals the line of the original wall. Above it, drawer fronts cut from a single 1x10 are screwed from behind to the drawers. Photo by Charles Miller.

the back allows the drawer to let go, rather than tighten up, as it slides home.

Partition alignment—Installing the partitions is the trickiest part of a site-built cabinet job like this one. I said earlier that you could save on materials by building the cabinet in place, but you can't save on time. After all, anyone with a table saw can build a square cabinet in the shop, but building one accurately in a closet or in an unfinished space under the rafters takes patience and thoroughness. The key to success is to establish a datum line, then lay out everything from this line, leaving the wedges of leftover space around the perimeters to be shimmed, trimmed, fudged and covered up as necessary.

In Genevieve's room, the existing baseboard provided a datum line in both horizontal and vertical planes. First, I divided the baseboard's length so that the four drawer fronts would lie directly below the shoji screens. I ran one screw into each supporting partition, about 1 in. below the top edge of the baseboard. Then I plumbed

the front edge of the partition and secured it with a second screw near the bottom of the baseboard. With the front edges located and the partitions standing straight, the next job was to align them to create parallel, square openings.

I built the new kneewalls 48¾ in. back from the inside face of the baseboard. This allowed me to run a couple of 1x4 straps horizontally across the studs to provide anchoring surfaces for the 48-in. partitions (drawing next page).

To align the partitions, I used hardboard cut to the full opening width (top left photo, p. 52). As long as the hardboard is cut square, and the partitions are secured so that the hardboard fits snugly between them, the resulting opening will also be square. I used screws to fasten the plywood flanges that held my partitions in place, just in case adjustment should be necessary.

When all the partitions were in place, I cut pieces of 1x2 to the exact dimension between each pair of drawer guides. Centered on the drawer fronts, the 1x2s are gauges that show how deep the grooves need to be in the drawer sides.

The bed slats also act as ties to link all the partitions together (bottom left photo, p. 52). I used dry 1x6 shelving pine for the slats, but almost anything that will span the distance between supports will do. I left an inch between the slats to keep the mattress well aired. I learned this the hard way when an early bed I built on a solid plywood platform developed mildew on the underside of the mattress cover.

Fitting the drawers—Before putting anything on top of the platform, I built and fitted the drawers. The drawers have ⅛-in. clearance between their sides and the partitions. The ⅜-in. projection of the drawer guide thus creates a ¼-in. interlock with the sides. All the drawers are 30 in. deep, but I let the sides extend 6 in. beyond the back of the drawer. The extensions support a drawer right up to the point where its back comes into view.

If time and budget allow, I use a router jig to dovetail the front of a drawer to its sides, but the back just has tongues cut on each end that are

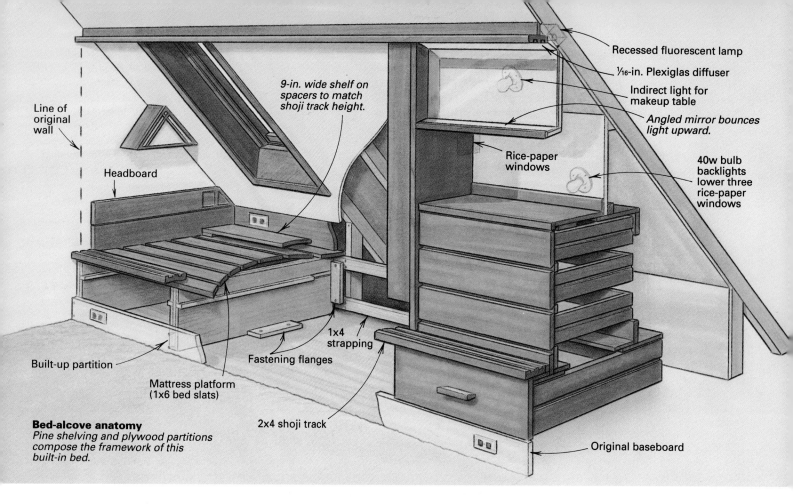

Recessed fluorescent lamp

1/16-in. Plexiglas diffuser

Indirect light for makeup table

Angled mirror bounces light upward.

40w bulb backlights lower three rice-paper windows

Rice-paper windows

9-in. wide shelf on spacers to match shoji track height.

Line of original wall

Headboard

Built-up partition

Mattress platform (1x6 bed slats)

Fastening flanges

1x4 strapping

2x4 shoji track

Original baseboard

Bed-alcove anatomy
Pine shelving and plywood partitions compose the framework of this built-in bed.

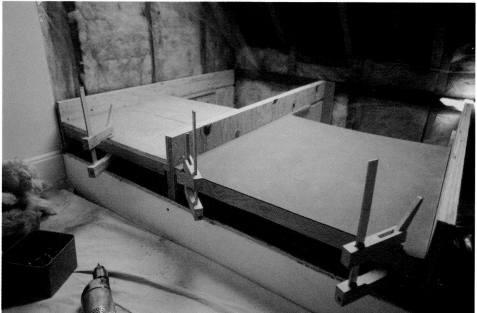

Aligning partitions. Load-bearing partitions made of three layers of 3/8-in. plywood separate the drawer bays under the bed and support the mattress platform. The drawer guides are sandwiched between the outer layers of plywood. The photo at left shows the hardboard panels that helped to align the partitions. Once the panels were in place, the partitions were screwed first to the baseboard and then to strapping along the stud wall. The 1x2s clamped to the leading edges of the panels are gauges that will be used to determine the depth of the grooves in the drawer sides.

Linked by slat. The partitions are tied to one another across their tops by 1x6 pine slats (bottom left photo). Spaces between the slats provide ventilation for the mattress. At the right side, the carcase for the vanity drawers sits directly atop the bottom drawer partitions.

Bookcase wall. Shelves deep enough for paperbacks are affixed to a 3/4-in. birch plywood panel between the bed and the vanity (photo below). The squares at the end of each shelf frame rice-paper windows that are backlit by bulbs behind the vanity drawers.

glued and nailed into dadoes in the sides (I take care not to put any nails where the groove for the guides will be plowed out). The drawer bottom rides freely in a groove cut in the front and the sides and is nailed into the bottom edge of the back, which is only as wide as the inside height of the drawer. Fastening the bottom here helps to keep the drawer square.

Fitting the drawers should present few problems if they are built square and true and if time and care have been invested in positioning the partitions. Don't try for too tight a fit, especially in the width of the groove. My guides were ¾-in. material, and I plowed out a ¹³⁄₁₆-in. dado in the drawer side. They're not sloppy.

On the other hand, you should be more stingy about the depth of the grooves. Remember, the guides have been planed to allow increasing clearance as the drawer slides home. Too much slop here can cause the drawer to bang about from side to side and actually hang up on the diagonal. You can always plow a groove out a little deeper. A router with a fence or a guide attached is the ideal tool for this because you can easily make very small adjustments. If things go wrong, you can glue a length of wood veneer tape into the dado, but it's nicer not to have to do that.

I dress the groove with paraffin wax, but only when I'm sure the drawer doesn't bind. Patience in working toward a fit has its reward here. The moment that a wood drawer on wood guides just slides into its opening and fetches up against its stop, expelling a little puff of air from the cabinet, is a moment that provides much satisfaction.

Beyond the footboard—With the drawers and the platform in, I had to decide what to do about the divider between the bed and the vanity. Here was where the self-imposed constraint of using the existing baseboard as the perimeter of the alcove began to bite. Because its height was determined by the slope of the ceiling, the mirror over the dressing table had to be as far forward as possible. But to bring it right up against the inside edge of the upper shoji track would eliminate the space required for a light above the mirror. And even that would put the top of the mirror at barely 6 ft. Temporarily derailed on the fast track, I tried to find other ways to light the mirror and kept coming back to the necessity of recessing a fluorescent fixture into the ceiling.

The fixture I used is a standard T-12 fluorescent fixture equipped with an Ultralume lamp (Philips Lighting Co., 200 Franklin Square Dr., Somerset, N. J. 08875; 908-563-3000). The lamp emits more lumens per watt than a standard cool-white lamp and has a higher Color Rendering Index, both important factors in getting an accurate reading on colors, like those at a makeup table.

Casting an even light across the face of the person standing at the mirror is important. So I put a narrow strip of mirror along the bottom edge of the large mirror, angled upward to bounce the light where it can fill in shadows.

Bookcase wall—As for the partition between dressing table and bed, my fast-track conviction that it could not be frame and drywall held up better. My daughter wanted more bookshelves, and the foot of the bed was a logical place to put them (photo facing page, lower right). I made the back of the bookcase out of ¾-in. birch plywood, which could be finished naturally on the book side and painted white on the dressing-table side to look like a wall.

To light the makeup table, I mounted a standard incandescent ceiling fixture in the space behind the mirror. On a playful impulse, I wired another of these lower on the sloped ceiling in the space behind the vanity drawer (the case for these has no back, so the fixture is easily accessible). Then, after carefully laying out the location of the bookshelf dividers and following a square-and-triangle motif suggested by the conjunction of the ceiling and the shelves, I jigsawed the holes in the birch ply and glued rice paper over them. This created little backlit rice-paper windows in the bookshelves. The dividers cover the edges of the paper. The only slight snag in this assembly is that the plywood thickness causes a shadow line, which can be seen where the backlighting travels at an angle through the window. If I'd thought of it in time, I could have easily eliminated the shadows by beveling these edges with a router.

The bedside reading light was more of a problem. Initially, I placed my standard ceiling fixture under the skylight as far down the slope of the ceiling as I could. I made a cardboard mock-up of the rice-paper shade that I had in mind to es-

Headboard. A reading light inspired by the bookcase's square-and-triangle motif lights up the headboard side of the bed. On the left, wooden tracks for shoji screens frame the alcove.

tablish just how big it should be—the trade-offs being the height of the fixture, the size of the shade and its proximity to errant elbows. I thought I had a satisfactory balance, so I went ahead and made the lamp. But Genevieve put her elbow through it the first night she slept in the bed. I forgave her and accepted the lesson. The second reading light ended up above the head of the bed (photo left).

What about the shojis?—The shoji screens have yet to be made, and it now seems unlikely they ever will be. Although she was initially keen to have them, Genevieve now believes they would get in the way, and I agree with her. We analyzed the patterns of opening and closing that might be required during a typical day and night. It became clear that in spite of the desirability of drawing a curtain over the unmade bed by day and the unfinished homework by night, this teenager would rather live and sleep in one room—at least for the time being—than be bothered sliding screens to-and-fro all the time. A feeling of confinement was also a factor. Having tried out the bed myself one night when she was sleeping at a friend's house, I too felt I might want more distance between myself and any enclosing screen.

I admit that this was something of a blow to my vision of the room. What about the function of the skylight as a backlight for the shoji? What about the square-and-triangle motif I was going to incorporate into the shoji lattice? Ah, well, at least I hadn't made them already. And the grooves in the bottom track appear to work perfectly as 9-ft. long pencil trays.

The rejected shojis and the difficulties I had with the makeup light and the height of the mirror were all results of my decision to keep the bed alcove within the area beyond the existing kneewall. If I had moved this line 6 in. to 12 in. into the room, I could have raised the upper shoji track a few inches, creating plenty of space to mount the mirror light, the reading light and the shoji screens. The amount by which this would have reduced the size of the room would have been insignificant in relation to the space gained by building in the bed and the dressing table—a case of choosing the wrong existing condition to work from.

At least the client is satisfied. The project was completed during one of the long dry spells that Vancouver is famous for. Finally, one morning when the spider webs were glittering and the earth smelled refreshed and autumnal, Genevieve appeared downstairs with a beatific smile on her face. "It rained on my skylight last night," she said. □

Tony Simmonds is a designer and builder in Vancouver, B. C., Canada. Photos by the author except where noted.

Facelift for a Loft

A curved wall, choice materials and a light-conscious design bring two rooms to life

by Richard Ayotte

It's not uncommon in New York City to find oddly shaped living spaces. They're usually the products of half-successful attempts at converting old industrial buildings and warehouses into living spaces. A recent project of mine involved such a space: a cramped, awkwardly arranged bathroom in a duplex loft apartment. The adjacent room—a dark, inhospitable space—didn't improve the livability of the apartment. My firm's task was to provide a more open space, rework the bathroom and create a casual sitting area that could double as a study. Making rooms feel bright was a key element of the program. Also, budget constraints dictated that the sauna and the apartment's

electrical panel remain in place. Though we were free to relocate the existing whirlpool, we had to reuse it as well as isolate its motor acoustically in order to address complaints from the downstairs neighbors.

Design solutions—The apartment's owners wanted to minimize any awkardness in having the main bathroom next to what is a public, social area. They also wanted to move the entrance to make it less conspicuous from the sitting space. We studied several possibilities, with an eye toward disguising the room's function when viewed from without. The solution was a curved wall between the two

rooms, flaring open to an enlarged entry area (drawing facing page). The wall's sensuous shape helps to soften the otherwise small, rectilinear spaces, and the glass block in the wall allows some passage of light between the rooms without compromising privacy (photo facing page).

We hoped to create a sense of expansiveness by creating an ordered, visually uncluttered space, so it was important to integrate all the disparate elements in the bathroom and to open up the floor space as much as possible. For example, the whirlpool bath was moved to the far corner of the room and set between existing walls to minimize its impact.

A habitable space. White walls, glass block and track lighting above the bookshelves serve to lighten the sitting area and create a feeling of relative spaciousness in a small room. *Photo by Charles Wardell.*

Traditionally free-standing elements, such as the vanity, were built in for the same reason. Mirrors were added to cover the walls over both the whirlpool and the vanity to expand the space visually. A custom towel rail hugs the wall, emphasizing its curve. Tile and accent colors are carried throughout the room (photo right).

Building in apartment buildings—As is typical with projects in apartment buildings, work was restricted to the apartment's interior, without recourse to access from adjoining apartments. Also, major plumbing lines had to remain in their existing locations, and work hours were kept from 9:30 to 4:30, weekdays.

The building has only one small elevator, which meant that many of the materials had to be walked up—six floors. The large bathroom mirrors proved especially difficult; we broke more than one en route up the fire stairs.

Inherited headaches—Construction problems, particularly in buildings originally designed for nonresidential use, can be complex. While the original structure may be sound, and accurate plans may exist for it, subsequent owners do not always document changes. To compound the problem, workmanship on these changes is often shoddy. Most of our difficulties were caused by such renovations.

Shortly after our contractors, Supply Side, Inc., began demolition, we discovered that the original bathroom ceiling, which we had wanted to keep, was supported on a metal stud partition we wanted to remove. It should have been suspended from the building structure, as the New York City Building Code requires. This necessitated additional demolition and new construction, not to mention the largest change order for the project.

Installing the new plumbing lines proved problematic as well. Although we didn't know the exact locations of joists, we thought we could assume (based on the orientation of the finish wood flooring) that they'd be perpendicular to the flooring. As it turned out, we discovered during demolition that the wood strip flooring had been installed over an earlier finish floor, and perpendicular to it. Resulting design changes were insignificant, but additional time was required to complete the more circuitous plumbing runs.

A custom shower base—The existing shower, which we were replacing, had a ceramic tile floor

Bright and open. To open up the bathroom visually, the contractors relocated the whirlpool and replaced the wall between the sitting area and the bathroom with a curved wall. *Photo by Vincent Laurence.*

Floor plan: after (detail)

Whirlpool — Shower

Vanity

Up

Bedroom

Electrical panel

Sauna

Floor plan: before

Shower — Vanity

Up

Whirlpool

Bedroom

Electrical panel

Bedroom

Sauna

set on a raised plywood base. Movement in the base, due either to inadequate structural support (causing excessive deflection) or to delamination of the plywood from repeated wettings, had resulted in frequent cracking of the grout. This had required nearly constant maintenance to prevent water leakage to the apartment below.

To avoid a recurrence of this problem in the new shower, we had planned to install a prefabricated cast-stone base. Unfortunately, we couldn't find a stock base to fit the odd-size space in which we had to work. Rather than alter the shower layout at this stage, we built a new plywood base and reduced the joist spacing beneath it to 12 in. o. c., thereby virtually eliminating deflection. Over the plywood, we placed a continuous layer of Bituthene (W. R. Grace Company, 62 Whittemore Ave., Cambridge, Mass. 02140; 800-242-4476), a rubberized membrane material used to waterproof roofs, walls and foundations. We ran the membrane up the walls approximately 12 inches to act as a "flashing," and down into the central drain to prevent any chance of leakage at the point of exit. Ceramic tile was installed over the Bituthene, using a mud base and thinset adhesive.

A close call—The most significant work delay we experienced involved one of our basic materials—the ceramic tile. The speckled, tan-colored porcelain tile intended for the flooring and some walls was impervious to water penetration, had excellent slip-resistance, and made a good color match with the existing whirlpool bath. The sole New York distributor assured us that the German manufacturer could deliver the quantities needed in plenty of time to meet our schedule. The contractor placed his order and put down a 50% deposit. Well into construction, the tile distributor vanished in apparent bankruptcy. All of the rough construction and fixture placement had been completed to accommodate the metric-sized tile. Consequently, switching to a readily available American tile would have incurred considerable additional work and compromised the quality of the project.

Fortunately, one of the apartment's owners, Richard Winger, was fluent in German and was able to speak directly to the manufacturer, who provided the tile for the balance that was owed on the order. □

Richard Ayotte is a principal in the firm Richard Ayotte Architecture in New York City.

Drawings: Karen Negri

From *Fine Homebuilding* (October 1991) 70:80-81

Found Horizon

Horizontal bands of oak casework create a tranquil atmosphere in a bedroom addition

by Philip S. Sollman

I've always felt that long horizontal lines suggest a certain calmness and tranquility. I'm most aware of this when I gaze across farmland at the distant horizon. Subtle interruptions, like trees, buildings or deeply plowed furrows add interest. These thoughts were in mind when I designed the interior of John and Joan Chernega's new bedroom addition. The strong horizontals became bed, cabinets, shelving and valances for indirect lighting, with grillework incorporated to create rhythmic contrast (photo above).

Set at the end of a residential street in State College, Pa., the house enjoys a private setting. The addition sits above the family room, and with lots of windows (photo facing page, top), it takes in the view that inspired it—fields and trees running over gentle hills to the horizon.

Philip S. Sollman is a designer and woodworker in Bellefonte, Pa.

Ribbons around the room—All rooms have an optimum organization plan. On this project, the best locations for such things as the bed, dressing area and lights were established by considering circulation, ventilation and views. My design fixed these elements and tied them together in ribbon-like fashion around the perimeter of the room. Vertical dimensions were established for the toe space, the countertop, and the tops and bottoms of both valances. These heights were crucial to the design and had to be rigidly adhered to. Any deviation would disturb the tranquility I was trying so hard to achieve.

Horizontal zones were established where electrical wiring surfaced to feed to lights, outlets and switches. Accurately locating the wiring involved constant collaboration with the builder and electrician. I visited the site often during the framing to make sure that things were in the right place. Luckily, everyone remained pleasant and cooperative throughout the project, though I wondered in the early going if my presence was welcome.

Building a bedroom in a bedroom—Ever since I became a woodworker, I've had to work in spaces that were impossibly small for the projects undertaken. I began in the damp cellar of a rented farmhouse, sharing a 10-ft. by 10-ft. space with my wife Jeanne, a potter. Ripping lumber meant holding the board steady and moving the table saw. Next, I moved to a rented garage, where I built a fair portion of our house. When I finished the house, I moved my shop into our future bedroom, where it remains today, awaiting the completion of a new shop.

Since I was accustomed to woodworking gymnastics, I knew I could handle the Chernega's extensive casework in my limited work space, provided I could move it out piece by

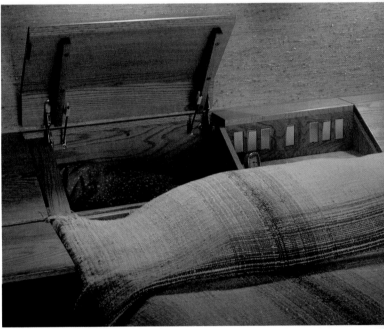

The gable end of this second-story addition (photo top) is nearly all glass, providing a view of the backyard and the fields beyond. Inside the addition, lights are controlled from a panel of switches recessed into the headboard. Headrests flip up to reveal storage compartments. Built as a separate unit, the headboard is supported by the built-in end tables.

piece on completion. We used red oak because it had been used extensively in the rest of the house. Oak-veneered plywood was used wherever possible for its strength, stability and speed in casework assembly.

The bed—The bedroom needed a focal point, and the bed with its built-in headboard naturally assumed this role. The headboard rests between flanking nightstands that help support it (photo above left). In the center is a recessed panel containing electrical switches that control lights throughout the addition. From here one can operate individual reading lights above the headboard, perimeter lights in the valances and an outdoor deck light, as well as lights in the hall and bathroom. We chose large toggle-type switches because they're easier to locate at night. The ones we used were from Leviton's Decora line (Leviton Mfg. Co. Inc., 59-25 Little Neck Pkwy., Little

Neck, N. Y. 11362, and two of them are touch dimmers, operated by holding down the switch as the light cycles from dim to bright. Then you release the switch when the light reaches the desired level.

I didn't want conventional plastic switch covers at the headboard, so I carved a highly figured piece of oak into a panel that fits over the switches (photo above right). I had to file crisp, straight edges around each switch opening to ensure a good fit. This little detail took a full day's labor, but added much to the finished appearance of the work. Because body heat could throw off its setting, the room thermostat was not placed in this panel. Instead, we mounted it above the bed.

On either side of the center panel, the headboard contains two deep storage areas under flip-up lids. Friction supports hold the lids in the open position for easy access to extra pillows and blankets. Closed, the lids double as

headrests for reading in bed. On each side of the bed, I built flip-up end tables into the nightstand. In the down position, they hang neatly under the shelf beside the bed on a pair of hinges, which are double-jointed. Regular hinges would have created a step at the edge when the tables were folded down. In the up position, the end tables are supported by folding metal braces, mounted underneath.

Maintaining consistent horizontal lines was tough in places, particularly at the bed. I had to abandon the idea of the bed overhanging the base because the extra-thick mattress and box spring measure 16 in., and it looked like I'd have only 15 in. above the toe kick to squeeze it into. So I built a base that angles inward 20° and at least hints at a toe kick. That let me lower the mattress just enough to make it level with the control panel.

The base of the bed is a plywood frame, mitered at the corners. Solid wood cross-pieces

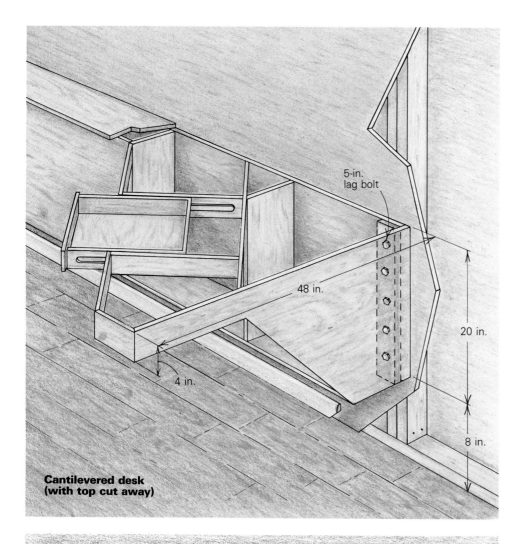

**Cantilevered desk
(with top cut away)**

5-in.
lag bolt

48 in.

20 in.

4 in.

8 in.

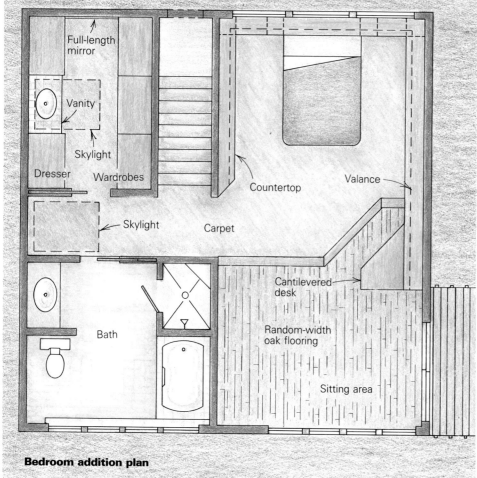

Bedroom addition plan

Full-length
mirror

Vanity

Skylight

Dresser

Wardrobes

Skylight

Bath

Countertop

Valance

Carpet

Cantilevered
desk

Random-width
oak flooring

Sitting area

inside help support the box springs.

In a number of locations, exact miters had to be cut on the ends of plywood panels. Since many of the pieces were quite long, this task would have been difficult on a table saw. I don't own a radial-arm saw, so I used a circular saw. Working with the good side of the plywood facing up, I scored the oak veneer with a knife along the cut-line. With the saw set at the appropriate miter, I started into the cut about ¼ in. and stopped to check that the saw kerf was at the exact edge of my knife cut. Without removing the saw, I marked the outside edge of the saw base with a pencil line. The distance from the line to the cut was marked at the other end of the plywood and a straightedge clamped between those points, against which the saw base would ride. I could then complete the cut without irregularities.

A sled bed—It was the end of January when I finished the bed. We managed to get the thing down the stairs from my shop and out the front door. I knew that it was too big to deliver in

In the dressing room above, dressers and a vanity line one wall, and wardrobes line the other. The full-length mirror at the end of the room is flanked by lighted grillework with translucent white plastic panels hiding the 100-watt fixtures. Unframed mirrors on three sides of the white tile vanity top help make the narrow dressing room seem bigger.

my Chevy Suburban, so I rented a large van.

As I turned into the slight uphill grade of our drive, the van's rear wheels began to spin on the snowy lane. After several attempts, I had advanced just 30 ft. When I got out and noticed the Florida plates and summer treads, I resigned myself to bringing the bed down the 1,000-ft. long lane to the van. But how? It was too heavy to carry that distance.

When I got back to the house, Jeanne jokingly suggested an idea that I thought might work. After carefully wrapping the bed for the journey, we tied two sleds under it. Our three dogs patiently pondered the situation as I loosely tethered them to the bed with baling twine. Then, in a flash, they were off—in so many different directions that my camera lens couldn't take it all in. Eventually, Jeanne and I pulled the bed down to the van ourselves.

Valancing act—Two rows of 12-in. deep lighted valances circle the bedroom. The first one, 5 ft. 3 in. off the floor, lights the cabinets below it and also serves as a display shelf. The second one, 7 ft. 10 in. off the floor, lights the display shelf below and is open above to reflect off the ceiling.

All the units are constructed of plywood and trimmed at the top and bottom with a solid strip of oak that extends beyond the face of the plywood, accenting the horizontal scheme. These edges also overhang the back of the plywood and provide a ledge for the removable grilles to rest on. I assembled these units with a Lamello plate joiner (Colonial Saw, Box A, Kingston, Mass. 02364). Thanks to this handy tool, the oak trim could be attached without screws or nails, and a consistent relief could be maintained.

The plans called for 150 lin. ft. of valance and nearly 200 lin. ft. of grillework. After finishing each unit, I stood it on end wherever I could find space. My shop soon became a forest of columns. They had to be finished and installed before I could start the next phase.

The underside of each valance is fitted with a grille made of ¾-in. by 2-in. by 8-ft. oak strips, radiused on their exposed edges. I ripped the cross-pieces ½ in. thinner so that I could let them into the lengthwise strips. I finished the pieces before assembling them, which was easier than having to force a brush or rag betweeen all the spaces later. I made a pair of 7-ft. tall A-frames out of scrap wood to use as drying racks for the 100-odd pieces. I drove finish nails, 3 in. apart, up one side of the A and down the other, then laid the strips on the nails spanning the two frames.

Next, I clamped the cross-pieces to a work table 20 or 30 at a time, and using a straightedge, routed ¾-in. wide slots into them. I fastened the pieces together from the back with drywall screws.

Where a valance passed over a window, I made the grilles narrower, leaving a space at the back to allow for a concealed drapery track. Where the faces of adjacent units butt together, a small piece of molding covers the joint. The grilles are supported by a lip at the front of the valance and screwed to the framework at the back. Where adjacent grilles butt together, I slipped a section of steel channel over the tops of each piece to keep them in line; otherwise, the ends might have warped or twisted out of alignment. The lights behind these grilles are on dimmer switches, and they create a soft, glowing atmosphere. Lights above the desk and bed are direct spots controlled by separate switches.

In the corners of the room, on either side of the bed, I built upright grilles, also lighted, but with the addition of translucent white plastic panels to hide the fixtures. These vertical elements add interest and help light the room. They also hide any problems in the woodwork that might have resulted from the corners of the room not being exactly 90° angles.

The cantilever tales—The bedroom is informally divided into a sleeping area and a sitting area. The angular border between the two is marked by the change from carpeting in the sleeping area to random-width oak flooring in the sitting area. This shape is reflected in a cantilevered desk that extends 4 ft. off the end of the cabinets.

The oak desk is 4 in. deep and includes a drawer. A grid-like framework, similar to a torsion box but without a bottom panel, forms the body of the desk and is lag-bolted into the wall studs (top drawing facing page). The desk is also supported by the triangular plywood end panel. It is suprisingly sturdy and will easily support a TV.

Dressing room—The plans included a separate dressing room opposite the bathroom (floor plan facing page). Along one side of the room, built-in dressers flank a vanity with a sink and ceramic-tile counter (photo facing page bottom). Mirrors are mounted on the three wall surfaces surrounding the vanity and give an illusion of greater space.

On the opposite side of the dressing room, I built wardrobes with hanging storage and open shelving. One of the wardrobe units is directly above the laundry room, so I included a laundry chute in its lower compartment.

In addition to natural light from a large skylight, the room has diffused incandescent lighting behind the grillework in the valances, over the dressers and on either side of the full-length mirror at the end of the room (photo top, facing page). Since you would be looking directly into grillework beside the mirror, I once again screwed white plastic panels to the backs. These grilles are 6 in. deep and diffuse the light provided by six 100-watt bulbs behind them. Recesssed cans for task lighting are set into the grillework over the sink. For maximum control, all of the lighting is controlled by dimmer switches.

Wherever possible, I integrated handles into the fronts of drawers and doors. I routed continuous pulls in the drawer fronts using a carbide drawer-pull bit from The Woodworker's Supply of New Mexico (5604 Alameda NE, Albuquerque, N. M. 87113). Blum European-style hinges (Julius Blum Inc., Blum Industrial Park, Hwy. 16—Lowesville, Stanley, N. C. 28164) were used for all doors. All exposed plywood edges were faced with oak. In most cases, I glued a single piece of solid oak between two plywood door blanks, then sawed through the middle, which saved lots of time.

The five dresser and wardrobe units provided some anxious moments for me during their installation. John and I easily hauled them up through the balcony door, only to discover their bulk prevented them from making the necessary 90° turn into the dressing room. John, who was taking time from work to help me, was very quiet at this point.

Taking some quick measurements, I decided on an alternate route through the new bathroom window. This involved standing on a rickety picnic table pulled up to the side of the house. John pressed his son into service, and the three of us, standing on the table, hoisted the awkward unit over our heads. Then two of us held, while John ran up to the bathroom window to pull the unit through. I could see his arms desperately groping for a handhold. The wardrobe finally went in, and from here, it was a straight shot into the dressing room. In this manner, all five units were neatly positioned side by side and fixed to the walls. We were all relieved that we didn't have to use our contingency plan—a crane lift through the skylight.

Finishing touches—We left the oak unstained so as not to detract from the fresh, bright appearance of the completed interior. Instead, I used a coat of Waterlox Transparent Sealer (Waterlox Chemical and Coatings Corp., 9808 Meech Ave., Cleveland, Oh. 44105), then a coat or two of polyurethane from the same company. Instead of carefully brushing it on, I applied it liberally with a paint roller and then lightly wiped it with a wad of paper towels.

When I do this, I'm careful not to apply more urethane than I can wipe before it gets tacky. This method works especially well on vertical surfaces where urethane tends to run and drip. One coat was enough in most places, but I applied two coats around areas that would get a lot of use, like door handles and countertops. Lightly sanded between each coat, it made for a fast and even finish. The final touch was a coat of paste wax. All of the woodwork received this treatment.

In the bedroom area, handwoven linen from Wolf-Gordon Inc. (132 W. 21st St., New York, N. Y. 10011) was applied to the walls above the countertop and between the valances. The fabric has a paper backing and is put up like wallpaper, with sizing and paste. It matches the color of the short-nap commercial-grade carpeting we used. Baseboards, window and door trim were painted to match the walls.

Finally, I designed and built a table and six chairs to complement the overall scheme. And a local weaver, Jean Giddings of Coburn, Pa., was commissioned to weave a custom spread that she designed for the bed. □

Jewelbox Bathroom

Ingenious framing and exotic glazing come together in a small bathroom tucked in a dormer

By Jeff Morse

As an architect who designs a fair amount of remodels, I believe that any changes made to a house should respect or rediscover its original style and individuality. Unfortunately, many of the houses here in Petaluma, California, where I work, have been added to poorly, becoming chaotic jumbles of styles and spaces.

Such was the case with the Rathkey place. John and Cynthia Rathkey own a late 19th-century bungalow near the center of town. Their house had been defaced by a flat-roofed 50s addition off the kitchen and a ramshackle bathroom that was tacked to the side-yard wall. They called me for advice about healing the house—taking away the grotesque additions and adding a garage that would include a master bedroom and a bath above it.

I told the Rathkeys that we could most likely squeeze their addition into the slightly trapezoidal space alongside the house. But keeping the two-story addition in scale with the original bungalow was a problem I immediately began to struggle with: A conventional two-story addition would dwarf the house.

Fortunately, the house had a wood-framed floor over a crawl space. Because the garage floor would be a slab-on-grade, its top surface would end up 30 in. lower than the floor of the house. To scale down further the two-story bulk of the addition, I proposed a story-and-a-half design with the top plate of the upper-story wall set 5 ft. 6 in. off the floor. A 7-ft. 6-in. garage ceiling would bring the top plate of the second-story wall within 2 ft. of the top plate of the original building.

Breaking the plate—Visually relating the addition to the house was as simple as using the same hip-roof form, with its unusual 7½-in-12 roof pitch. The low plate would bring the ceiling planes much closer to the floor than is typical, creating a dynamic and sheltering space. And to emphasize that volume, I designed the roof to transfer its loads without the need for posts or collar ties that would detract from the space. The low plate, however, created a problem with the windows—

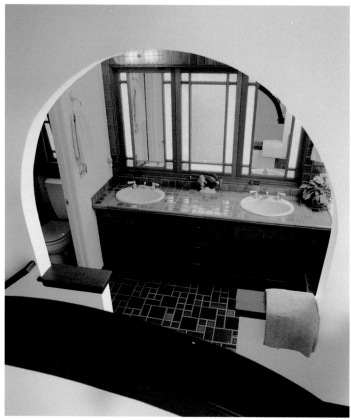

Bath alcove. An archway inspired by the headboard in the foreground frames the bath, which includes a separate enclosure for the toilet. The mirrors over the sinks are the interior panels of dual-glazed windows.

especially in the bathroom. Lifted as high as possible, the upper glass line was still well below standing eye level. As important as the low plate was in scaling down the addition, I felt it was equally important to break the plate somewhere to get a standing eye-level view and avoid an oppressive feel to the low roof near the walls.

A shallow-hipped dormer was the perfect device to open up the bathroom and scale down the somewhat monolithic form of the addition's exterior, but it presented an interesting structural dilemma. Because there are no posts to hold up the ridge beam and no collar ties to keep the walls from spreading, the hip rafters take on the load in compression while the top plates act as a tension ring to contain the thrust of the hips.

It doesn't take a genius to figure out what would happen if you broke the plate of such a roof, but it did help to have one on hand when I decided to try it. Richard Hartwell, an engineer and a good friend of mine, devised a scheme to

transfer the tension load in the top plate around the window and door openings at the north and south dormers. By installing small glulam columns at either side of the opening, we were able to transfer the tension load in the wall plate to the header and the sill plate at the opening, then back to the opposing wall plate (top left drawing, facing page). Simpson HD2A hold-downs transfer loads from the double plate to the columns, and framing straps transfer it from the column ends into the header and sill plates (right drawing, facing page).

An open plan—Keeping an open and airy feel to the upstairs addition was something we all wanted, so the Rathkeys readily agreed to opening the bath and the vanity to the main bedroom space (photo left). This also allowed the bathroom to feel expansive well beyond its rather modest dimensions. The bathroom is tucked into a space that is merely 5 ft. wide and 13 ft. long (bottom left drawing, facing page), and about half of that space is taken up by the counter and the bathtub. The arched entry to the bath repeats the shape of the bed's headboard, creating a rhythm of arcs at the top of the stairs.

Exotic windows—I thought it was important to have some good-sized operable windows in the bathroom to balance the light and provide some cross ventilation. Unfortunately, large bathroom windows facing the street are usually ill-advised. Another strike against the windows was that the vanity would be right in front of them. My first thought was to work mirrors into the glazing, but the backside of a mirror isn't exactly a handsome exterior detail.

Then it occurred to me that iridized glass would probably work well. Iridized glass has a thin metallic coating on it that gives it a shimmery, rainbow look resembling a film of oil on water (photo, p. 62). This bathroom has two kinds of glass with the iridized coating—water glass and opal glass (Spectrum Glass, P.O. Box 646, Woodinville, Wash. 98072; 800-426-3120).

Drawings: Gary Williamson

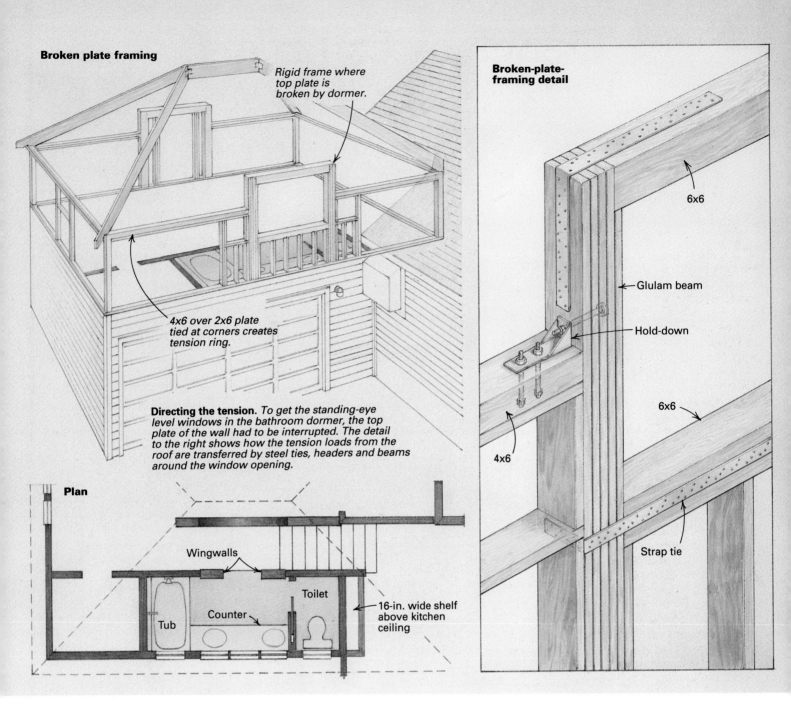

Broken plate framing

Rigid frame where top plate is broken by dormer.

4x6 over 2x6 plate tied at corners creates tension ring.

Directing the tension. *To get the standing-eye level windows in the bathroom dormer, the top plate of the wall had to be interrupted. The detail to the right shows how the tension loads from the roof are transferred by steel ties, headers and beams around the window opening.*

Plan

Wingwalls

Toilet

16-in. wide shelf above kitchen ceiling

Tub

Counter

Broken-plate-framing detail

6x6

Glulam beam

Hold-down

6x6

4x6

Strap tie

Water glass is clear with a wavy pattern. But once the glass is iridized, its reflective quality renders it completely obscure to vision from the outside during the day when the light is brighter outside than in, and vice versa. Opal glass, on the other hand, has milky, opaque white swirls in it that abstract images from either side, no matter what the lighting.

There are three windows over the lavatory. Two of them are centered over the sinks and glazed with mirrors on the inside and iridized water glass on the outside. The window in the middle also has iridized water glass on the outside, but the interior side is glazed with Spectrum's "hammered" glass—an obscure glass that has a rippled surface. Each window has nine lites: one large pane in the middle bordered by narrow strips of iridized water glass and iridized opal glass.

The final piece of the bathroom-window puzzle was the need for tempered glass in the tub area. Much as I tried, I couldn't find anyone who

would temper iridized glass. I was told that it simply couldn't be done. So we decided to use glue-chip glass for the center lite of the windows over the tub and the toilet. Glue-chip glass has patterns etched into its surface that look like frost. Glass artisans make the patterns by applying hide glue to a piece of glass. When the glue dries, it peels thin chips of glass away in complex, feathery patterns that let in light while obscuring the image on the other side. Best yet for our purposes, glue-chip glass can be tempered after the patterns are created in it.

Specialty glass isn't cheap. The iridized glass cost about $9 per sq. ft.; hammered glass cost $5.50 per sq. ft.; and the tempered glue-chip glass came in at $9.50 per sq. ft. But used judiciously in a prominent place, a spot of expensive glass can easily carry its budgetary burden.

Like the other windows in the addition, the perimeter lites in the tub and toilet enclosures are just a fraction under 3 in. wide. This allowed

us to use iridized glass because the code accepts nontempered glass 3 in. in width or less near tub enclosures.

So who would we get to make such bizarre windows? We decided early in the design to stay with wood sash and jambs (in spite of the additional cost) because they are an important element in defining the character of the project, and they're a link with the original bungalow. I got bids from three window companies: two large manufacturers and a custom-window builder that I had been using on other projects. To my surprise and delight, Dave Ferguson of B&D Window and Sash Co. (B&D Window, P. O. Box 424, Clearlake Oaks, Calif. 95423; 707-998-3717) could not only provide the true divided-lite sash at a price equal to the least expensive production windows, but he could also do it in clear heart redwood. He was also able to handle our strange glazing requirements. Ferguson built the nine-lite windows so that the center lite was

Flush-framed dormer. **The author prevents the addition from overshadowing the original house by keeping the second-floor walls a mere 5 ft. 6 in. high at the top plate. A dormer over the vanity provides headroom and space for a trio of windows, which are glazed with iridized glass (detail below).**

double glazed, and the edge lights were single glazed (drawing right). This allowed a reasonably narrow muntin size, which matches the other windows. For one final wrinkle in the window saga, the mirrored lites over the sinks extend all the way to the top and the bottom of the sash.

Toilet and tub—To complete the bathroom-as-alcove idea, the toilet was given its own small room (3 ft. by 5 ft.) with a door. The wall of the toilet enclosure on the side of the original house fortuitously abuts the old attic. The attic amounted to unused space, so we carved a 16-in. deep linen storage area into it that is tall enough to fit three shelves.

The tub was set at counter height to provide an easy view out the window. But because of the low plate height, raising the tub was accomplished only by extending the ceiling upward into the 12-in. deep rafter recess, giving adequate headroom to comfortably use the shower. Contractor Larry Volat doubled the rafters on either side of the headroom recess and put 2x4 drywall backing on edge between them to keep the ceiling as thin as possible.

The tub we settled on, the Tea for Two by Kohler (Kohler Co., 444 Highland Ave., Kohler, Wisc. 53044; 414-457-4441), has a nice combination of ingredients. It was the smallest (32 in. by 60 in.) double-ender I could find, and it comes with or without whirlpool jets. It's the perfect tub for conservation-minded, hedonist couples with space limitations.

Laying out the tile—Whenever I look at tilework, the first things I notice are the mistakes—the "Oh, didn't quite fit" cuts. Tile can be pretty unforgiving. It can also be expensive and way too plain in shape, color, texture and finish for

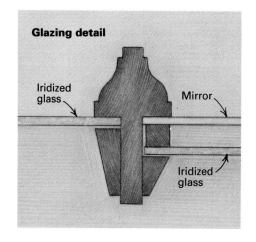

Glazing detail

Iridized glass

Mirror

Iridized glass

my taste. These factors all influenced the approach we took to the tilework in the Rathkey bathroom, which was executed with care and precision by tilesetter Eugene Dolcini.

Tilemaker Bob McIntyre runs a modestly sized porcelain and stoneware tile manufacturing operation in a couple of warehouses just off the railroad tracks in Healdsburg, 40 miles north of Petaluma (McIntyre Tile, Inc., 55 West Grant St., P. O. Box 14, Healdsburg, Calif. 95448; 707-433-8866). He produces some of the most beautiful tiles I have seen. What I like best, however, are his seconds. These are tiles that are rejected for a variety of reasons: too wide a color range for the given glaze, iron spotting or perhaps some slight warping. To me, most of these seeming imperfections add interest and character. The cost of the seconds is a quarter to a third of the firsts, which is also appealing. The trick to using them is being able to cope with the usually limited quantities of seconds available in any given size with a particular glaze.

To that end I've taken to mixing sizes within a field. Since many of McIntyre's tiles are modular, such as 3 in. by 3 in., 3 in. by 6 in. and 6 in. by 6 in., they can be combined into larger patterns to create a random ashlar effect. We used all three sizes on the blue floor (photo facing page). On the shower wall and tub surround, the green tiles are 3 in. by 3 in. and 6 in. by 6 in. We had enough of the smaller tiles to use them as borders, thereby outlining the field tiles and avoiding tapered cuts in the larger ones. Where the 6 in. by 6 in. tiles abut one another, they are always offset by the width of at least one of the smaller tiles to avoid a static, heavy spot of tile in the field. Similarly, the light and dark tiles are distributed around the wall to keep distracting dark or light patches from developing. The only drawback I have found to mixing sizes in the field using seconds is that they vary slightly in thickness and therefore take more care (and more time) to set.

Once we had the tile and the layout in mind, we measured for trim pieces, such as surface bullnose and quarter-rounds. One of the nice things about working with a custom tilemaker like McIntyre is the possibility of special orders. For example, the step into the Rathkeys' tub has an "S" curve to its front, allowing one to stand in front of the lavatory near the tub. I sent a template to McIntyre's production foreman, and he shaped the appropriate quarter-rounds so that we could achieve a smooth curve without cutting the trim into small pieces. The rounded edge of the bullnose is easy on the feet while getting in the tub, and the step makes an equally good place to sit after a soak. □

Jeff Morse is an architect based in Petaluma, Calif. Photos by Charles Miller.

Squares, triangles and curves. A tub raised atop a low platform occupies its own niche in the bathroom, where it is framed by a complex arrangement of roof lines, archways and wingwalls. Note how the ceiling over the tub is recessed for showering headroom. By carefully laying out different size tiles that share the same module, Morse was able to use discounted tiles to create rich geometric compositions.

Wide-Open Kitchen Remodel

It took some bright ideas to get 21 windows and skylights into this 200-sq. ft. addition

by Matthew Adams Longo

Form follows function. A peninsula with a 30-in. deep countertop helps define the cooking area; to the left, a pass-through with operable shutters unites the kitchen and the living room. Photo taken at A on floor plan.

Stove, sink, refrigerator. Cabinets overhead, linoleum down under. When it comes to residential design, conventions often produce a formulaic kitchen. So when Eve and Jeb Wallace called me to remodel their kitchen, I sensed an opportunity to try something unique. I felt this because Eve and I had grown up together, attending the same schools where the visual arts, creative thinking and nature studies were emphasized. After spending the better part of an afternoon discussing what the Wallaces really wanted, we decided to do some things that would break free from convention.

Eve and Jeb were very attached to their property—close to the ocean, with mature trees, streams and rock outcroppings—but frustrated by their house. They bought the 1960s ranch, located in historic Manchester-By-The-Sea, Massachusetts, before they had children. As their family grew, Eve and Jeb felt more and more boxed in by their house. The 8x12 galley kitchen was especially brutal with its two 18-in. aluminum sliding windows crouching between the base cabinets and the overheads. But the Wallaces needed more than light and space. I felt their new kitchen should be the center of activity in

their house. It should reflect and support their love for their site and their enjoyment of family and friends.

Open inside and out—We bumped out the kitchen on two sides—5 ft. 4½ in. at the back of the house and 8 ft. at the side—and added a new dining room (drawings, p. 66). A 3-ft. 6-in. bump out at the back (photo, p. 67) allowed room in the kitchen for a eating nook. The new construction added 200 sq. ft. of kitchen space.

By doing away with upper cabinets, we opened up space in the cooking area for windows and

From *Fine Homebuilding* (December 1992) 78:62-65

The greenhouse effect. By day, plenty of windows and skylights showcase the landscape and make for well-lit work surfaces; by night, track lighting provides illumination. Note the fir trim tacked to the track between the fixtures on the window header. Photo taken at B on floor plan.

skylights (photo above). The new kitchen is open to the rest of the house as well, but the Wallaces can close it off with shutters and doors on the interior wall (photo facing page).

The Wallaces wanted three things from their kitchen: a place to cook, a place to eat meals with the family and a place to entertain. These activities should be related but separate. So I designed a kitchen where cooking, entertaining and sitting/eating areas overlap. The cook is surrounded by 30-in. deep, U-shaped counters, which provide plenty of work surface, but across the counters are the eating nook and the enter-

taining area. The host can stay socially involved while cooking; guests can chat across the living-room pass-through.

All of this had to be built with a budget in mind. Expanding the existing kitchen instead of relocating it and using as much of the old roof as we could saved money. Standard windows, stock cabinets and a little creative thinking also helped keep costs under control.

Design challenges—Having settled on the plan, I could now deal with its problems. First, I was running out of headroom. Extending a roof that

was already at its minimum pitch for skylights left me with a 6-ft. high ceiling at the new eaves wall. But when I checked the Uniform Building Code (UBC), I found that 50% of a kitchen may have a sloped roof below 7 ft. This meant the roof over the counter could be built with its eave 6 ft. off the finished floor. With the 30-in. deep countertop projecting from the exterior wall, headroom at the edge of the counter turned out to be an adequate 7 ft.

I was also concerned with the Wallaces' comfort while their new kitchen was under construction. So we did everything—excavating for the

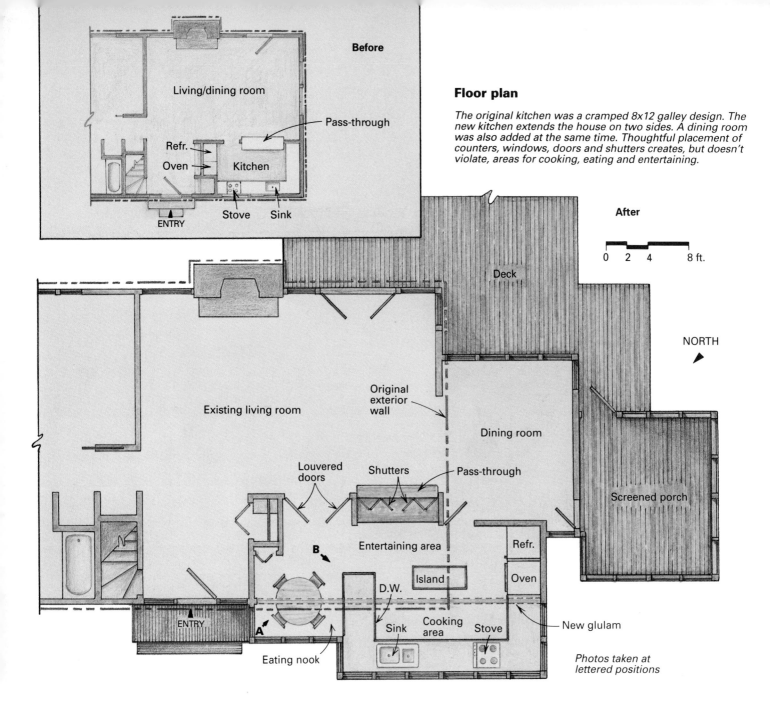

Before

Living/dining room

Pass-through

Refr.

Oven → Kitchen

Stove Sink

ENTRY

Floor plan

The original kitchen was a cramped 8x12 galley design. The new kitchen extends the house on two sides. A dining room was also added at the same time. Thoughtful placement of counters, windows, doors and shutters creates, but doesn't violate, areas for cooking, eating and entertaining.

Deck

After

0 2 4   8 ft.

NORTH

Original exterior wall

Existing living room

Dining room

Louvered doors

Shutters

Pass-through

Screened porch

Entertaining area

Refr.

B

Island

Oven

D.W.

Sink Cooking area Stove

New glulam

ENTRY

A

Eating nook

Photos taken at lettered positions

footings and the 3-ft. crawl space, building the block foundation, running the 2x8 floor joists and framing the walls and the roof—all with the existing exterior wall still in place. The house stayed dry during construction, and it was easier for the builders to maintain the existing roof pitch.

Next we had to align the window framing and the skylight framing. Rough openings for the windows were larger than those for the skylights. The contractors for the job, C&S Builders, laid out and built the eaves wall first. They framed the window openings with doubled trimmer studs between them, then lined up the new rafters on the centerlines of the window framing. The skylights are narrower than the windows, so the rafters could be blocked out to create the rough openings for the skylights. To extend the existing roof, bird's mouths were cut in the new rafters to fit over the top plate of the original eaves wall, which at this point was still in place. The carpenters threaded the new rafters in between the old ones and coaxed them up on edge. Each new common rafter consists of a pair of 2x6s spaced

with ½-in. plywood, like a header, and runs all the way to the ridge beam for added strength.

Finally, there was the problem of insulating the cathedral ceiling. Code requires that newly constructed roofs provide an R-value of 33, which is easily achieved with batt insulation between 2x10 or 2x12 rafters. But the existing roof was framed with 2x6s, and we couldn't afford to tear it off and replace it. Because Jeb planned to reshingle the entire roof, we met the R-33 requirement by using 6-in. batt insulation between the rafters plus 2½-in. rigid insulation (polyisocyanurate panels) layed on the existing roofing (drawing facing page). This was covered with ½-in. plywood screwed through the insulation into the existing sheathing. When this plywood sandwich met the skylight framing, there was a 3½-in. change in level. To bring these two conditions in line, ripped 2xs between pieces of plywood were nailed on top of the doubled 2x6 rafters that framed each skylight opening.

With the framing complete, the builders removed the old kitchen walls. They shored up the

roof with a temporary beam 3 ft. behind the original eaves wall and cut out the studs and the top plate, leaving an open span of 24 ft. The existing house has glulam purlins, so I called for a 6½-in. by 16½-in. glulam to replace the old eaves wall and support the roof. The new beam was only 7ft. 6 in. off the finished floor, so C&S's five-man crew was able to heft the 1,500-lb. glulam into place. Built-up studs at each end support the beam. The glulam works well with the rest of the framing members. The extra-thick rafters and built-up window header create a series of coffers that balances the dimension of the glulam. When cased in fir, the sunlit coffers produce a warm glow from the trim's natural color.

Big countertops, stock cabinets—When we decided to go with skylights and windows instead of upper cabinets, the loss of storage space was minimized in part by making the countertops 30 in. deep. This provided additional work surface and storage at the back of the counters for items previously hidden in cabinets.

Drawings: Bob Goodfellow

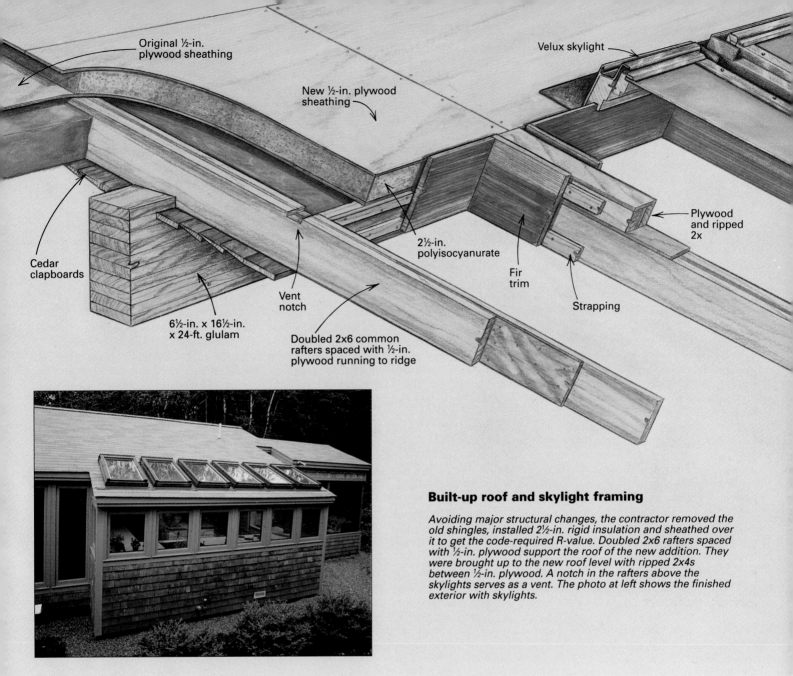

Original ½-in.
plywood sheathing

Velux skylight

New ½-in. plywood
sheathing

Plywood
and ripped
2x

2½-in.
polyisocyanurate

Fir
trim

Cedar
clapboards

Strapping

Vent
notch

6½-in. x 16½-in.
x 24-ft. glulam

Doubled 2x6 common
rafters spaced with ½-in.
plywood running to ridge

Built-up roof and skylight framing

Avoiding major structural changes, the contractor removed the old shingles, installed 2½-in. rigid insulation and sheathed over it to get the code-required R-value. Doubled 2x6 rafters spaced with ½-in. plywood support the roof of the new addition. They were brought up to the new roof level with ripped 2x4s between ½-in. plywood. A notch in the rafters above the skylights serves as a vent. The photo at left shows the finished exterior with skylights.

Custom cabinetry was not realistic for the budget. To receive the oversized countertops, 24-in. stock cabinets were anchored to a 2x4 kicker spiked to the floor 4 in. from the wall, then the cabinets were screwed into the counter. A 2x4 ledger runs along the window sill and supports the extended countertop. Cherry edgings customize the countertop and the stock cabinets. A 24-in. deep island with doors on both sides separates the cooking and entertaining areas. A 30-in. deep peninsula between the cooking area and the eating nook has factory-made custom end and back panels.

We created the pass-through that separates the kitchen from the living room with back-to-back cabinets. On the kitchen side, we used 24-in. deep stock cabinets, but on the living-room side we built a 12-in. deep solid cherry cabinet. This creates a transition between the casual quality of the kitchen and the formal nature of the living room. Louvered shutters, hung in the pass-through opening, provide the option of closing off the kitchen.

Wood from floor to ceiling—For the Wallaces' kitchen, I chose materials that imply a nautical theme congruent with Manchester-By-The-Sea's ocean environment. Boats docked in the nearby harbor are framed with wood beams and have lapstraked hulls. Their decks and rails are often a natural wood finish, with white rigging and hardware in contrast. The kitchen's solid-oak floor, white cabinetry with cherry trim and cedar ceiling punctuated with round, white light fixtures establish the nautical tone. Although an oak floor is not common in a kitchen, I reasoned that it was cheaper than tile, it required no unusual subfloor conditions, and it made a strong continuity with the existing wood floors in the house. The ceiling is actually exterior cedar clapboards nailed to the rafters.

Besides the round light fixtures, we used lots of track lighting, one of the least expensive solutions available for this kitchen design. Track lighting requires only a single power point per track, and additional fixtures, if needed, can be easily plugged into the existing track. Originally, we

wanted sconces at each of the window mullions above the kitchen counters. However, wiring became expensive and complicated and therefore, once again, track lighting proved to be the best solution. The track was mounted horizontally to the window head casing. After placing a fixture above each window mullion, we covered the track with a fir trim board, cut to fit between fixtures, and nailed it through the center of the track where there are no wires. This creates the effect of individual lights for each mullion.

This project shows that trying new ideas is not necessarily expensive. Standard products and sizes ensured a high level of quality at a realistic price—about $85 per sq. ft. The richness of this kitchen comes from sensitivity to the surrounding landscape and from the materials chosen, not from decoration or heroic detailing. ☐

Matthew Adams Longo is an associate architect with Benjamin Thompson and Associates in Cambridge, Mass., and free-lances residential work. Photos by Joel Gardner except where noted.

Custom Kitchen Remodel

From the wrap-around buffets to the built-in breakfast nook, an old kitchen gets a new look

by Paul D. Voelker

Deborah Schultz and Penn Fix were planning an extensive kitchen remodel. They wanted something that would blend with their 1926 California-Moorish home and its high-coved ceilings, niches and arches. Architect/builder Gerry Copeland drew the plans; my role was to collaborate with the owners on the layout details, offer ideas for building materials, and then, with a lot of freedom in detailing, create something unusual and artistic (photo facing page).

After seeing quartersawn oak in the front door and in the floors, I suggested quartersawn oak for the cabinets. And once I'd explained to them the difference between quartersawn oak and the more common plain-sawn oak (see sidebar, p. 73), the Fix-Schultzes agreed. We settled up on the other details –the built-in seating, the roll-out shelves and the tambour-door appliance garage –and my brother, Jerry, and I started work.

Taking the bad with the good—The first challenge was to find quartersawn white oak locally—shipping costs from the East coast are horrendous. After calling several suppliers here in Washington, I located one with some in stock. Of the 500 bd. ft. I received, about 100 was totally worthless—firewood to heat the shop. The supplier agreed to ship an additional 100 ft. at no cost, but there were still some major defects to deal with.

Many of the boards showed sticker stains— black stains deep in the wood caused by using stickers of too high a moisture content. To make matters worse, whoever dried the lumber did not place the stickers directly over each other, which resulted in permanent deflection of some boards—more firewood. Furthermore, the lumber was sawn improperly at the mill, resulting in many boards too thin to dress to a full ¾-in. thickness. As a result of all the defects, 500 bd. ft. yielded about 350 bd. ft. of usable stock.

Jerry and I straightened out most of the remaining stock by clamping it to a straight-line ripping jig (see *FHB* #53, pp. 58-61) and running it through the table saw. Then we ripped most of it into 2½-in. to 3½-in. widths (we saved some wider stock for drawer fronts). We ripped it to narrow widths for

three reasons. First, opposing bends could be glued up to straighten each other out. Second, many boards showed quartersawn figure on one side and appeared rift-sawn on the other. We wanted the quartersawn boards for the highly visible areas like door panels, end panels and countertops. And third, the floor in the dining room was also mixed and we wanted to match it.

Cabinet construction—Our first step in building this set of cabinets was to measure the room, including the locations of windows, doors, radiators, light switches and so forth. Back at the shop we cut story sticks to wall or cabinet-run length and transferred all the pertinent measurements—the location and size of windows, doors, chimney, etc.—to them.

We use story sticks because they eliminate mathematical errors in measuring and give us a standard against which to double-check all dimensions. For instance, we cut a story stick the length of the sink wall, located the windows on the stick and centered the future

Shelf-peg holes are drilled in the side of a wall cabinet with the use of a special sliding-table jig, mounted under the drill press. Working the lever with his knee, Voelker advances the table in evenly spaced increments.

sink-base cabinet under its window. Next we marked 24 in. to the right of the sink for the dishwasher. Then we jumped to the end and located the breakfast-nook seat under the second window. The space between the dishwasher and the seat determined the width of the drawer cabinet. The dimensions of the cabinet to the left of the sink were determined the same way.

Standard cabinet elevations have their own sticks, which we keep for repeated use. These sticks are cut to the height of the cabinet side piece and show the location of dadoes for shelves and for cross supports under drawers. We use these cross supports to stiffen the face of the cabinet, take the bow out of the plywood sides (if there is one) and keep drawer stacks a uniform width, top to bottom. They also can be useful for supporting the drawer slide while fastening it to the cabinet side.

Using the measurements taken from the sticks, we wrote up cutting lists for tops, bottoms, sides and partitions. The pieces were cut from ¾-in. birch plywood and marked with a letter to identify the cabinet to which they belonged. We then put the dado blade in the table saw and did all necessary rabbeting and dadoing (drawing, p. 71).

Next we drilled the shelf-peg holes in the sides of the upper cabinets. This is a common operation in our shop, so we have a special jig for it (photo left). On the feed table under the drill press, we installed a jig that rolls on sliding cabinet-door hardware. On the front edge of the jig, we screwed a shelf standard as an index stop. A spring-loaded kneeboard with a bent screwdriver tip in the end engages holes in the shelf standard to ensure a uniform 1-in. spacing of the peg holes.

We assembled the carcases with Franklin Titebond yellow glue and pneumatic fasteners—staples where they wouldn't show and finish nails where they would. After assembling the cabinet sides, bottoms, partitions and cross members, the cabinets were measured for backs, which were then cut from ¼-in. birch plywood and attached with staples and hot-melt glue. We used oak plywood for the backs of the wrap-around buffets; they

From *Fine Homebuilding* (February 1990) 58:36-41

Curve clamping details

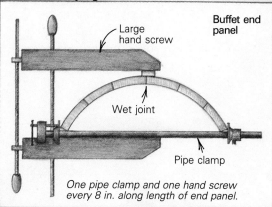

Buffet end panel

- Large hand screw
- Wet joint
- Pipe clamp

One pipe clamp and one hand screw every 8 in. along length of end panel.

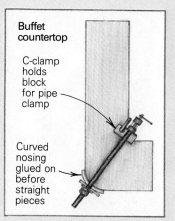

Buffet countertop

- C-clamp holds block for pipe clamp
- Curved nosing glued on before straight pieces

Clamping sequence for half-round countertop

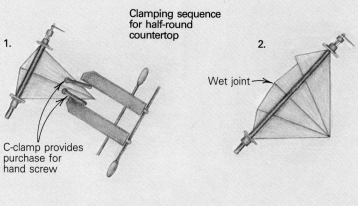

1.

C-clamp provides purchase for hand screw

2.

Wet joint →

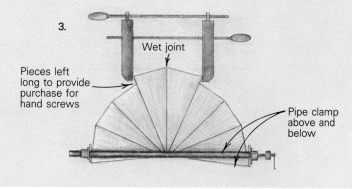

3.

Wet joint

Pieces left long to provide purchase for hand screws

Pipe clamp above and below

The tilt-front bin and the roll-out drawer on full extension slides provide easily accessible storage under the kitchen sink (photo left). Glued up from pie-shaped pieces of quarter-sawn oak, the round counter beside the stove (photo below) was roughed out on the band-saw and finished with a router mounted in a circle-cutting jig. The nosing was cut the same way, but the thin walnut inlay was flexible enough to bend around the curve.

have glass doors so the inside of each cabinet would be fully visible.

Next, base supports were attached and strengthened with glue blocks. The base supports are ¾-in. plywood, 4 in. high and were set back 3½ in. from the finished face of the cabinet. This allowed a 2¾-in. deep toe space after the finished kick was installed. The finished kick covers any shimming of the base cabinets made necessary by uneven floors and provides some leeway (¾ in.) for the finished flooring. We ripped the finished kicks from ¾-in. oak plywood and made it ¼ in. less than the height of the toe space so they could be easily slipped into place. These pieces were stained and lacquered in 8-ft. lengths. They were cut to size on the job and installed by Copeland's crew after the floor tile had been laid.

We faced the carcases with strips of oak ripped and planed to ⅜ in. thick. We used ⅜-in. stock because it is strong enough to scribe where a cabinet butts into a wall and thin enough to be trimmed with a router. We let the facings extend ¹⁄₃₂ in. past the outside edge of the cabinet sides. This created a ¹⁄₁₆-in. gap between adjoining cabinets and permitted a tight face joint when attaching carcases together.

Cabinet doors—Our first step in making the raised-panel doors was to glue up ⅝-in. thick panels, oversize 1 inch in width and 2 inches in length, and set them aside for a week or so to give them a chance to shrink or swell before being cut to finished size. Panels were of randomly selected quartersawn stock to correspond to the oak floor; the owners liked it that way.

In the meantime, we ripped rail and stile stock (once again, slightly oversize) and cut it to length. We cut the rails in each line of cabinets from a single board for continuity of grain and color. Wherever we could, we did the same with adjoining stiles.

Stiles were cut to door height plus ⅛ in., and rails were cut to exact length, plus ¹⁄₁₆ in. The rails were coped (the ends were cut on a shaper to be a negative image of the pattern later shaped on the inside edge of the frame) with a cope and pattern set (#MC-50-030) from the Freeborn Tool Co. (E. 3355 Trent Ave., Spokane, Wash. 99202-4459). That removed ¹⁄₃₂ in. from each end, shortening them by ¹⁄₁₆ in. overall.

Next we cut an ogee pattern on the inside edges of the stiles and rails using the shaper. This molding process also cut the panel groove in the edge of the stock. Then we moved the stock to the table saw and ripped it to 2⁹⁄₁₆ in. wide. This extra width, along with the ⅛ in. added to the stile length, allowed for trimming ¹⁄₁₆ in. off the door on all four sides to clean and square it up, resulting in 2½-in. wide rails and stiles. We take these extra steps because on most jobs we use matched rails and stiles, and one ruined piece may mean a lot of extra work.

The pieces were moved to our horizontal-boring machine and drilled for dowels at the

Drawings: Michael Mandarano

joints. We once used two dowels per joint, but have found that one is plenty if done right. We use ⅜-in. dowels, fluted spirally and longitudinally. As with shaping and coping, we keep the stock face down so that any variation in wood thickness will not misalign the cope with the pattern.

Next we returned to the panels, which we cut ⅛ in. undersize to allow a ¹⁄₁₆-in. gap between the edges of the panel and the bottom of the groove in the door frame. This gap allows the panel to shrink and swell during seasonal humidity changes.

We sanded the panels flat and shaped the edges with a panel-raising cutter on the shaper. Then we sanded the edge profile with a finish sander and eased the edges for easier installation. Because the panel fits snugly into the grooves, the easiest sequence for assembly seems to be stile, rail, panel, second rail, second stile. We centered the panel in the frame by wedging a short piece of ⅛-in. thick balsa wood into the bottom of each groove before the panel was installed. After they had been glued up, the doors were cut to final size, and the edges and corners were routed with a ³⁄₁₆-in. radius quarter-round bit and finish sanded.

Drawers and tambours—We made the sides, front and back of the drawer carcase of ½-in. ApplePly (States Industries, Inc., P. O. Box 7037, Eugene, Ore. 97401)—an excellent product. It's extremely dense nine-ply alder-core plywood, with no voids. It comes in a variety of face veneers; I use maple. We used ¼-in. birch plywood for the bottoms. The sides were rabbeted to accept the front and back, with the bottom held in a dado set up ¼ in. from the bottom. We glued and stapled the drawer carcases together. The bottoms were fixed in place with ⅝-in. brads. Rather than install adjustable shelves behind the double-door base cabinets, I built roll-out drawers for them (left photo, facing page).

The drawer faces are simply solid oak boards with the corners and edges radiused to match the doors. Whenever possible, adjoining or stacked drawer faces were cut from a single board. We attached the faces to the drawer carcase with Mepla drawer-face adjusters (Mepla, Inc., P. O. Box 1469, High Point, N. C. 27261). These are 25mm dia. by ½-in. thick ribbed plastic inserts that house a steel nut (detail drawing, this page). They are installed in a 25-mm dia. hole drilled ½-in. deep in the backside of the drawer faces. After the adjusters are tapped into place (friction fit), a machine screw is run through the drawer carcase into the nuts in the adjusters. They allow about ³⁄₁₆-in. movement of the face until the screws are tightened, which allows enough play to adjust the faces precisely.

For this set of cabinets we used KV 8505 side-mount drawer slides, full extension plus 1-in. overtravel (Knape & Vogt Manufacturing Co., 2700 Oak Industrial Dr. N. E., Grand Rapids, Mich. 49505). Admittedly, these are overkill for cabinet drawers because the slides

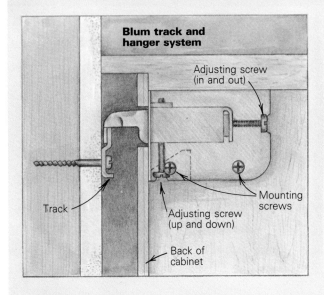

Blum track and hanger system

Adjusting screw (in and out)

Track

Adjusting screw (up and down)

Mounting screws

Back of cabinet

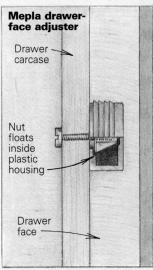

Mepla drawer-face adjuster

Drawer carcase

Nut floats inside plastic housing

Drawer face

Cabinet construction

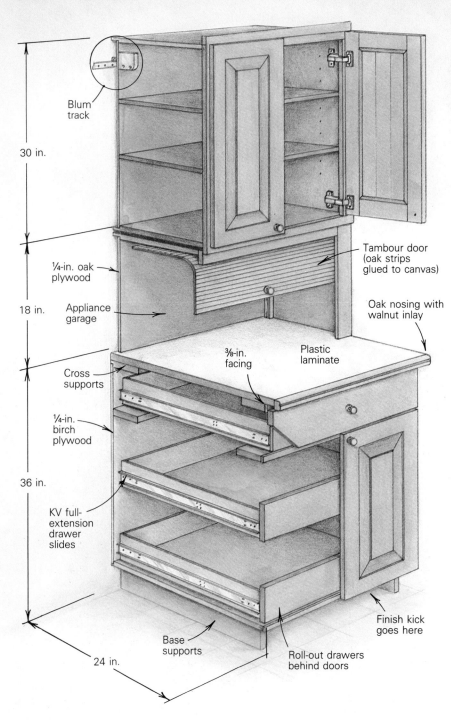

Blum track

30 in.

¼-in. oak plywood

18 in.

Appliance garage

Cross supports

¼-in. birch plywood

36 in.

KV full-extension drawer slides

24 in.

Base supports

Tambour door (oak strips glued to canvas)

Oak nosing with walnut inlay

⅜-in. facing

Plastic laminate

Finish kick goes here

Roll-out drawers behind doors

Built-in window seats and a freestanding trestle table create the breakfast nook at the back end of the kitchen (photo above). The walnut grilles behind the righthand seat back and in the toe space allow heat from a hidden radiator to circulate. Although the wrap-around buffets and the round counter beside the stove have oak tops, the main work areas, such as around the sink (photo below), have plastic-laminate countertops, which are more serviceable.

have a load rating of 150 lb., but they are excellent, heavy-duty, smooth-acting slides, allowing easy access to the back of drawers. They are simply screwed to the sides of the drawers and to the insides of the cabinets.

Most people store their blenders, toasters and other appliances on top of the counter, so we built an additional cabinet between the upper and base cabinets, just to the right of the stove, expressly for this purpose (left photo, p. 70). It's called an appliance garage, and like a garage, it has an overhead door. I made the tambour door, using ¼-in. thick by ¾-in. wide strips of oak glued to a piece of canvas. Rather than routing a track in the cabinet sides, I used plastic track from Outwater Plastic Industries (4 Passaic St., Woodridge, N. J. 07075). The track is dark brown, comes in straight and curved sections, and is simply nailed in place.

Wrap-around buffets—Where the dining-room buffets wrap around the sides of the arched opening into the kitchen, we had to make curved end panels for the two cabinets. Oak veneer glued to curved plywood backing would have been the easiest construction method, but would not have matched the door panels. Instead, we glued up the curved panels from 3-in. rippings of solid stock, clamping them in pairs (with a combination of pipe clamps and large hand screws) until the full curve was completed (drawing, p. 70).

The outsides were sanded to a smooth curve with a belt sander run diagonally—an effective method if done carefully. We then cut the pieces to length on the table saw and routed a rabbet on the inside of the ends to accept a ¾-in. plywood top and bottom. Then we attached the unit to the buffet. The process was fairly time-consuming, but well worth it.

Countertops—Although the main work areas have plastic-laminate countertops (bottom photo) with ¾-in. medium-density particleboard substrate and oak nosing, there were four tops made from 4/4 oak: the breakfast-nook table, a half-round top for the cabinet to the left of the range, and one each for the two wrap-around buffets. The basic construction was pretty straightforward. First, we edge-glued the boards (Titebond, again) into rough size, sanded the glued-up panels flat and trimmed the edges on the table saw. The curves were then roughed out on the bandsaw and trimmed to final size with a 3-hp plunge router attached to a circle-cutting jig with an adjustable pivoting arm.

Next we ripped the 8/4 nosing, glued and splined it to the tops. The curved nosings were roughed out on the bandsaw in quarter-arc segments, then they were clamped to the workbench and the inside edges were routed with the same jig. We carefully shortened the cutting arc by exactly ½ in. to compensate for the width of the ½-in. dia. router bit. We mitered the ends of the curves, adjusting the angle slightly as needed for a tight fit, then glued and pipe-clamped the pieces in place.

We attached the straight edging pieces in the same way. The outside edges of the curved nosings were cut with the router and jig after the tops were assembled.

After sanding the nosings flat we routed the groove for the walnut inlay using a face inlay bit (Norfield Tools and Supplies, P. O. Box 459, Chico, Calif. 95927), which cuts a channel ½ in. wide by ³/₁₆ in. deep. We then cut and planed walnut strips ⁷/₃₂ in. thick by a hair over ½ in. wide. We sanded the inside edges slightly, cut them to length, put glue in the channel and carefully pounded in the strips, using a block of wood and a hammer. With the snug fit, no clamps were needed. The thin walnut would bend around the larger radiuses, but we had to bandsaw curved pieces for the smaller ones. We sanded the inlay flush, routed a ½-in. radius on the top and bottom of the nosings and finish-sanded all the tops.

The half-round top to the left of the stove differed from the others in that the front was made of wedge-shaped pieces of solid oak (right photo, p. 70). The wedges were glued together in pairs, then the pairs were glued together (drawing, p. 70), as with the curved end panels. The piece was then sanded smooth, the curve roughed out on the bandsaw and finished with the router and circle-cutting jig.

As a general rule, when working with solid wood it is not advisable to band end grain as we did by running solid nosing on the ends of the countertops. Wood movement is greater across the grain than it is along it, so banded end grain will often crack, split, or swell and cause the edging joint to fail. We got away with it because the oak was quartersawn, dried to 6.5% moisture content, and the length of the banded end grain was, for the most part, relatively short.

The breakfast nook—Dimensions for the window seats in the breakfast nook were adapted from guidelines in *Architectural Graphic Standards* (John Wiley & Sons, Inc., 605 3rd Ave, New York, N. Y. 10158, 1988; 8th edition). The guidelines call for a seat height of 18 in., so we built the seats 16 in. high, allowing for 1 in. of compression when sitting on a firm 3-in. thick cushion. The top of the back is 36 in. high to correspond to the height of the kitchen countertop. The front facing was extended ½ in. above the seat to prevent the seat cushion from sliding forward. We built the seat as a single unit, but made the back in two pieces and screwed them to the seat on the job site.

Because there was an existing radiator behind one of the seats, we made walnut grilles and installed one in the kick space under the seat and one in the top behind the seat to allow for air circulation.

Instead of using hinged tops to gain access to the storage space under the seats, we opted for drawers, which were constructed in the same fashion as the other drawers. The only differences were that the window-seat drawers had angled front faces, and the oak faces were extended about ½ in. below the bottom of the seat to be used as handles,

since we didn't want any protruding hardware for people to bump with their legs (top photo, facing page).

Finishing and installation—To finish the cabinets, we first wiped on Watco natural oil and let it stand for a few minutes before wiping the surface dry. It's important that the oiled wood be allowed to dry for at least three days before lacquering, otherwise the oil interferes

Quartersawn oak

A cross section of a tree will show the obvious annual rings and the less visible medullary rays, which are groups of cells that conduct moisture to and from the sapwood. For economic reasons, most lumber is plain-sawn—cut from a tree by squaring a log and cutting several boards from one side, then rotating the log 90° and repeating the process. An end section of a plain-sawn board will show the annual rings roughly parallel to the face and the medullary rays perpendicular to the face.

Quartersawn lumber can be sawn from a log in several ways. One way is to quarter the log, then saw the quarters into boards with the face of each board being at right angles (or nearly so) to the annual rings. The medullary rays are then nearly parallel to the face. These rays are well pronounced in oak so that when they appear on the face of the board at a slight angle they produce the beautiful figure for which quartersawn oak is so well known.

In addition to being beautiful, quartersawn lumber is also very stable. When wood dries, the greatest shrinkage occurs in the direction of the annual rings. A plain-sawn board will experience the most shrinkage in width, with very little in thickness and a negligible amount in length. A quartersawn board, on the other hand, will shrink mostly in thickness and very little in width. As a result, tops and panels laid up of quartersawn boards will be very stable. Also, a plain-sawn board upon drying and shrinking may cup, whereas a quartersawn board will not. —*P. D. V.*

with the lacquer and results in a blemished surface. Next we applied three coats of pre-catalyzed semi-gloss clear lacquer—a durable finish—lightly sanding between coats.

We installed the wall cabinets first, using the Blum track and hanger system (Julius Blum, Inc., Blum Industrial Park, Highway 16—Lowesville, Stanley, N. C. 28164). The hangers are fastened inside the cabinets in the upper corners, and a metal arm protrudes through a rectangular hole cut in the back (left detail drawing, p. 71). The track is screwed to the wall, and the cabinets are simply hung on the track. The hangers, which slide along the track, have adjustment screws to move them up and down, in and out. With adjoining cabinets, we hung them loosely on the track and screwed them together with 1¼-in. drywall screws run through the sides, just behind the facings. Then we snugged them to the wall as a unit. The hanger system simplifies installation considerably, saving more than enough time to pay for itself (hangers cost me $1.70 each and rail runs $5 for 6 ft.).

The base cabinets were installed after the uppers. We removed the doors and drawers, set the carcases in place, shimmed them up as necessary to keep everything level and screwed adjoining units together. These assemblies were then screwed to the wall. We checked the faces with a framing square to make sure that the cabinets hadn't been twisted when fastened to the wall. Where they had, we shimmed between the back of the cabinet and the wall or between the floor and the base of the cabinet. If the cabinet faces are out of square it is difficult to adjust the doors and drawers for equal spacing between them.

We then set the countertops in place, scribing them to the wall with 36-grit paper in a belt sander. Since the backsplash covered any small gaps, a tight fit was needed only where the front edge of the top touched the wall. We fastened the tops to the cabinets from underneath, screwing through the cross members.

After the tops were set we replaced the drawers and doors, adjusting for even spacing between them. We used Blum concealed hinges with opening angles of 125° or 170°, depending on the application. Their use requires boring a 35mm dia. hole in the back of the door, and they are considerably more expensive than conventional cabinet hinges. But the advantages are several. The door can be removed simply by pulling up a little tab, and reinstalled by snapping the hinge back onto the hinge plate, which makes for easier moving and installation. And the hinges are adjustable in six directions—an important feature when you consider that there is a ⅛ in. or so gap between all doors and drawer faces.

Next we installed the door and drawer pulls (through both the drawer face and carcase), put plastic caps (also from Outwater Plastic Industries) over the heads of the visible screws, then cleaned and polished everything.   □

Paul D. Voelker is a cabinetmaker in Chewelah, Washington.

The Heart of the House

Merging a small kitchen and a separate breakfast room

by Bill Mastin

The story began when Tom and Kathy bought a two-story house in one of the older neighborhoods in Oakland, California. Its Spanish Colonial style was generally quite to their liking, with heavy wood beams and a dark tile floor in the entry hall. But the parts of the house where they and their teenage daughter Maja anticipated spending the most time were lacking. The existing kitchen had barely adequate storage space, felt cramped, and was isolated from the formal dining room, the breakfast room and the backyard. Usable outdoor space was at a premium on their upslope lot, but we saw the potential for a pleasant garden area in the several terraces that divided the backyard into narrow flowerbeds. Unfortunately, the terraces were reached by a circuitous route that passed through a dreary doorway next to the garbage cans on the concrete stoop.

So the questions that complicated the story were: How do you transform a small kitchen into a room that aspires to become the heart of the house? How can cramped spaces feel more open? How can a steep backyard be made more accessible?

Planning for openness—The answers to some of these questions are obvious: if you want more openness, you take out a wall. But how much wall do you remove? The first solution that I envisioned included a pass-through opening between the kitchen and breakfast room (drawing below). This option would have allowed the existing wood floor and cabinets to remain in the breakfast room and held the potential for counterspace and storage below the pass-through. Also, the wall separating the breakfast room from the kitchen concealed a forced-air heater riser that fed the upstairs registers. If we kept the existing wall, we would probably save a couple of thousand dollars by not having to match floors and cabinets and move heating ducts. While this approach had its practical benefits, the pass-through didn't fit Kathy's image of a large, open space—a "farmhouse kitchen." We ended up following her instinct, therefore, and created a 7-ft. wide opening crowned by a wood beam (photo facing page). A new tile floor linked the kitchen and breakfast room.

This "one big room" solution promised more spaciousness, but meant we'd have to find other places for storage, and create a suitable beam over the opening to match those found throughout the house. We found our storage space in the hallway near the basement stair (floor plan, p. 76). The washer and dryer originally occupied a spot next to the flue—near the back door. We moved them to the basement and converted their places to pantry space. The larger of the two pantries has heavy-duty pull-out bins that can hold a lot of canned goods.

Tying the kitchen to the yard—The connection between the garden and the kitchen reflected an era that relegated the rear of the house to utility functions, not socializing. Flanked by steps on both sides, the rear stoop was a precarious little perch at the crossroads of three paths. The paths stayed, but we did away with the awkward stair topography by building a small deck over them. The kitchen floor now flows out to the deck, making a smoother transition to the yard (floor plan, p. 76).

This connection with the outdoors was further emphasized by the height of the new windows on the back wall of the kitchen. Skylights were precluded by the upstairs floor, so we made the new windows taller than normal, reaching within 4 in. of the 8-ft. 4-in. ceiling. This significantly increased the feeling of spaciousness because it made it possible to catch a glimpse of the upper yard from the kitchen. The high windows also allow filtered afternoon sun to fall across the floor to form shadow patterns on the tile pavers.

My experience has taught me to shelter doors exposed to the weather (such as this one) with some type of canopy to keep them from leaking. Such canopies are usually opaque, and I had originally envisioned this one covered with a couple of rows of mission-barrel tiles. But we wanted our canopy to let in the light and to become a gracious portal to the garden. The solution turned out to be rustic redwood brackets (photo, p. 76) topped with a translucent fiberglass panel called Filon (B. P. Chemicals Inc., Filon Products, 12333 S. Van Ness, Hawthorne, Calif. 90250; 213-757-5141). Woodworker Richard Shaw shaped the awning brackets from 4x material and tied them to the existing wall with steel angles and lag bolts (bottom drawing, p. 76).

Selecting the colors—The colors we chose are sympathetic to the existing tile and wood, but lighter in value. The predominant color in the two rooms is the rich honey tone of the Douglas fir cabinetry, shelves and trim. The pav-

Pass-through opening

Removing a wall allowed a once isolated breakfast room to share space with this recently remodeled kitchen in Oakland, California. The wood and tile surfaces are in keeping with Spanish Colonial details found throughout the house.

ers are also warm to the eye, but we didn't want to overuse the tone; it's important to know when to stop with a color, and sometimes it takes a judgment call as things are being assembled. In this kitchen, we had imagined facing the doors of the new refrigerator with a pair of Douglas fir panels to unify it with the new cabinetry. Once the unit was pushed in next to the cabinets, however, the consensus was, "Enough warmth, already!" So we decided not to use the wood panels, continuing instead with the grey plastic laminate already picked out for the main countertop. No one's regretted it.

Balancing the warmth of all the Douglas fir are fields of creamy white on the walls and ceilings, grey windows and doors, and a strip of deep blue tiles on the counter backsplash. This ribbon of blue tiles makes its way atop the base cabinets around the room—above the stove, and atop the base cabinets in the hall and breakfast room. To accent the room further, we worked a spare pattern of blue tiles turned at 45° into the field of pavers.

Refining the details—One of the first challenges facing contractor Bill Jetton was to fashion a rustic beam to span the opening between the breakfast room and the kitchen. He knew that a recently milled 10x10 purchased at the local lumberyard would almost surely twist and shrink soon after installation, so he searched instead for a salvaged timber. At a used building-materials yard, he found one that had seen previous duty as a highway shoring timber. The beam was dry, but gouged and dirty. Jetton had it cleaned up by a sandblasting outfit and cut off a couple of 18-in. pieces for the corbels. We took the pattern for the corbels' decorative profiles from one of the existing beams in the entry hall, and Jetton cut out the shapes on a big bandsaw. Then both beam and corbels were sealed with a couple of coats of clear lacquer before installation. The beam is decorative, and it's affixed by way of bolts to the 4x8 header above it. The corbels were then toenailed to the new beam. Once the trimmers were in-

stalled beneath the corbels and the drywall was furred out to give the impression of a thick wall, the beam had the visual bearing to appear old and not out of place.

There are at least four different casing details around windows and doors throughout the house. The one that seemed right for the kitchen (found conveniently at the existing breakfast-room window) is a head and jamb formed by curved plaster. To build them, our drywall and paint expert Dave Richards beveled the framing members to conform to the curve. Then he covered them with expanded metal lath and shaped the layers of wet plaster with a sheet-metal screed he made to form the 3-in. radius. With this detail complete, the daylight in the room softened, creating just the feeling we wanted.

Paver floor—Hexagonal paver tiles cover the original entry and hall of the house, so it seemed quite natural to cover the floor of the new kitchen and breakfast room with them.

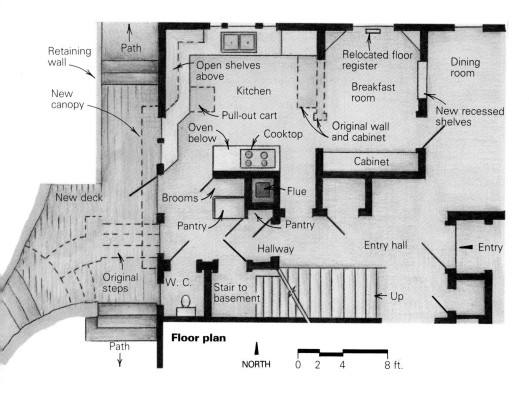

Floor plan

Retaining wall

Path

New canopy

New deck

New recessed shelves

Open shelves above

Kitchen

Pull-out cart

Oven below

Cooktop

Brooms

Pantry

Pantry

Original steps

Path

W. C.

Stair to basement

Hallway

Relocated floor register

Breakfast room

Original wall and cabinet

Cabinet

Flue

Entry hall

Dining room

Entry

Up

NORTH   0 2 4   8 ft.

Rather than use hexagonal tiles, however, we chose to use 12-in. by 12-in. square tiles for simplicity and to emphasize the boundaries of the rooms.

I must admit that some of the highest anxiety on the job came with the installation of the pavers and the way we colored them. Jetton had his tile sub install the raw Mexican pavers, with the idea that the water-base pigment could be applied later once we'd seen the whole floor alongside the new wood cabinets. The theory was sound, but applying pigment is an additive process, and it has to be done with a very light touch. Also, the tiles look darker when they are wet, so you can spend plenty of time waiting for them to dry out to see their true colors. Sure enough, we went too far with it, and the tiles ended up being too orange. Our tile sub brought us back to square one by using an orbital sander to take the tiles back to their original pinkish color, and we started over. It goes almost without saying that the next time I got involved in a paver-tile floor, I recommended prefinished tiles. Tinting them *before* they're installed is another option.

Cabinets and floating shelves—Our cabinetmaker John Sitko followed the basic layout of the counters and cabinets that I had devised, adding furniture-grade touches here and there to elevate them above the ordinary. In

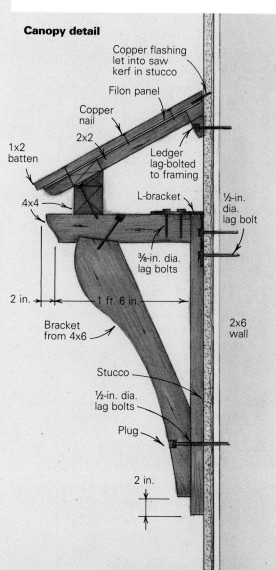

Canopy detail

Copper flashing let into saw kerf in stucco

Filon panel

Copper nail

1x2 batten

2x2

Ledger lag-bolted to framing

4x4

L-bracket

½-in. dia. lag bolt

⅜-in. dia. lag bolts

2 in.

1 ft. 6 in.

Bracket from 4x6

2x6 wall

Stucco

½-in. dia. lag bolts

Plug

2 in.

Shelter and sunlight. Natural light is in short supply along the back wall of the house, so architect Mastin called for a canopy over the door with a roof of translucent fiberglass.

particular, the heavy bullnose along the counter and the lighter weight edging above the toe space help to relate the cabinets to the rounded plaster jambs.

In the interest of not cluttering the space we decided against an island counter between the stove and the sink. Tom and Kathy thought a small pull-out cart would be useful, however, for occasions when extra chopping space was required. Sitko built the cart from my sketch—a simple design with a maple top and open storage below mounted on casters, so it could be moved where needed. Contrary to our intention, it has stayed more or less permanently parked in its space under the counter. When they began using the kitchen, Tom and Kathy found that a slightly longer chopping block they already had was more useful. There's a lesson about utility and portability in this: the chopping table they use is open underneath, so it doesn't affect the feeling of spaciousness the way a fixed island cabinet would, or even the more substantial roll-away cart that never gets used.

Our openness extends to the storage above the counters. Tom and Kathy wanted to avoid closed cabinets, preferring instead to look at the detail of their best crockery and the spines of their favorite cookbooks. Our goal became sleek shelves with no visible means of support (photo below right).

The L-shaped shelves are 2x12 Douglas fir boards mitered at the corners. To anchor them securely at the miters, Sitko glued the pairs of shelves together with three Lamello wafer splines and a pair of threaded rods that reach across the miter (drawing below). To support the short legs of the shelves, hidden grooves cut into the back edges of the shelves fit over ledgers affixed to the wall. The long legs of the shelves bear on the 6-in. stubs of 12-in. by ½-in. dia. lag bolts with their heads removed. The bolts were driven into the studs after the drywall had been hung. Sitko made sure they were horizontal by drilling a ½-in. dia. guide hole in a 6x6 block with a drill press. Held flush against the drywall, the guide block made it easy to drill the pilot holes for the lag bolts.

Because the shelves had to be slid onto the hidden ledger, slots had to be cut in the back of the long shelves to accommodate the bolts as the shelf made its travel. Sitko used the drill press with a ½-in. dia. bit to cut 6-in. deep slots, 1½ in. wide in the backs of the shelves. He next scribed each shelf to match the contours of the wall. Finally, before placing them onto the bolts and sliding them onto the ledgers, Sitko packed each slot with Bondo, a commonly available auto-body putty. The Bondo filled the remaining space in the slots as the shelves were driven home, making a sturdy installation that hasn't budged. □

Bill Mastin is an architect living in Oakland, California.

Plan of open shelves

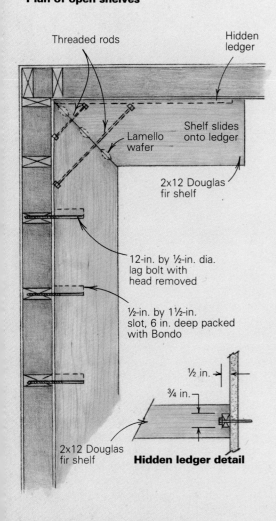

Threaded rods

Hidden ledger

Lamello wafer

Shelf slides onto ledger

2x12 Douglas fir shelf

12-in. by ½-in. dia. lag bolt with head removed

½-in. by 1½-in. slot, 6 in. deep packed with Bondo

½ in.

¾ in.

2x12 Douglas fir shelf

Hidden ledger detail

Pots, cookbooks and coffee cups are stored on a trio of open shelves with hidden supports. The bullnose trim on the cabinets and shelves reinforces the rounded feel of the window jambs.

New Kitchen for an Old House

Cherry cabinets form an island where cooking is the center of attention

by Philip S. Sollman

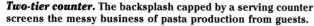

Two-tier counter. The backsplash capped by a serving counter screens the messy business of pasta production from guests.

Island kitchen. The freestanding cherry cabinets perfectly suit the lifestyle of the owners, who love to cook and entertain. The kitchen works like a bar in a restaurant. Guests can gather around on the outside without being in the way of those working on the inside.

I don't usually take three years to design a kitchen. But Gerry Lang and Jennifer Tucker had an existing kitchen that worked and they kept inviting me over for wonderful meals of homemade pasta and wine, during which we would discuss the design of the new kitchen. I encouraged them to take their time, not to rush the process, and offered to come over for as many meals as it took.

Lang is a great cook and an enthusiastic host, so the new kitchen was bound to be the hub of social activity. Lang and Tucker wanted to talk with guests while cooking, but not feel crowded by them. We decided to keep guests entirely out of the kitchen by making the work area small, but the views into the kitchen expansive. This meant the kitchen couldn't be obscured by a refrigerator or by overhead cabinets. Also, Lang collects old photographs, so he wanted to preserve the wall space surrounding the kitchen for hanging them; this ruled out overhead storage. Being so exposed, the kitchen had to look good, too. From the outside we wanted it to look like a piece of furniture; from the inside we wanted it to work efficiently.

All of these elements created several design problems. Views toward the kitchen counters had to be screened from guests seated in the living and dining areas. Also, overhead stor-

age space had to be recouped somewhere else. And finally, we had to find a place for the refrigerator.

An island kitchen—The final plan included freestanding base cabinets rimmed by a two-tier countertop: a lower one for working and an upper one for serving (the upper counter also screens the lower counter). The refrigerator stands just outside the working core, recessed into a 7-ft. long wall with cabinets above and beside it. By creating perimeter corridors around the kitchen, we eliminated traffic flow through it. Essentially, the kitchen works like a bar where guests can gather on

From *Fine Homebuilding* (December 1991) 71:42-45

one side without getting in the way of cooks working on the other side (photo above).

With a freestanding kitchen, providing access to the inside corners of base cabinets proved to be easy: we filled the corners with drawers that open to the dining room and to a corridor behind the range. The deep drawers make up for some of the lost overhead storage.

Commercial sink and range—A freestanding commercial sink, which Lang got second-hand, stretches 7 ft. along one wall of the kitchen. With a 12-in. high backsplash on the back and both sides, it was beautiful but threatened to dominate the kitchen. To remedy this,

I surrounded the sink with cabinetry and matched adjacent countertops to the level of the backsplash.

A serious cook, Lang chose a commercial six-burner gas range (Garland Commercial Industries, Inc., 185 E. South St., Freeland, Pa. 18224; 717-636-1000). Because we knew it would put out a lot of heat, we placed the range as far away as possible from the living/dining area. Plain cherry panels, which cover the back of the range, are removable so that the range can be pulled for servicing.

In order to come flush with the raised vent panel along the back of the range, the upper counter on this side of the kitchen had to be

18 in. above the lower one. This added height gave me enough space to build a shallow spice rack beneath the upper counter (photo facing page).

Behind the spice shelf was enough space for a wire raceway with an outlet every 12 in. and a light track (Lightolier, Inc., 100 Lighting Way, Secaucus, N. J. 07096-1508; 201-864-3000), studded with small incandescent bulbs. These provide working light at countertop level without illuminating the whole room.

Beading: variations on a theme—Throughout its 160 years, this old farmhouse had undergone many changes, few of which were

Before painting. Sollman used electrican's tape and a screen-splining tool to mask the valleys on either side of the drawer beads.

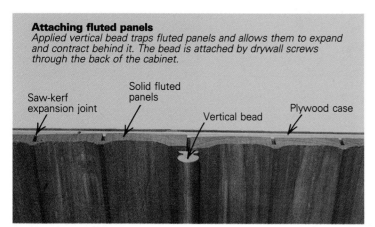

Attaching fluted panels
Applied vertical bead traps fluted panels and allows them to expand and contract behind it. The bead is attached by drywall screws through the back of the cabinet.

Saw-kerf expansion joint

Solid fluted panels

Vertical bead

Plywood case

Drawering a bead. Here, black wire pulls are integrated into the horizontal beads that adorn the drawers. Rather than metal drawer slides, these drawers have grooves in their sides that ride on ¾-in. wood strips screwed to the cabinet sides.

well executed. Soon after moving in, Lang and Tucker completely gutted the place (they had to sleep in the barn for four months). Except for the beaded edge detail on the exposed underside of the floorboards, the timber frame lacked any embellishment. I subsequently used the bead as a decorative element elsewhere in the house, and we felt beads should also carry over into the kitchen design. I used beaded detailing around the nosing of the upper counter, on the drawer faces, between cabinets and between sections of the fluted panels that decorate the backside of the cabinets.

I built the basic casework using ¾-in. plywood fastened together with biscuit joinery and drywall screws. To save money on materials, I used cherry plywood only where the cabinet interiors were exposed, and used birch plywood where they were hidden (partitions between drawers and under countertops, for instance). The vertical dividing panels between cabinets were edged with solid cherry and then routed with a ⅜-in. radius beading bit.

Drawers and doors—I tailored the drawers to fit the most frequently used items. For instance, the top drawer beside the stove is big enough to hold a large frying pan. Four separate banks of drawers fill in the "ell" to the right of the range. The cabinets that separate the kitchen from the dining area feature conventional storage space behind doors.

I like to integrate handles and pulls into cabinet design. On these cabinets, a ⁵⁄₁₆-in. dia. bead, painted black, runs along the top edge of the drawers. The number of horizontal beads on each drawer increases from one on the top drawers to two on the middle drawers and three on the bottom drawers (photo above right). This sets up a pleasing horizontal rhythm. Into these beads I set black wire pulls: the pulls become extensions of the beads. For each drawer, I mounted the pull in the center of the bottom-most bead. This kept the mounting screws away from the fragile top edge of the drawer. Mounting the pulls as low as possible also keeps knuckles and fingernails from getting crunched if the drawer above isn't fully closed. On the upper drawers, which have only a single bead, I routed the bead 1 in. down from the top edge.

I have never liked metal drawer slides. I think wooden slides look better and work just as well. On these drawers, I routed ¾-in. slots into the sides and screwed ¾-in. wood runners to the cabinet sides. It's a simple system that works just fine. I assembled the drawers out of cherry, with half-blind dovetails in front and full dovetails in back. Half-in. plywood forms the drawer bottoms.

It was important for the appearance of the kitchen that the drawer faces fit very closely, yet I had to maintain enough clearance around them that they wouldn't bind against each oth-

er or against the case. To accomplish this, I cut the drawer faces a bit oversize and cut the front dovetails deep enough to allow the drawer face to flare out along its edges. A bit of delicate belt-sanding after assembling finished this flare nicely. In all, I built 34 drawers, and as you might guess, they took a long time.

I glued up cherry planks for the cabinet doors and ran the grain horizontally to minimize binding caused by shrinkage and expansion. Cherry-plywood doors were ruled out because we didn't think the thin veneer would hold up under traffic. I could have cut my own veneers and laminated them over plywood, but that would have been too labor-intensive and too costly. This grain pattern runs continuously from one door to another, interrupted only by the black vertical beads.

After gluing up the doors, I cut horizontal saw kerfs into the backs but stopped the kerfs short of the doors' edges. These kerfs act as expansion joints for seasonal movement of the wood. Vertical cleats screwed to the inside of the doors make up for the strength lost to the saw kerfs. I cut horizontal beads into the top and bottom edges of the doors, and installed wire pulls into the beads along the top.

Painting the beads—Except for the bead on the upper counter, all the beads were spray-painted with black enamel to contrast the warm-figured cherry. To assure a glossy,

Cook's-eye view. The kitchen is open to the living/dining area, but the lower—working—countertops are screened from guests by the upper counters. The lower counters are of a manmade material called Fireslate, which is composed largely of portland cement and is highly heat resistant.

smooth bead, I finished the cabinets and drawers first, using Waterlox Transparent and Waterlox Satin Polyurethane (Waterlox Chemical and Coatings Corp., 9808 Meech Ave., Cleveland, Ohio 44105; 216-641-4877).

When the time came to paint the beads, I masked the area between the beads carefully because I wanted to paint only the beads themselves, not the valleys between them. Through trial and error, I finally found that with a splining tool (used to install screening in doors and windows), I could roll plastic electrical tape between the beads (top left photo, facing page). Then I trimmed away the excess with a utility knife, masked the rest of the drawer or door with newspaper and spray-painted the beads.

Fluted panels—Because the cabinets are essentially freestanding, their exposed backsides had to be dressed up. The design called for cherry panels with vertical flutes, positioned between black vertical beads. The panels are made up of ⅞-in. thick cherry boards, glued up with biscuits. I positioned the biscuits toward the back edge of each board so the router wouldn't hit them when I began fluting.

To add interest to the overall composition, I varied the width of the flutes across each group, or wall, of panels. The flutes on either end of a given wall are the widest, and those in the middle are the narrowest. This meant that the spacing of each panel had to be marked carefully before routing. More passes with the router were required as the width of each flute increased. I used various sizes of core-box bits to do this, and ground a scraper to finish the bottom of the flutes.

After the panels were sanded and finished, I cut a series of deep saw kerfs into the back of the panels where the ridges of the flutes occurred. This prevents any cupping of the wide solid-wood panels. The completed panels stand side by side against the ¾-in. plywood backs of the cabinets. The black vertical beads, which I milled individually on a router table, cover the joints between panels and hold the panels in place (bottom left photo, facing page). The beads are attached to the case from behind by drywall screws. Because the beads overlap the edges of the fluted panels, dimensional changes go unnoticed. I provided the cabinets with a firm-footed appearance by running a generous baseboard around the outside. This provided a small horizontal ledge into which the black vertical beads terminate.

A couple of countertops—The upper countertop runs around three sides of the kitchen (four if you count the windowsill over the sink), capping the black vertical beads and fluted panels. I built this counter out of 1¼-in thick solid cherry and cut a large bead in the outside edge.

I couldn't resist cutting a curve into the edge of the cherry counter that faces the dining area. I knew people would congregate along this counter and felt the curve would be a little friendlier.

After considerable research, Lang decided on a manmade material called Fireslate for the lower countertops and backsplashes (Fireslate 2, Inc., Hamel Rd., Lewiston, Me. 04240; 207-784-8746). Composed largely of portand cement, Fireslate has been marketed for years as a material for laboratory countertops, but it's also used for kitchen counters, flooring, thresholds and windowsills. Fireslate is available in grey, green, brown and white. Lang chose the dark grey finish because it complements the black highlights in the cabinetry.

Highly heat resistant, Fireslate runs about $18/sq. ft., making it more expensive than plastic laminate but considerably less expensive than solid-surface materials. On the downside, Fireslate is porous and will stain (citric acid is the biggest culprit). But Lang has been rolling out his pasta on these counters for a couple of years now and is pleased with them. Though the counters show some staining, the blemishes aren't obtrusive and haven't hurt the taste of the pasta. □

Philip S. Sollman is a designer and woodworker in Bellefonte, Pennsylvania. Photos by Kevin Ireton.

A Cantilevered Kitchen Addition

Solving structural problems with steel, wood and ingenuity

by Robert Gleason

A cantilevered frame. To enlarge the kitchen and family room, a 4-ft. by 30-ft. addition was hung from the rear of this house. Finishing the new exterior before removing the old one minimized disruption to the household.

Photo: Charles Wardell

Why bother with an addition that's only 4 ft. wide? Because it can make a dramatic change in a small, dark room. A small job isn't always a simple one, however. In fact, when Ed and Mary Weinsoff asked me to build a 4-ft. by 30-ft. addition onto the back of their two-story, gambrel-roof house, I knew from having worked for them before that their plans would demand some creative work.

The Weinsoffs planned to combine their kitchen and family room into a new space that would include an enlarged kitchen and lots of glazing to bring in natural light. The two spaces would be unified by a continuous ceiling plane, with no exposed beams. Extending the foundation was out of the question, though. Not only did the Weinsoffs want to keep their existing basement plan, but the fact that the yard bordered on some wetlands meant that foundation work would require an expensive and lengthy approval process. So

instead, we built a 4-ft. by 30-ft. addition that cantilevered from the back of the house, 8 ft. above grade (photo above).

Selecting the windows— The addition would face east—perfect for catching some morning sun during breakfast. Unfortunately, several large trees (which the Weinsoffs wanted to keep) limited the amount of direct sunlight that would hit the windows. To compensate, we decided to incorporate four roof windows into the addition. To add even more daylight, the kitchen would get a double casement window and the family room would have a 13-ft. long custom Marvin unit consisting of five double-hung windows mulled together. Having five windows joined at the factory yielded more glass area for a given space than installing them separately would have. The single unit was also much easier to finish, both inside and out.

The problem with the five-window unit was that it would go into the wall that was out on the end of the cantilever, and a 13-ft. header would have put too great a concentrated load at each end of the opening. So to distribute the load, we had Marvin build two stud pockets into the window framing. Doing so reduced the longest header span to about 5 ft., reducing the concentrated loads to a point where our cantilever design could easily handle them. Even with the stud pockets included, the window still had more glass than five separate units.

Calculating loads— Our floor system would have to support an 80 lb./sq. ft load (a 40-lb. roof load and a 40-lb. floor load). To compensate for the vertical shear load at the foundation wall, we'd need 45 2x10 joists. To reduce bending force imposed by the 4-ft. cantilever, the joists would have to extend 12 ft. under the

Drawings: Bob LaPointe

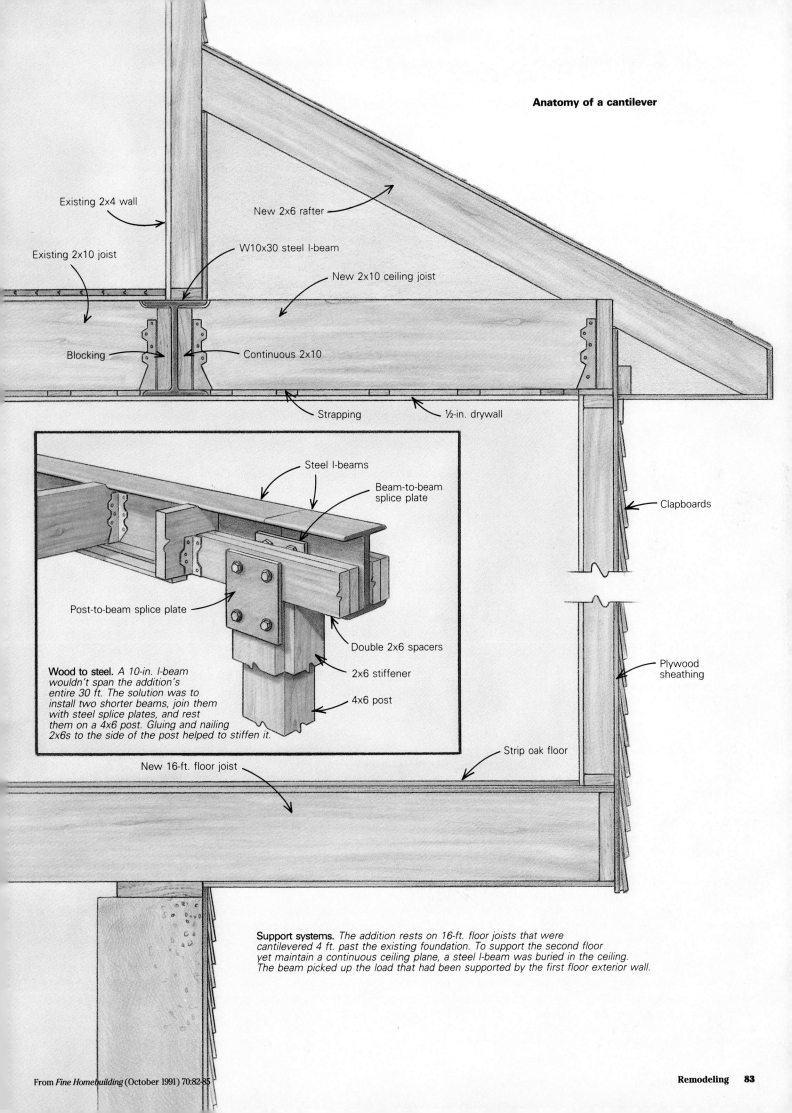

Anatomy of a cantilever

Existing 2x4 wall

New 2x6 rafter

Existing 2x10 joist

W10x30 steel I-beam

New 2x10 ceiling joist

Blocking

Continuous 2x10

Strapping

½-in. drywall

Steel I-beams

Beam-to-beam splice plate

Clapboards

Post-to-beam splice plate

Double 2x6 spacers

2x6 stiffener

4x6 post

Plywood sheathing

Wood to steel. *A 10-in. I-beam wouldn't span the addition's entire 30 ft. The solution was to install two shorter beams, join them with steel splice plates, and rest them on a 4x6 post. Gluing and nailing 2x6s to the side of the post helped to stiffen it.*

New 16-ft. floor joist

Strip oak floor

Support systems. *The addition rests on 16-ft. floor joists that were cantilevered 4 ft. past the existing foundation. To support the second floor yet maintain a continuous ceiling plane, a steel I-beam was buried in the ceiling. The beam picked up the load that had been supported by the first floor exterior wall.*

house. Nailing a new 16-ft. joist on either side of each existing joist met all these requirements.

Extending the house meant removing the existing exterior wall and finding an alternate way to support the second floor. To support such a heavy load over such a long span, we decided to use structural steel beams (drawing previous page). But we wouldn't be able to span the full 30 ft. with a single piece of steel. The need to bury the beam in the ceiling (to maintain an unbroken ceiling plane) limited us to a beam 10 in. deep. Besides, a single 30-ft. beam would have been too heavy and cumbersome to handle.

Calculations showed that a W10x22 steel I-beam could span the 12½-ft. kitchen, and a W10x30 the 17½-ft. family room. The outboard end of the latter beam would fall over a doorway that led from the family room to the garage (an existing fireplace on the same wall determined the door location). That end would rest on a 3-ft. long steel-door header. To support the inboard end of each beam, I designed a hidden support post into the kitchen cabinets (top photo facing page).

From the outside in—To minimize disruption to the kitchen, my crew and I finished the exterior before tearing out the existing wall. After removing the clapboards, plywood and band joist at the base of the wall, we installed our new 2x10 joists, then snapped a line across their outboard edges and trimmed them in place.

We installed the joists crown *down* to oppose the cantilevered floor load. But with no foundation to anchor the ends of the joists, it was impossible to align them with the top of the cantilever's band joist. I started wishing that I had rejected any noticeably crowned joists, even if that had meant buying twice as many in the first place. The solution was to keep the band joist as the high point, to level it as best we could, and to shim any joists that fell below it. After sheathing the underside of the overhang with ½-in. plywood, the problem was no longer noticeable.

The pitch on the addition roof had to match that of the main roof. An 8-in. space between the new roof and the existing second-floor window sills left enough room for one row of clapboards and an 8-in. wide strip of flashing. I always have trouble making roll flashing look good when I have to bend it, so I had the flashing fabricated in a sheet-metal shop. The .040 bronze/bronze aluminum flashing almost perfectly matched the color of the step flashing supplied with the Velux roof windows, resulting in a neat, uniform appearance.

With the roof tight we were ready for our doors and windows. We centered the kitchen casement in the new back wall, just high enough above the countertop to leave room for a 4-in. backsplash. The five-window unit was a bit more complicated. The tops of all the door and window casings had to line up. But we had framed the window openings before the five-window unit was ready—and before I knew its exact dimensions. As a precaution, I framed the sill 1 in. too low. The day before delivery, I measured the window at the lumberyard, then ripped out a filler piece on the job site. The filler piece raised the window just enough to align it with an adjacent door. Wood shims placed beneath the vertical jamb locations made the final adjustments.

Installing temporary supports—Before removing the existing exterior wall, we would have to shore up the ceiling (and the second floor of the house). My feeling on temporary support: you can't have enough of it. If I notice any sagging or movement, I reinforce or add to the supports. On this job, we began by laying planks on the existing floor to distribute the loads and protect the hardwood. We stood jack posts on the planks every 8 ft., spanned them with 4x6s, then jacked the posts up enough to snug the 4x6s tight against the bottoms of the old ceiling joists. We then carefully plumbed the posts and put just enough pressure on them to take the load off the old wall, yet not enough to raise the ceiling.

We used the same system on the second floor to support the roof and ceiling loads (though had the roof borne directly on the wall to be removed, I would have braced the top plates or the rafter ends to keep the roof from thrusting outward).

Steel and wood—We were now ready for the steel beams. We got them into the house through the garage-to-family-room door opening. Because the longer piece weighed 525 lb., and because only two of us were on the job at this point, we rented a hoist that was designed to remove engines from cars. The hoist could be disassembled, making it easy to get it into the house; it was on wheels, so we could move it around, and it had the needed capacity and lifting range. The hoist's lift arm was equipped with a chain. Wrapping the chain around the center of the steel beam let us lift it about 6 feet off the floor. After supporting both ends of the beam, we removed the chain, repositioned the hoist arm under the beam's center point and raised the beam to its final height. The next step was to move the beam horizontally into place. Now, 18 ft. of steel I-beam is not something you want swinging around in cramped quarters, so we built a temporary wood frame beneath each end of the beam. Cross pieces on the frame let us slide the beam into position.

After positioning both pieces of steel, we bolted a splice plate across the joint and put two temporary posts beneath each side of the joint (drawing previous page). We then installed a 4x6 post from the foundation sill to the bottom of the splice point, and glued and nailed 2x6s onto the 4x6 to stiffen it.

The next job was to tie the old ceiling joists to the steel blocking. We attached 2x10 blocks to the web of the I-beam between each existing joist. These 14-in. pieces were then "shot" onto the I-beam's web with a power hammer (also called a powder-actuated fastening tool) and attached to the existing ceiling joists with joist hangers. On the addition side of the beam, we were able to fasten one continuous 2x10 to the web. We fastened the ends of our new ceiling joists to this web piece with hangers. The steel beam measured 10 in. high, and the 2x10 ceiling joists only 9¼ in. We achieved our continuous ceiling plane by aligning the tops of the joists and the I-beam, then nailing strapping across the bottom of the joists.

A problem floor—Placing the steel was tricky, but perhaps the most challenging part of the job was adding on to the strip oak floor. The oak ran perpendicular to the outside wall and had to be extended 4 ft. To keep costs down, we wanted to save as much of the existing floor as possible. We decided to weave the new oak into the existing oak by removing every strip back to its first butt joint (bottom photo, facing page). Each existing oak strip was ripped into three pieces with a circular saw. This made it easy to remove the center and groove pieces, as only the tongue section was nailed. We then carefully pried the tongue section loose and pulled any remaining nails.

Installing the new strips was fairly conventional where the old floor stepped back. We simply slipped the new strip over the old tongue and drove it up tight with a floor nailer. After a series of step-backs, a piece would have to be driven in from the end. Luckily, these pieces made a tight joint with both the new and old strips. We had planned on face-nailing these areas, but the fit was so good that we let the tongue and groove do their thing.

After laying the first 8 ft. of flooring, we noticed a big problem. The farther along we went, the harder it got to pull the far end of each strip up tight to the preceding strip. Stretching a string across the floor confirmed my worst fear: the new strips weren't maintaining a straight line with the old. As it turned out, the new strips were about 2/100 in. narrower than the old, a variation that was small enough to leave a tight fit when each new strip was slipped between two old strips, but large enough to cause a significant variation over the length of the room. We'd already lost about ¾ in. over an 8-ft. distance.

We considered replacing the entire floor, but it ran through the hallway into the dining room. I finally decided to order some custom-made oak flooring strips from a local millwork shop. The strips were 2¼ in. wide on one end (the same as the existing strips) but 2½ in. wide on the other end. I had them made in 10-ft. lengths, the longest length that we could use. Installing three of these strips over the first 18-in. stretch got us back on track. We then worked in a custom strip every foot or so to keep from losing more ground as we went along. Though I could distinguish the custom-made strips from the stock ones, the difference certainly wasn't obvious. After the floor was sanded and finished, even I couldn't find most of the special pieces. □

Robert Gleason is a remodeling contractor from Boxford, Massachusetts.

Opening up. A support post for the steel beams in the ceiling was built into the cabinets. Roof and wall windows were used to bring in lots of light. The result shows how a little space can go a long way. ***Photo by Charles Wardell.***

A problem floor. While weaving in the new floor, the author discovered that the new strips were slightly narrower than the old, so they were steadily veering off course. His solution was to order custom flooring strips that were slightly wider on one end. Inserting one of these every foot or so brought everything into line. ***Photo by Robert Gleason.***

Recipe for a Kitchen Remodel

Natural materials, top-shelf hardware and tasteful leftovers accent an Arts and Crafts motif

by William E. Roesner

In 1979, my wife and I were the lucky winners of a Scottish-Baronial/American Arts and Crafts-style house in Newton Centre, Massachusetts. At least, it seemed that way when our sealed bid on the house beat out the competition. The robust three-story house, designed in 1912 by prominent Boston architect James H. Ritchie for himself, was replete with dark-stained beamed ceilings, Tiffany windows, quartersawn white oak floors, a Grueby tiled fireplace, an oak-paneled den and other details that placed it stylistically in that period.

Strongly emphasizing class distinction, the Scottish-born Ritchie divided the house into two distinct domains: a simple, functional kitchen and pantry with a bedroom and bathroom above it for the servant (who did all the cooking), and the rest of the house for himself and his family. The two domains were clearly distinguished by their level of detailing. For in-

stance, all the doorknobs in the main part of the house are made of crystal. In the servant's section, they're plain white porcelain. Also, a separate stair, spare in detail, links the kitchen with the servant's quarters. The owner's staircase, on the other hand, is embellished with an artful balustrade, complete with a hand-carved newel post.

For our purposes, however, we thought the servant's bedroom would make a perfect guest room. But for the kitchen to assume a prominent and complementary position in our house, a major remodel was in order.

Once the domain of servants, the kitchen was refurbished to meet contemporary demands and to reflect the Arts and Crafts detailing found in the rest of the house.

Cooking up the plan—Having practiced architecture for more than 25 years, I had always worked to fulfill the wish lists of others. Now I had the chance to design something for myself. The only "client" I had to satisfy was my wife, Elizabeth, who generously volunteered to stay clear of most aesthetic decision making. As a gourmet cook, though, she had plenty to say about how the kitchen would be organized, including how and where food would be prepared, where the dishes would be washed and where storage would be provided.

With Elizabeth's stamp of approval, I organized the kitchen into a food-preparation area and a dishwashing and storage area, with an island counter in between (photo above). The food-prep area has a double sink set in a 6½-ft. long counter, with a refrigerator on one side and a microwave and cookstove on the other. Opposite this sink, the island stores common foodstuffs and portable appliances.

As food is prepared, it's placed on the island counter and then moved to either the small dining table for two located at the end of the island or to the formal dining room. Dirty dishes are returned to the single sink on the opposite side of the kitchen and loaded into an adjacent dishwasher. Dishes and silverware are stored on this side of the kitchen as well as in the pantry (bottom photo, p. 89), which also provides storage for table linens, liquor and wine.

My design brief called for the extension of the Scottish Arts and Crafts tradition into the kitchen through the use of details influenced by Charles Rennie Mackintosh, Scotland's premiere turn-of-the-century Arts and Crafts designer (see FHB #54 pp. 36-41). This meant fitting the cabinets with white-colored door and drawer fronts, cross-shaped door pulls and leaded-glass panels, as well as introducing to the kitchen dark wood doors, casings, trim and other finish details. The cabinets would be European-style; they're more accessible than standard cabinets.

The new kitchen appliances would be supplemented with several of the old ones from the original kitchen, including a six-burner, two-oven Magic Chef gas stove dating from about 1930, a kitchen-window exhaust fan dated 1912, a 6-volt intercom system and an old hot-water radiator.

Lighting would be provided primarily by rheostat-controlled, low-voltage incandescent fixtures and by fluorescent fixtures mounted beneath the upper cabinets. Other amenities would include display niches (top photo, p. 89), granite countertops, stainless-steel sinks and chrome-plated faucets.

Of course, my detailed plans would be futile without the handiwork of top-flight craftspersons. I chose Nathan Rome, a member of the Emily Street Woodworkers Cooperative in Cambridge, Massachusetts, to build the cabinets. On Rome's recommendation, I hired William Iacono of Thorpe Construction (also a member of the cooperative) as general contractor. Iacono's team included foreman John Patriquin, a master furniture builder and finish carpenter, and cabinetmaker Jonathan Wright, who would be responsible for most of the shop-built millwork such as doors, jambs and baseboards.

Roughing it out—Iacono's first step was to gut the existing kitchen and pantry down to bare studs and joists. Even the subfloor was removed. It was replaced with ¾-in. exterior-grade plywood panels installed between the joists; the panels were glued and screwed to 2x ledgers fastened to the sides of the joists, positioned so that the tops of the panels are flush with the tops of the joists (drawing at right). This effectively dropped the subfloor about 1 in., allowing the new terra-cotta tile floor to finish out coplanar with the adjacent hardwood floors.

The 8-ft., 1-in. high kitchen ceiling was too high to butt the upper cabinets against, so an 11-in. high soffit was framed around the perimeter of the kitchen. The soffit not only drops the upper cabinets to a convenient height (18 in. above the countertops) but also serves as a plumbing chase for the rooms above and is a means for introducing mahogany trim at the ceiling, thus generating a visual relationship with the beamed ceilings in the living room.

With the soffit completed, the exterior walls were insulated with 3½-in. fiberglass batts, then covered with a 4-mil polyethylene vapor barrier. The ceiling and most of the walls were finished with ⅝-in. gypsum blueboard and skim-coat plaster.

Originally, the cookstove's two ovens were vented into a small duct inside the wall that ran up through the house and out the roof. During demolition it was discovered that sometime in the past, the wall framing had charred slightly from overheating, though somehow it had never caught fire. The building inspector insisted on fire-resistant construction behind the stove and directed us not to hook up the old exhaust duct. The plastered wall behind the cookstove received a double layer of ⅝-in. fire-rated drywall affixed to ⅞-in. metal furring channels nailed to the existing studs. Then we installed an exhaust hood over the stove to absorb heat from the open stove duct.

After the plastering was finished, the existing windows were refurbished. This included straightening the existing zinc weather stripping, installing new wooden guides and replacing the old counterweight ropes with copper-dipped, 75-lb. steel "bag chain." The bag chain (available from Turner & Seymour Manufacturing Co., P. O. Box 358, Torrington, Conn. 06790; 203-489-9214) cost $26.20 for a 100-ft. length, the minimum amount available. Also, a few cracked window lights were replaced with antique glass, saved during demolition, to preserve the wavy view through the windows.

Coved baseboards and fumed oak—While the rest of the work was in progress, Rome and Wright were busy with the millwork. Doors, casings, baseboards and soffit trim were made out of African mahogany to match existing details in the house.

The coved baseboards (photo below) were milled from 1¾-in. by 4⅜-in. stock. The cove was produced by plowing a 1½-in. dia. flute down the length of the stock using a shaper, and then running the stock top-edge-down through a table saw to rip the baseboard to finished thickness. The roundover at the top was produced by routing a 45° bevel along the top edge and then easing it with rasps and sandpaper. Almost all the millwork and cabinetry were prefinished in the shop with three

The coved mahogany baseboards were produced by using a shaper to plow a 1½-in. dia. flute down the length of solid mahogany stock, then ripping off the excess with a table saw. The roundover at the top was shaped by hand using rasps and sandpaper. All the millwork was prefinished with three coats of urethane lacquer.

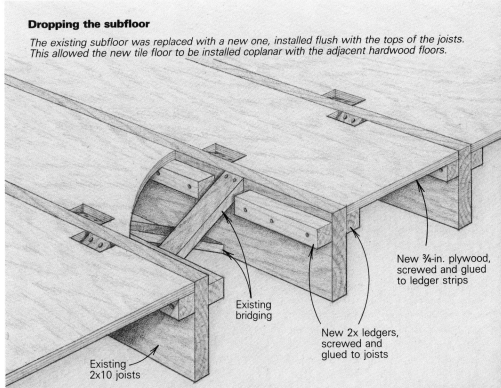

Dropping the subfloor

The existing subfloor was replaced with a new one, installed flush with the tops of the joists. This allowed the new tile floor to be installed coplanar with the adjacent hardwood floors.

New ¾-in. plywood, screwed and glued to ledger strips

Existing bridging

New 2x ledgers, screwed and glued to joists

Existing 2x10 joists

Drawing: Vince Babak

coats of Lacthane quick-drying, water-resistant urethane lacquer (Eastern Chem-Lac Corp., 1100 Eastern Ave., P. O. Box 266, Malden, Mass. 02148; 617-322-8000) prior to installation.

Wright also milled a supply of unfinished quartersawn white oak door thresholds as well as floor boards for the maid's-stair landing, where the oak would alternate with African mahogany (left photo, next page). To replicate the dark coloration of the existing oak floor, I placed the oak flooring inside a large plastic-bag tent out in the yard overnight and slipped in a small pan of powerful ammonia (ammonium hydroxide) from my blueprinting machine. The tannin in the white oak reacted with the ammonia fumes to produce a rich brown color that, when finished with polyurethane varnish, turned a beautiful golden brown. This is by and large the same principle used by Arts and Crafts artisans at the turn of the century. Please be forewarned, though, that this ammonia is extremely powerful stuff and should not be used indoors or without protective respirators, goggles and gloves.

Composing the cabinets—The cabinets in the kitchen and pantry are built out of a combination of solid African mahogany and mahogany plywood. Complete with sturdy dovetailed drawers and bridle-jointed doors, ball-bearing, full-extension drawer slides and concealed hinges, they're furniture-quality inside and out. Special features include a spice drawer, a bread drawer, an under-the-counter wine rack, a tray-storage cabinet with vertical dividers and two appliance garages tucked into the end of the island (top right photo, next page). Each garage contains a MEPLA mechanical swing-up shelf supplied by Frederick Shohet, Inc. (51 Concord St., N. Reading, Mass. 01864; 508-664-5775): one supporting a food processor and the other a mixer, plugged in and ready for use. Roll-out drawers below hold the accessories.

I originally wanted the Mackintosh-inspired, cross-shaped door and drawer pulls to consist simply of four square holes, each big enough for a finger to slip through. My wife objected, though, so I decided instead to notch 1x crosses into single square openings and to cover the backs of the openings with ¼-in. mahogany plates screwed to the door and drawers (top right photo, next page). The solid-mahogany

A pair of display niches, formed out of mahogany and granite, are illuminated with low-voltage incandescent fixtures. A continuous stainless-steel plugmold, concealed beneath the upper cabinets, gives maximum flexibility in the placement of countertop appliances.

Adjacent to the kitchen, the pantry (photo above) echoes its detailing except that its countertop is of African mahogany instead of granite. The original 6-volt intercom seen in the foreground still works. In the kitchen (photo facing page), the dining table consists of a 2¼-in. thick slab of African mahogany supported by a carved mahogany column. The existing gas cookstove was protected for years by a layer of grease. Scrubbed clean, it's as good as new.

doors and drawer fronts were painted by Johnson Brothers, a furniture-restoration shop located here in Newton, with multiple coats of white lacquer to maintain the wood-grain texture and the bridle-joint "read through."

The leaded-glass inserts for the upper cabinet doors were fabricated and installed by Lyn Hovey Studio in Cambridge, Massachusetts. The glass is imported, hand-blown restoration glass. This "antique" glass has the character-

istic distortion of old handmade glass, but it's actually new. It's made by hand-blowing molten glass into cylindrical shapes and then cutting the cylinders to length while they're still hot. After cooling, each cylinder is cut lengthwise, reheated in a furnace and flattened into rectangular sheets that measure approximately 24 in. by 36 in. The glass, typically used for colonial restoration, averages ⅛ in. thick. Apparently, the glass is hard to find. Ours was made in Germany and imported by S. A. Bendheim Co., Inc. (61 Willett St., Passaic, N. J. 07055; 800-221-7379). The restoration glass was set in 5/16-in. lead came, matching in profile that found in the den, but the new came was also given a copper-colored decorative foil face.

Base cabinets were fitted with continuous plywood tops to support granite countertops (African mahogany countertops in the pantry) and to allow the sinks to be mounted under the granite in routed openings. There's a dining table for two at the end of the island opposite the appliance garages (see photo facing page). It's simply three 2¼-in. thick African mahogany boards edge-glued to form a 28-in. by 33-in. slab. The slab is supported on one end by a cleat screwed to the face of the island and on the other by a single column of white-painted mahogany, carved to match in abstracted form the existing newel post at the foot of the main stair.

Both table and column are notched to slip together, and the base of the column is secured by a ⅛-in. steel pin set into the tile floor.

Topping with granite—With the cabinets in place, the most expensive phase of the remodel— fabrication and installation of the countertops—could begin. After weighing the virtues of both granite and marble, I picked granite because it's four to six times harder than marble, and hence is less likely to chip or stain. The granite would also be used for backsplashes, sidesplashes and window stools.

It was important that the countertops complement the African mahogany, the white-colored walls and cabinets, and the tile floor. After a trip to the stoneyard, I settled on a ¾-in. thick, $18 per sq. ft. stone called "Turquoise," which was quarried in Saudi Arabia, cut and polished in Italy and fabricated in Charlestown, Massachusetts, by Louis Mian

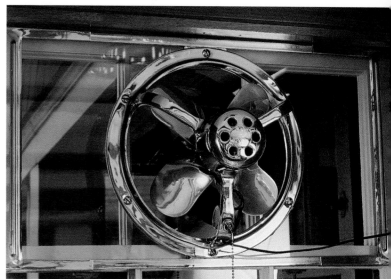

The solid-mahogany door in the kitchen corner conceals a stairway that leads to the old servant's quarters upstairs. Above the door a radiused recess in the soffit, trimmed with mahogany, accommodates the swing of the door. The landing consists of African mahogany alternating with ammonia-fumed white oak.

Floating in a sea of terra-cotta tiles, the European-style cabinets harbor a number of amenities, including the spice drawer, appliance garage and full-extension storage trays shown in the top photo. The original kitchen fan (photo above), dating from 1912, was restored and chrome-plated by a local shop. The job cost $200.

Inc. (547 Rutherford Ave., Boston, Mass. 02129; 617-241-7900).

Because of the complexity of the granite work, I had Thorpe Construction produce in place full-size, ¾-in. plywood templates complete with sink cutouts, sills for the display niches, window stools and splashes. The templates consumed five sheets of ¾-in. CDX plywood and took 149½ hours to make. Mian was called in to review and approve the completed mock-up. I also photographed it and produced a mounted photo montage that was used with the templates for reference back at Mian's shop.

Mian was responsible for shipping, handling and installing the granite. Each of the 29 pieces was fabricated slightly oversize so that it could be ground to an exact fit on the job site. Finish grinding was accomplished outside the house with the use of portable angle grinders fitted with #60 industrial-grade diamond-grit wheels, which cut the granite like it was wood. Once Mian's stoneworkers achieved a perfect fit, the pieces were bedded in epoxy. Installation took two stoneworkers two days to complete.

Oiled terra-cotta—The final phase of construction was the installation of the terra-cotta tile floor. I ordered French-made, unsealed Coverland tiles, called CMPR—French Terra Kotta, from Tile Creations (400 Arsenal St., Watertown, Mass. 02172; 617-926-0559). The rich golden hue of the tiles was achieved by heating them in an oven to about 350° F, removing them with the aid of a pair of insulated ski gloves, and then immediately applying boiled linseed oil to the tops of the tiles with paper towels. The paper towels allowed me to apply the oil in controlled doses, preventing the oil from dripping over the edges, which would have inhibited the grout bond. The oil was absorbed by the tiles to a depth of about ⅛ in., effectively sealing the tiles and preventing them from staining.

The tile was set on a 1½-in. thick mortar bed reinforced with expanded metal lath set perpendicular to the floor joists. The only special concerns during installation were to create a pleasing color pattern and to maintain directionality (the tile has a distinct grain pattern created by machine extrusion and wire cutting). Unlike most terra-cotta tile, French Terra Kotta has a smooth surface, which we maintain by applying an occasional coat of Butcher's Wax Bowling Alley Paste (The Butcher Co., 120 Bartlett Street, Marlborough, Mass. 01752-3013; 508-481-5700). It's a turpentine-based carnauba wax that's wiped on, allowed to dry and then buffed to a shine.

Saving the best for last—For the most part, all that remained was to restore the original stove, fan, intercom and radiator. We were delighted to discover that the Magic Chef cookstove had been thoroughly preserved by a thick layer of cooking grease. Once we dismantled, cleaned and reassembled it, it looked almost like new.

The kitchen fan (photo above right) was restored by William Sweeney of The Yankee Craftsman in Wayland, Mass. Sweeney scrubbed it clean, polished it, installed a new cord, replaced its cracked glass and, finally, sent the fan to a local shop for chrome-plating. The total cost of the job was $200.

The 6-volt house intercom (bottom photo, previous page) simply needed polishing and it was ready to use for calling the basement, guest room or upstairs hall. The hot-water radiator was delivered to Tim Harney at T. O. C. Finishing Co. For $100, he sandblasted and refinished it. The radiator (photo, p. 86) was relocated in the kitchen next to the back door.□

William E. Roesner is an architect in Newton Centre, Mass. Photos by Bruce Greenlaw.

A Screened-porch Addition

Simple detailing and inexpensive materials provide a shelter from the swarm

by Jerry Germer

Screened porches have graced our homes since horse tails were first woven into screens in the mid 1800s. On hot summer evenings, people would sit on the porch, perhaps in a swing hung from the roof, and pass the time with family, friends and neighbors. But in the middle of this century,

Roof structure. A three-tiered 15-in. fascia conceals a very shallow-pitched shed roof constructed of pressure-treated framing and corrugated, fiber-reinforced plastic (FRP) panels.

when postwar builders were faced with the need to build massive numbers of houses quickly and economically, they built smaller houses on smaller lots. Large outside porches no longer fit the houses or the lots. Lifestyles changed, too: People were spending more of their free time inside and in front of the television.

Recently, however, screened porches have been making a quiet comeback. Has television lost its charm, or are people rediscovering the outdoors? I'm not sure, but for our family, a screened porch (photo previous page) was the only way we could enjoy the

beauty of our rural New Hampshire site without being assaulted by hordes of pesky insects.

Making plans—The north side of the house off the living room seemed the obvious location for the new porch. Snugged against the house on its shadiest and most private side, the porch could project over the small bank that drops away to the backyard. A 3-ft. wide walkway could run along the back wall of the house, connecting the porch with the back door near the kitchen. That way, we'd be able to bring food out onto the porch without hav-

ing to negotiate steps or pass through the living room. Steps would lead from just outside the porch deck to the lawn.

To economize on materials, I decided to lay out the plan on a 3-ft. by 3-ft. grid, yielding a 15-ft. by 9-ft. deck floor—just about right for barbecue equipment, a small table and a few chairs. An existing window and the wall section below it would be cut out of the living-room wall to provide a passageway to the porch from indoors. A screen door would link the porch to the stairs and to the deck/walkway.

Getting the deck to float—The bank at the rear of the house drops off about 5 ft. right away. If I built the new porch at the same level as the living-room floor, the open space below the porch would range from 1 ft. to 4 ft. Closing off this space with open, lattice-type skirting would have been tricky, and a solid foundation seemed an even less attractive alternative—I didn't want to stand in the backyard and see a 4-ft. high wall of parged concrete block.

A simpler and more elegant solution was to cantilever the floor structure over the sloping bank, supporting the joists on a perpendicular 4x10 beam 6 ft. from the house (drawing p. 93). The beam rests atop two 4x4 posts, which bear on concrete footings resting about 3 ft. below grade. The posts are spaced 9 ft. apart, so the beam cantilevers out 3 ft. at each end. I used 2x8s on 3-ft. centers for floor joists, fastening one end of each joist (with a joist hanger) to a 2x8 ledger bolted to the house sill. The floor of the porch consists of 2x4 boards in continuous lengths, spaced ½ in. apart and screwed to the joists. All structural members, as well as the decking, are pressure-treated Southern yellow pine. The effect, with the house's skirtboard wrapping around the joists, is of a porch that floats out over the bank.

With no foundation walls to which I could attach screen, though, I needed to find another way of maintaining continuity of the insect barrier. The only solution that came to mind was to screen the floor. That's why I stapled fiberglass screen over the tops of the joists, before screwing down the decking. It worked; bugs can't get up through the bottom of the deck. But after two years of summertime use, the porch revealed the flaw in my scheme. Bits of debris, ranging from dust to pencils, fall into the cracks and get trapped by the screen. Vacuuming has been only partially effective in cleaning out the cracks, but then again, our aging Electrolux no longer has the suck it once did. Nevertheless, if ever I have occasion to build another screened porch, I'll take the to come up with a solution that allows for periodic cleaning of the screen.

Daylight and privacy—I wanted the walls of the porch to be as light and open as possible, yet still offer some privacy. Because the roof structure would be very lightweight, supporting posts were kept lean as well—2x4s on 3-ft. centers. Two posts meet at the corners so that neither post overlaps the inside face of the other. I stapled 36-in. widths of black fiber-

From *Fine Homebuilding* (February 1992) 72:81-83

glass insect screen to the inside face of each post, then secured 1x2 wood strips over the stapled edges with drywall screws.

Black screen over regularly spaced posts doesn't make for a very interesting wall surface, however, nor does it provide much in the way of privacy. Hoping to take care of both of these problems, I wrapped 30-in. high panels of 1x2 balusters around three sides of the porch. The panels are screwed to the outside faces of the posts, which allows removal of the panels for maintenance and repainting. The effect though, with all balusters spaced approximately on 5-in. centers, is of a continuous rail.

Keeping rain out, letting light in—Most roofed porches have a downside. In providing a sheltered space outdoors, they shade the windows, darkening the rooms. While summers here are short, winters are long, and gray days abound. When I remodeled our house, I tried to maximize passive-solar gain. By adding more windows on the south side of the house and removing non-bearing interior partitions on the first floor, I'd been able both to warm the house and to make it feel lighter and more cheerful. But in my zeal for energy efficiency, I had also eliminated some north-facing windows. I didn't want to block out light remaining from the north windows by shading them with an opaque porch roof.

"Why not design a roof that would allow light to pass through?" I thought to myself. If I could find the right material, the idea might have promise. Glass was ruled out immediately as being too expensive. Options in plastic included double-skinned polycarbonate sheet (such as Exolite) and corrugated fiber-reinforced plastic (FRP). Exolite would work but isn't cheap. FRP would be cheap, but in order to drain properly, the panels would have to overhang the eave. The exposed ends, undulating like a washboard, would fit better on a shed or a chicken coop—not at all in keeping with the character of our house. If I were to use the FRP, I would have to come up with an eave detail that hid the corrugated panel ends without impeding drainage.

A shallow pitch concealed—The two challenges confronting me were how to make the porch roof seem to belong to the house and how to hide the corrugated ends of the FRP from view. A shed roof that matched the pitch of the house's roof would run smack into the second-floor windows. And a shallower pitched roof would seem an afterthought. A completely level roof, on the other hand, would underscore the house's horizontal eave and frieze board. But I still needed to provide some slope for

Behind the fascia. Vertical cleats nailed to the joist support the fascia. Flashing and an angled 1x6 protect the fascia boards from runoff.

Section through porch

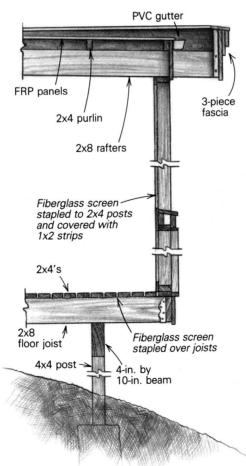

PVC gutter

FRP panels

2x4 purlin

2x8 rafters

3-piece fascia

Fiberglass screen stapled to 2x4 posts and covered with 1x2 strips

2x4's

2x8 floor joist

4x4 post

4-in. by 10-in. beam

Fiberglass screen stapled over joists

drainage. A solution was suggested by the roofing material itself.

Because the panels are 12 ft. long, I'd be able to use them full-length (no horizontal lap joints), all but eliminating the chance of wind-driven rain getting up under my roofing. I figured I could get by with a minimum pitch for drainage—say, ¼ in. per ft. Later, I could wrap a fascia around the three exposed sides of the roof to hide the rafters, the result being a flat-looking roof with good drainage (photos left and facing page).

Because my goal was to let in as much light as possible, I left all roof framing exposed. The 2x8 rafters, spaced 3 ft. o. c., run perpendicular to the house, dropping 3 in. in 12 ft. The high ends of the rafters are fastened to a 2x8 ledger lag-bolted to the house. The lower ends of the rafters extend 15 in. past the top of the outer wall, to carry the fascia. I also ran 2x4 purlins (22 in. o. c.) 15 in. out to support the fascia at the side walls. Two ⅛-in. cables run diagonally under the rafters, corner to corner, to brace the roof against racking. The FRP roofing panels were then attached to the purlins with aluminum roofing nails and rubber washers. The nails are spaced 6 in. to 8 in. o. c. (I had to predrill the panels).

Details, details—Concealing the rafters and the FRP would require a 15-in. wide fascia, which, I felt, would be overly heavy-looking if installed in one piece. Some horizontal lines would be necessary to reduce the apparent width of the fascia and to add a little interest to an otherwise plain façade. So I built a three-leveled fascia, with layered boards of diminishing size.

Behind the fascia, the FRP panels project over the porch's front wall by about an inch. A PVC gutter attached to an interior fascia above the screen wall collects runoff and carries it to downspout tees at each end (photo above). Rather than run downspouts down the corners of the porch, where they would have messed up the corner-post detail, I elected to let the water drip directly to the ground.

The translucent roof panels function well in winter, allowing a great deal of northern light into the house. In the summer, the porch is shaded by the house throughout the day, except for early in the morning and late in the afternoon. But the late afternoon summer sun was a nuisance. Hoping to resolve the problem simply and inexpensively, I draped sheets of burlap on 1x1 battens from eyehooks screwed into the purlins, a solution that has worked quite nicely. According to my wife, an architect never knows when to quit. □

Jerry Germer is an architect and writer living in Marlborough, N. H. Photos by Vincent Laurence.

Drawing: Bob LaPoint

Frugal Four-Square Fixup

Bumping out a wall and adding a porch
bring light and air to a turn-of-the-century classic

by Linda Mason Hunter

The new space. Though only bumped out 42 in., the entryway lets in light through a skylight and sidelights, opening up the dining room considerably. The pair of wide openings between dining room and porch links an indoor room with an outdoor room, and the house to the backyard.

When it was built in 1910, our house stood alone, surrounded by cornfields; it was a rural homestead on the Iowa prairie. Today it's only one of many houses on a tree-lined boulevard in Des Moines. The house is known as a "four-square" (photo, p. 97), and more specifically as a "homestead house." A four-square is simply a house that is predominantly square in plan (for more on four-square architecture, see the sidebar on p. 97). A homestead house is a type of four-square sold as a mail-order-kit house by Sears, Roebuck and Co., as well as by many lumberyards, from 1908 to 1913. The cost ranged from $733 to $853, including plans and all materials down to the nails.

Our house is really the quintessential farmhouse—a sturdy, unpretentious shelter that's simple in design, construction and decoration. Our remodeling aimed only to improve the house, not transform it.

Nice, but not perfect—The house was designed for 20th-century living, so it already fit our needs well. The kitchen, for example, wasn't a tiny afterthought designed exclusively for servants, as is often the case in houses built before 1900. Also, the house was originally plumbed, wired for electricity, and outfitted with central radiant heat (steam radiators), one of the simplest, healthiest means of heating. Finally, the floor plan is largely open, and it even included the original closets.

But our tidy house was not without problems. The interior was dark and the rooms were small. Our dining room couldn't comfortably fit more than six people at a time, making family celebrations cramped affairs. In the 1970s we made matters worse by stuffing an ancient air-conditioner into the only rear window in the dining room, making the room darker still and obscuring the backyard while eliminating any natural cross-ventilation. Also, though oriented well toward the front of the house, passage between the indoors and outdoors in back was inconvenient, making the backyard largely an unused space (top photo, next page).

Gradually, over a period of nearly a year, the design for a small addition evolved in my mind, a design that would remedy all of our house's shortcomings and create a more pleasant, livable space. I thought that by bumping the rear dining-room wall back 3 feet and making that space a light-well I would be able to brighten the entire first floor. To accomplish this I figured on fitting the new rear wall with French doors and sidelights, and adding a long horizontal skylight and sidewall windows. Finally, we would add a gazebo-like back porch, with access through the new French doors. Our new rear porch would mirror the front porch in style, materials, and detail. Though a relatively small project (photo above), it promised to open up the house to the backyard as well as provide my husband and me with a place to sit, read and talk.

An outdoor room realized. **The back porch looks as if it had been built with the house. Most important, though, it provides a measure of privacy outdoors at home.**

Paring and honing—I commissioned Bill Wagner, a long-time family friend and an experienced preservation architect, to work out the kinks in my design and come up with working drawings. Bill envisioned the bumpout as more of an entryway than an integral part of the dining room. To define the distinct functions of the spaces, he called for a pair of recessed-panel oak kneewalls to frame the passageway between dining room and entryway, the kneewalls mimicking those already separating living room from dining room.

Craftsman-style oak columns would be added at the inside ends of the new kneewalls to further reinforce the distinction between interior and transitional areas, as well as to add a little drama to the design (photo facing page). Across the top of the passageway an oak head jamb would tie the kneewalls and columns together visually while disguising the header.

Sitting around our oak dining-room table in February, Wagner, builder Bill Warner, and I worked out the details of the project. By substituting footings and piers for a foundation,

A dismal backyard. Before the porch and bump-out addition, the backyard wasn't much of a sight, and getting there required an awkard trek through the kitchen and pantry. This photo shows the layout of batter boards and stringlines.

A roof for the long haul. To support the roof sheathing, 2x10s were needed for strength. The exposed rafter tails were made thinner to give them a real delicate appearance.

Structure and sheathing. Many old porches have hollow columns supporting their roof, which is one reason you see so many saggy old porch roofs. To maintain the same look as the front porch yet give the back porch a considerably longer life, carpenters supported the roof with 4x4s notched and lag bolted to the joists. Scraps of 2x4 provide spacers and nailers for the red wood sheathing.

we'd be able to save a couple of thousand dollars at the outset. The new back porch would be built largely of redwood, as were the front porch and siding. The porch ceiling would be beadboard, painted sky blue ("to keep the flies away," according to an old homesteader myth). Interior trim would all be oak, finished to match the existing woodwork.

After carefully studying the plan, Warner submitted an estimate of $14,000, plumbing and electrical included. This was more than we'd wanted to spend, but we liked the design and details and felt we'd already eliminated everything we could. Because we wanted some landscaping, furnishings for the porch, and a financial cushion for whatever might go wrong, we secured a loan of $16,000—enough, we hoped, to cover all exigencies. With that in hand, we were ready to begin construction. Six weeks before we were scheduled to begin, we ordered the doors, sidelights, and skylight. Delivery can take a while, and we wanted these materials on site when they were needed.

Getting started—Like many remodeling projects, this one had its surprises. The first order of business was to have the electrical service and meter moved, as these were located on the wall to be razed. City building code, however, requires that whenever incoming power service and the meter are moved, all house wiring must be brought up to code. So we hired an electrician to identify and remedy any violations, and to move the service and meter.

Before we could begin laying out the porch or pouring the footings, we had to tear out the old back steps. In the process of removing them, Warner and his brother Craig discovered why our pantry leaned into the yard: a corner of the foundation was laid directly onto the ground—with no footings—and had settled over time. To halt the settling, Bill and Craig removed the problem foundation wall, dug a hole 4 ft. deep for a 10-in. square footing and rebuilt the wall on top of the footing.

After we attended to that unforeseen problem (and expense), it was time to begin the new construction. Bill and Craig laid out the addition with string and batter boards, then dug nine holes 4-ft. deep for the porch's 12-in. square footings.

Because the exterior bump-out wall wasn't going to be load-bearing, the new joists didn't have to be tied in to the existing floor joists. Instead, we lag bolted a ledger board to the existing band joist and attached the floor joists using joist hangers. To support the framing forming the porch's perimeter, we located 8x8 posts over each of the footings.

To support the porch roof, we used 4x4s, notched and lagged to the floor joists. Bill and Craig later wrapped each of these 4x4s with 1x8 redwood, using 2x4 blocks as spacers and nailers for the redwood sheathing (bottom right photo, facing page). Building porch-roof rafters and ceiling joists was relatively straightforward. The ends of the rafters were notched and ripped to 3½ in. where they would extend past the fascia to give them a lighter appearance that would

be more in keeping with the scale of the rest of the porch (bottom left photo, facing page). To keep the 20-in. overhang on the sides of the roof from sagging, 2x4s laid flatwise were laid into notches on the top of the two outermost rafters. Three of these outriggers, on 4-ft. centers, were used on each side to stiffen up the overhang framing. To give the end of the shed roof somewhat more character, Bill added a small gable.

Exterior detailing—To make brackets that would match those on the front porch, Bill and Craig traced the profile of one of the originals onto a piece of 1x12. Then, using the 1x12 as a pattern, they cut three 5/4x12-in. pieces of redwood for each bracket and laminated them together. The top and bottom pieces, which frame the brackets, are 4x4s with the ends beveled 45° on all four sides to form a point.

We duplicated the front-porch railing on the new porch. The top rail is 2x4 redwood with a 20° bevel on both sides of a 2-in. wide flat section that runs down the middle. The bottom rail is 2x4 redwood, laid on edge, with edges chamfered on both sides of a ¾-in. wide flat section. The slats are 1x4 redwood, 18 in. high, spaced an inch apart. These sit on the ¾-in. flat spot in the center of the bottom rail and are toenailed to it. Two pieces of cove molding, one on each side of the slats underneath the handrail, anchor the top of the slats to the handrail.

Bumping out—After stripping the exterior dining-room wall down to the studs, we were ready to cut the opening for the bump-out. Bill braced the ceiling temporarily with a 2x6 header on 2x4 "legs." With this support in place, he and Craig worked quickly to remove the old studs and frame in the new opening.

We built the two new kneewalls only 22 in. deep instead of 29 in. like the originals, so as not to block the view to the French doors. All other kneewall details and dimensions are the same as the original, including a bevel on the edge of the sill and on the top lip of the baseboard rail. We used cove molding over the panel, along the inside of the stiles and rails to match the original.

The core of each of the two columns is a 4-in. by 4-in. vertical box made of ¾-in. plywood. The box was toenailed to the oak sill; then, solid oak boards—the finish surface—were nailed to the plywood and to each other. Butt joints were used instead of miters to match the newel post in the front hall.

When the woodwork was done, it was my job to finish it, filling the holes with wood putty, sanding, staining, and varnishing. Having stripped, sanded, stained and finished all original woodwork 10 years before, I was able to get nearly an exact color and texture match with the new woodwork. □

Linda Mason Hunter is the author of The Healthy Home: An Attic-To-Basement Guide To Toxin-Free Living *(Pocket Books, 1990). Photos by author except where noted.*

Square architecture
by William J. Wagner

For practical reasons, square structures have long been popular. Perhaps the principal attraction of the square structure is that it possesses greater square footage than a rectangular (nonsquare) house with the same perimeter length. A 24-ft. by 40-ft. rectangle and a 32-ft. by 32-ft. square both have sides totaling 128 ft., but the square holds 1,024 sq. ft. as compared with the rectangle's 960 sq. ft.

Cubes and near-cubes are also very rigid structures. And because all angles are right angles, square houses are easy to lay out and economical to build. They're also very adaptable structures, permitting almost any kind of addition to the central plan without upsetting the design.

Doubtless, the square house's strength, economy and adaptability all account for some of its popularity as the four-square. With the advent of balloon framing the four-square blossomed in the U. S. Principal supporting members in balloon-frame houses are closely spaced 2x4 or 2x6 studs, which extend from floor to roof, and are used for both the exterior and key interior walls. The four-square lent itself beautifully to this new framing technique, with three rooms on the first floor (including the living room across the front half), a stair leading to four rooms on the second floor, and a third-story attic. Sills, joists, and studs were precut to size, then exterior walls and partitions were laid out on the deck and raised to a vertical position. Windows and doors were stacked above each other, so as not to waste any long studs in window or door areas.

The balloon-framed four-square was adapted to many different architectural styles in the early part of this century. From 1890 to 1920, the heyday of pattern-book architecture in the U. S., four-squares were the most popular style. These houses dot the countryside all over the Midwest and in the northern tier of states.

The most common manifestation of the four-square was as a hip-roof Prairie-style house (sometimes called an American Foursquare), although even Modern and International-style houses have adapted the practical four-square plan. Also, the basic four-square design would often take on secondary features of Mission-style and Italian Renaissance homes.

William J. Wagner has an interest in preservation, restoration and adaptive additions. He is restoration architect for many of Iowa's historical sites.

Big Ideas for Small Spaces

This freestanding addition collects a houseful of thoughtful details into 768 sq. ft.

by Howard Katz

Adding to match. Green battens applied on a 16-in. grid unify the cross-gabled, three-story addition (right in photo) with the existing cottage, which sports a 24-in. grid. A belt of green shingles girdles the first floor of the addition to anchor the building visually.

"**S**oon to be completed is a screened pavilion on the southeast side of the house." That's how I concluded my article "House in the Woods," which appeared in issue #43 of *Fine Homebuilding*. Turns out, I was wrong.

The article recounted the design and construction of a 2½-story, energy-efficient cottage for my two children, my wife, Ruth, and me. Built on a 2-ft. module, the cottage (photo facing page, left side) originally had a living area, a dining area and a kitchen on the first floor, two bedrooms and a half bath on the second floor and an office in the attic. The module is revealed outside by green, beveled pine battens nailed on a 2-ft. grid to white ½-in. AC plywood siding.

We're happy with the playful exterior, but we quickly tired of sharing one tiny bathroom and of eating at a counter. Also, our library and our Spaulding and Roseville pottery collection quickly outgrew every available space. We scrapped the pavilion idea in favor of a more ambitious project: a three-story, freestanding addition. This would add just 768 sq. ft. to the house, but the figure is deceiving. We'd use innovative built-ins, exquisite materials and proven design tricks to wring the maximum utility out of the three small stories while enlarging them visually.

Rearranging the floor plan—Located 12 ft. south of the cottage, the addition is a 16-ft. square tower with a living room/library on the first floor, a master bath and a dressing area on the second floor and a master bedroom on top. Concurrent with its construction, we revamped the cottage by converting the living/dining area into a dining room, the master bedroom into an office and the office into a third bedroom. The original two-tier deck on the south end of the house links the two structures at the first and second floors, and a spiral stair joins the new master bath to the bedroom above it. For privacy, the bilevel master-bedroom suite is isolated from the living room below.

The addition is laid out on a 16-in. module (two-thirds the scale of the cottage). We applied a 16-in. grid to its exterior to unite the two structures visually.

Finding a builder—Five years ago we obtained the building permit for our cottage by submitting a sketch on the back of a junk-mail piece. Now our township employs a part-time building inspector who goes by the book. Nine pages of plans and two county inspections later, we had a building permit for the addition.

Still, we had no builder, which wasn't surprising. This project would demand painstaking attention to detail that would border on exasperating. The rough openings for the windows, for instance, couldn't vary by more than ⅛ in. vertically or horizontally without upsetting the exterior grid. Luckily, we eventually found Tuck Elfman, a builder with his own millwork shop, who saw the project as a challenge.

Variations on the theme—Elfman broke ground in November of 1989. The construction of the addition resembles that of the cottage, except that the addition has a radon-venting system beneath the slab, platform-framed walls

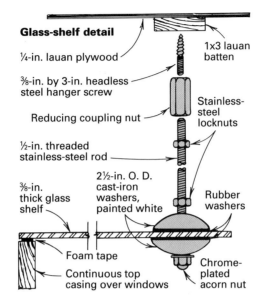

Glass-shelf detail

¼-in. lauan plywood

⅜-in. by 3-in. headless steel hanger screw

Reducing coupling nut

½-in. threaded stainless-steel rod

⅜-in. thick glass shelf

1x3 lauan batten

Stainless-steel locknuts

2½-in. O. D. cast-iron washers, painted white

Rubber washers

Foam tape

Continuous top casing over windows

Chrome-plated acorn nut

Surrounding shelves. **The first floor is a living room, a library and a solarium. It's surrounded on three sides by awning windows, a continuous built-in bookcase with drop-in planters and a continuous glass shelf that hangs from the ceiling to hold ceramic collectibles.**

Drawings: Michael Hiotakis

instead of complicated balloon-framed ones, 2x10 floor joists instead of site-built exposed beams and a cross-gable roof (four gables instead of two). The passive-radon-venting system is simply a vented loop of 4-in. PVC pipe placed just inside the foundation walls, 4 in. beneath the slab. The cross-gable roof is a result of our inability to decide how to orient the gable ends; we avoided the problem by having four.

Because the addition is three stories instead of two, we shingled the bottom 10 ft. of its exterior to create a little variety and to produce correctly proportioned wall spaces above for the applied grids. Stained green, the cedar shingles are laid 7 in. to the weather over Tyvek housewrap and ½-in. CDX plywood.

The grid areas have ½-in. AC plywood, "A" side out, over ½-in. foam insulation and housewrap. We fastened the 1x3 grid battens (which are beveled 30° on the edges) to the plywood with 6d galvanized nails, bedding the battens in DAP acrylic caulk. This time, though, we used lauan instead of pine for the battens because lauan is more weather resistant than pine yet costs a lot less ($1.05 per bd. ft. vs. $2.50 per bd. ft.).

I won't use exterior AC plywood for siding again. The plywood on the cottage has football patches made of filler, not wood, and they shrank. The plywood on the addition has stable

wood patches, but two of the sheets delaminated after just a few months of exposure to the weather. We replaced the two bad sheets and have had no problems since. But if there's a next time, I'll use medium density overlay (MDO), an exterior plywood finished with a fiber resin.

Oil-base or latex?—According to the September 1990 issue of *Consumer Reports*, "Nearly all exterior paints contain a mildew-fighting agent,

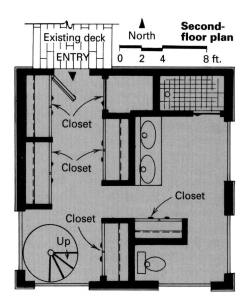

but the latexes as a group offer superior protection." This verdict prompted us to finish the addition, including plywood, grids, fascias, doors and four turned acorns at the eaves, with exterior latex paints. The cottage was originally finished with oil-base paint, so we refinished it with the same oil-base paint when we painted the addition. This will provide a good test for oil-base vs. latex paint. (I'll try to report back in a few years.)

Nightmare roof vents—The only comment I have about the roof concerns its continuous, corrugated-plastic ridge vents, which were made by a company that's now out of business. The vents were designed to be shingled over, but there was no provision for capping the ends. That was good news for our local southern flying squirrels, which just fit through the uncapped openings. These squirrels are nocturnal and seem to enjoy keeping people awake at night.

Elfman worked very hard to drive several squirrels from our vents, then nailed and caulked the ends shut. We were careful to seal the addition against other woodland creatures whose space we invaded, but until this episode I had only thought of the flying squirrel as Bullwinkle's pal. The moral of the story: Before you install this type of ridge vent, make sure that end caps are available for it.

Winding up. **A steel spiral stair links the master bath to the master bedroom above. A unifying theme on the second floor is the 1x6 T&G pine paneling, which is capped by a simple continuous crown molding. Photo by Ruth Anderson.**

Designer vanity. **A custom-made vanity is the heart of the master bathroom. Installed back-to-back with a 7-ft. high closet, the vanity is topped with a black granite slab that holds a pair of stainless-steel sinks. The recessed medicine cabinet above has a defogging central mirror plus outlets inside for recharging appliances.**

Continuous built-ins—Inside the addition, Ruth combined astute detailing with scrumptious materials to make the most of small rooms.

The bottom story is a living room, a library, a greenhouse and a gallery, all tucked comfortably into 256 sq. ft. (photo p. 99). The floor is a slab on grade paved with 8-in. square, black slate tiles (American Olean Tile Co., 1000 Cannon Ave., Lansdale, Pa. 19446; 215-855-1111), a big improvement over the crudely scored concrete slab in the cottage. A band of Andersen Perma-Clad awning windows installed in all walls but the north one creates the feel of a sunroom. Measuring 4-ft. square, the low-e, double-glazed windows are the only stock Andersen units that fit the grid. The inexpensive ceiling is ¼-in. lauan plywood underlayment with 1x3 lauan battens applied to it on the 16-in. grid.

The two neatest features in the room, though, are the continuous built-in bookcase installed below the windows and the continuous glass shelf that's suspended from the ceiling above the windows. The bookshelves have ¾-in. plywood sides, bottoms and shelves; 1x lauan face frames and toe kicks; and 1-in. thick lauan tops. The tops are split into front and back rails spaced 6½ in. apart to hold drop-in Bo-Kay fiberglass planter boxes (Molded Fiber Glass Tray Co., East Erie St., Linesville, Pa. 16424; 800-458-6090). These planter boxes are filled with a variety of house plants that serve as natural air fresheners.

The glass shelf for our pottery collection consists of 16, ⅜-in. thick, float-glass panels installed end-to-end, ¾ in. apart. We used glass for the shelves so that our pottery would be visible from underneath; glass shelves are also less obtrusive in a small room. The backs of the panels are supported by a continuous top window casing, and the fronts by custom hangers that go between the shelves and screw to the ceiling battens (drawing p. 99). I made the hangers out of industrial components that I bought from a local fastener supplier. We held the glass panels about 10 in. shy of the room's corners, allowing ceiling-mounted lamps to pass through.

Designer bathroom—The second floor has 7-ft. high partitions and closets surmounted by an 8-ft. ceiling. This not only makes the master bathroom and dressing room seem bigger, but also allowed us to apply an uninterrupted lauan grid to the ceiling, keeping our theme intact. The partitions and the closets, as well as the bottom 7 ft. of the exterior walls, are paneled with 1x6 T&G pine capped by a simple continuous crown mold. Called pine fencing, the 1x6s are grooved down the middle to simulate 1x3s.

The bathroom has a sort of 1930s country-train-station motif (photo facing page). The custom-made vanity has a black granite top that holds two stainless-steel kitchen undermount bowls, the appearance of which we prefer over ceramic bathroom sinks. The classic cross-handle faucets are from Artistic Brass (4100 Ardmore Ave., South Gate, Calif. 90280; 213-564-1100), while the reproduction chrome drawer and door pulls came from Antique Hardware Store (R. D. 2 Box A, Route 611, Kintnersville, Pa. 18930; 215-847-2447).

Third-floor plan

North

0 2 4   8 ft.

French
Dn doors

French
balcony

Above the vanity we installed a Mirror Plus flush-mounted medicine cabinet (Robern, Inc., 1648 Winchester Road, Bensalem, Pa. 19020; 215-245-6550). It has interior outlets for recharging appliances plus an electric defogging mirror that's activated by flipping a switch inside the cabinet. A pair of linear incandescent lights separates this central mirror from two outer mirrors. All this doesn't come cheap—the cabinet cost $1,900.

Doors to nowhere—The master bedroom is reached from the second floor by way of a simple, space-saving steel spiral stair (left photo, facing page) made by Mylen Industries (650 Washington St., Peekskill, N. Y. 10566; 914-739-8486). The bedroom features French doors that lead to nowhere (photo below). Passage through them, however, is restrained by a French balcony, which is not to be confused with a balcony you can walk on. Called a Hand-I Rail (another Robern product), it's a metal rail that's bolted to the exterior side of the door opening. The rail conveniently demounts from four brackets so that large furniture can be hoisted into the room.

The multifaceted cathedral ceiling in the bedroom is covered with the same 1x6 T&G pine used on the second floor. The ceiling is one of the few wood surfaces in the addition that has a natural finish. Ruth tired of the varnished wood that dominates the interior of the cottage, so she was determined to limit natural wood in the addition to a few areas. The ceiling finish is a nonyellowing blend of 20% white oil-base paint and 80% paint thinner, which we wiped on with rags. The white-oak flooring in the bedroom (and on the untiled portion of the second floor) is finished with a bowling-alley urethane that's supposed to resist yellowing (M. A. Bruder & Sons, Inc., 600 Reed Road, P. O. Box 600, Broomall, Pa. 19008; 215-353-5100).

Off-peak heat—Our highly refined addition wouldn't be complete without energy detailing to match. Besides low-e windows and substantial insulation (R-19 in the walls and R-30 in the ceilings), we installed the same high-tech heaters that inhabit the cottage. Sized by our local utility, each electric thermal storage unit contains ceramic bricks that are heated by electric resistance during off-peak hours (from 5 p. m. to 7 a. m. in our case). When heat is called for, a fan blows air through the bricks and into the room. The system is very economical; our off-peak rate is 2.8¢ per kilowatt hour, less than half the standard rate. □

Geometry in the ceiling. Folded like origami, a cross-gable cathedral ceiling crowns the master bedroom. The French doors (left in photo) open to a French balcony, which is simply a metal rail that's bolted across the outside of the door opening.

Designer Howard Katz lives in Riegelsville, Pa. Photos by Tom Crane except where noted.

Taking a Load Off

Three basic shoring techniques for making structural repairs

by W. Whitie Gray

On my last three jobs the clients were more impressed by my shoring methods than by the repairs I made. Not that there was anything wrong with my work; they liked that well enough. But in each case, selling the clients on the shoring techniques convinced them I could do the job in the first place. In this article I'll describe the shoring techniques that I used on each of the three jobs. These methods are low-tech—they don't require much equipment—but they get the job done quickly and safely.

Simple shoring—The first job involved simply raising the ceiling and roof of a 70-ft. long veranda so that, among other things, new porch columns could be put in place. For this job, I used a simple shoring technique (drawing right).

My crew and I were restoring Helmwood Hall, a 150-year-old house in Shelby County, Kentucky, that's on the National Historical Register. Everything had to go up evenly, smoothly and gently. We didn't use hydraulic or screw jacks to raise the roof because they would have been in the way of our work. Also, with hydraulics it's easy to pump one time too many and break something, and these were brittle timbers we were dealing with.

Because the porch was a trabeated structure—that is, designed to transfer the weight of the structure to the foundation down each column—and because we had to lift this weight to make our repairs, we dug 2-ft. wide holes for temporary footings about 4 ft. in front of the porch. Then we built wood footings, using a layer of 2x10s. The 2x10s bear on a series of spiles driven into the ground at an angle so that the bottoms of the jack posts could be cut square. Spiles are long stakes that we make from 2x4s or 2x6s and sharpen by cutting a taper on one edge at an acute angle of 15° or 20°. When driven into the ground with the tapered edge up, spiles compact the soil beneath them.

We notched the tops of the jack posts with a cut like a bird's-mouth cut to engage the bottom corner of the fascia at the juncture of a ceiling joist and a rafter; we positioned them at such an angle that we could work conveniently under and around them. The jack-post angle can vary, and the safest angles are those that are closest to plumb—the farther away from plumb, the greater the hazard. Of course,

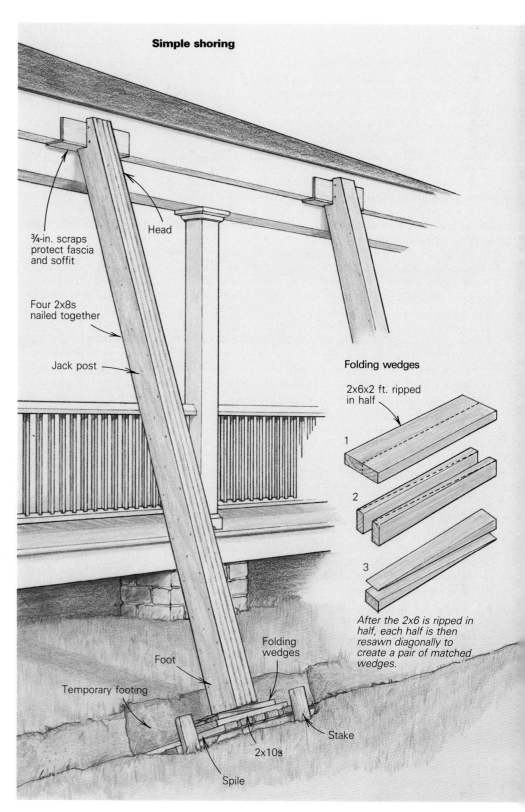

Simple shoring

Head

¾-in. scraps protect fascia and soffit

Four 2x8s nailed together

Jack post

Foot

Temporary footing

2x10s

Spile

Folding wedges

Stake

Folding wedges

2x6x2 ft. ripped in half

1

2

3

After the 2x6 is ripped in half, each half is then resawn diagonally to create a pair of matched wedges.

all shoring methods are potentially dangerous, and safety is the most important consideration. Sizes of timbers must be designed with a large safety factor in mind.

The jack posts were designed to be strong enough to lift the weight without distorting. We laminated them out of four 2x8s nailed together so the posts would have a wide foot to stand on. Leonardo Da Vinci long ago discovered that a bundle of saplings bound together would support more than a solid post of the same diameter.

Folding wedges—Wedges used in opposing pairs, called folding wedges, are the key to all of our shoring methods. In this case, we inserted them under the feet of the jack posts and used them to raise the roof. The wedges are sawn from yellow pine 2x6s at least 2 ft. long (detail drawing, previous page). We rip the 2x6s in half giving us two pieces of wood 2¾ in. wide. Each of these is then resawn diagonally, which gives us a 2¾-in. wide wedge with a long slope and a low rise.

The wedges are cut and used in pairs. This pairing assures that the lifting occurs evenly. The wedges are made so they can be hammered in or out (at some point we trim them blunt on the thin end) and are held in place by gravity and friction. They must be removed as carefully as they are inserted.

After the heads of the jack posts were put in place (we use duplex nails to hold them temporarily) and the feet set on wedges and footings, we were all set to raise the roof. This was done by driving the opposing wedges into each other (depending on the load, we'll drive wedges with anything from a 22-oz. framing hammer to a 10-lb. sledge). We did this at each jack-post location, raising the entire roof a little at a time and monitoring the progress by measuring with rule, story pole and stringlines. We only wanted to clear the new columns by ½ in. As each new column was placed we simply backed out the wedges and allowed the weight to settle.

Crib shoring—On my next job I had to raise and level the interior floors of the oldest house in Eminence, Kentucky. Inside this 150-year-old structure, doors wouldn't close, plaster was cracked and furniture wouldn't stay put.

Under the house was a crawl space and a tiny hand-dug basement. Walnut sills, girders, and sleepers supported 2-in. by 12-in. roughsawn poplar joists (girders that carried other girders were called sleepers). The dirt within the rock foundation was powder dry and very fine.

I decided to raise the floor with crib shoring (drawing below) and leave it in place permanently. I had seen my engineer father employ this same method to shore up floors under heavy equipment in an old mill. Crib shoring, which involves layers of crisscrossed timbers, works on the same principle as snowshoes; it distributes weight over a larger area, thus sustaining a big load on a soft surface.

On this particular job we used pressure-treated 6x6s to make cribs (sometimes we use 4x4s or landscape timbers). Crib design and timber sizes are custom-fitted to the job. Here the bottom timbers were 4 ft. long, and those in each successive tier were about 6 in. shorter than the previous ones. As each crib was assembled, we toenailed the timbers together. Under the house, we moved the timbers about easily with rope and a small sled called a stone boat. Made of two 2x4 runners about 4 ft. long and two 2x10 crosspieces about 2 ft. long, we used the sled to move all manner of tools and materials in the tight spaces.

After all the cribs were strategically located under the sagging timbers, we used 2-ft. folding wedges to raise the floor. Wedges were nailed to hold them in place, but nailed sparingly so additional repairs could be made in the years ahead. In this case the girders and sleepers were laid out in a grid of 12-ft. squares, and the joists changed directions at every grid. But it was easy to see where the girders had failed: generally in the center of their span. This is where we placed a crib. In places, we used two or more cribs with a beam between them.

When we collected our pay, all the door locks worked again and the floors were level, flat and stable.

Rake shoring—The third job that I'll describe was the most difficult and required the most sophisticated use of low-tech shoring methods. I was asked about a problem wall by a client living in a manor house built in 1864. The walls were solid brick, which had been molded and fired on the site. On the south side of the two-story house a brick pilaster had shifted about 1 inch on the cut-stone foundation, thus allowing the weight of the brick wall to break the limestone lintels over two windows.

To compound the problem, the soft inner brick of the three-layer wall had crumbled and settled. This caused two things to go wrong simultaneously. The outside of the wall bulged 6 in., and indoors the sculptured plaster ceilings, with pierced leaf molding, were beginning to break and fall. The inner layer of brick was all that held the ceiling up and the wall in place. It too had moved about ¾ in.

Two architects and one engineer had diagnosed the illness as terminal and could only recommend razing the wall and rebuilding it. I convinced the owners that it could be saved and corrected with rake shoring (photo facing page) at less than one tenth the cost of rebuilding.

The procedure was similar to the simple shoring mentioned previously, but with a few important differences. Our temporary footings were dug and ditched so they would drain after a rain. They were placed at a distance from the house that gave the jack posts an angle to the grade of about 60° (drawing facing page). This angle was critical because we were trying both to lift and push the wall at the same time.

After the footings were done, we nailed together wall pieces to lie vertically against the house and distribute the horizontal thrust of the jack posts. These wall pieces were made up from six 2x4s on edge.

We planned to push and lift the wall at two locations above and below the second-floor joists. We left holes in our wall pieces at these levels and made corresponding holes in the outer brick, so we could penetrate the wall with short needle beams. Each needle beam acts as a chock for the upward force where the jack posts meet the brick wall.

We used two pairs of jack posts—each pair consisting of an upper and lower post—positioned on either side of the windows with the broken lintels. We connected the upper and lower jack posts with 2x6s.

In this case, the upper jack posts were made of three 2x8s sandwiched so that the center 2x8 could slide between the two outer 2x8s. The two outside pieces were connected with 2x4 ties top and bottom every 3 ft. In addition to lifting the entire jack post with folding wedges placed on the footing, we inserted another set of wedges at a joint in the center 2x8, about 4 ft. up from the footing. Only the

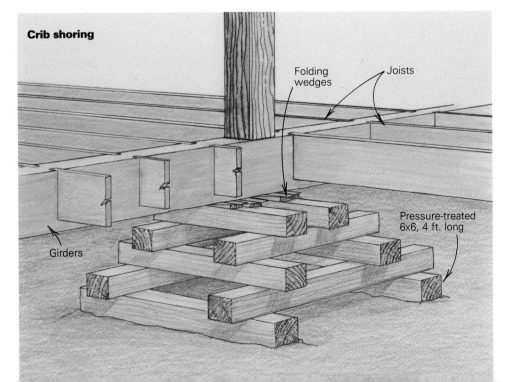

Crib shoring

Folding wedges

Joists

Girders

Pressure-treated 6x6, 4 ft. long

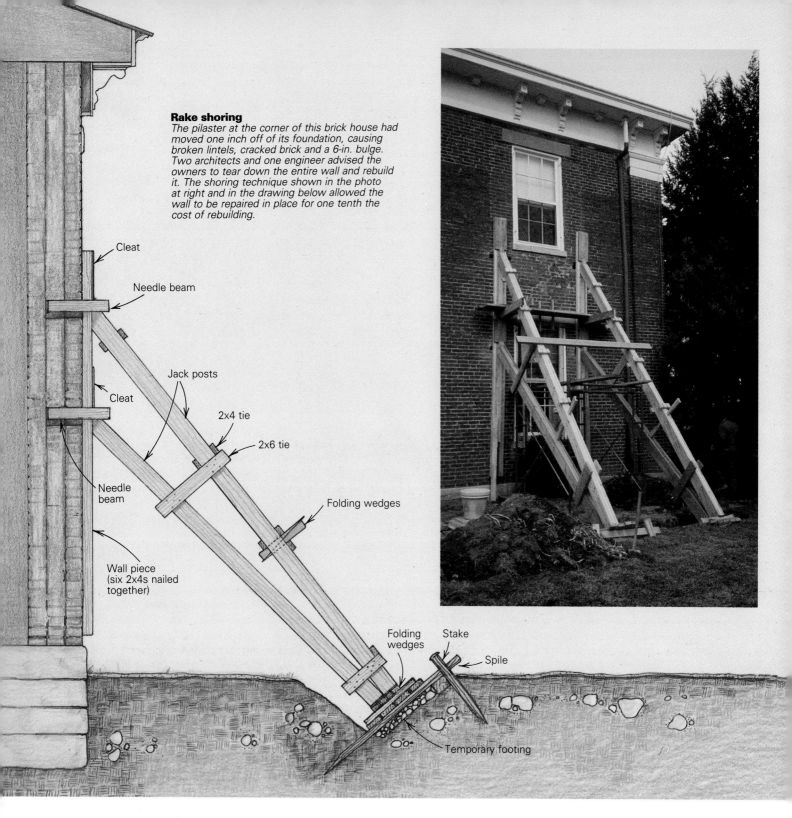

Rake shoring
The pilaster at the corner of this brick house had moved one inch off of its foundation, causing broken lintels, cracked brick and a 6-in. bulge. Two architects and one engineer advised the owners to tear down the entire wall and rebuild it. The shoring technique shown in the photo at right and in the drawing below allowed the wall to be repaired in place for one tenth the cost of rebuilding.

Cleat

Needle beam

Jack posts

Cleat

2x4 tie

2x6 tie

Needle beam

Folding wedges

Wall piece (six 2x4s nailed together)

Folding wedges

Stake

Spile

Temporary footing

center 2x8 raises the needle beam. The side 2x8s push against the wall piece and, with wedges and blocking, hold what is gained by the center 2x8. When all was at the ready we tightened the wedges to hold the wall and prevent any more movement.

Repairing the wall—With the shoring taking up the load of the wall, the next task was to put the brick pilaster back in place on the stone foundation. This we accomplished by building a bulkhead 4 ft. from the house. Then we placed two 25-ton screw jacks and short 6x6 posts between the bulkhead and the brick to push the pilaster back into place.

To keep the foundation from shifting again

we excavated the dirt beside it and poured a concrete buttress against the pier, just below the finish grade line. We wanted no evidence of tampering with the original foundation. We gave the concrete a weekend to cure and then began the serious work of pushing the wall back plumb.

There had been a few periods of rain as work progressed, and we had tightened the wedges in our shoring after each rain to compensate for the softening of the earth at the temporary footings. When we checked the wall and ceiling inside they were back in place, and only one 6-in. piece of leaf molding had fallen.

The next days were spent removing lintels and rebuilding the brick wall in rake or stair-

step fashion. Instead of using limestone lintels, we cast new lintels from portland cement and sand, reinforced with ½-in. rebar. To duplicate the marks on sawn limestone, we stroked the green concrete with a rubbing stone.

All the bricks were tuckpointed to a depth of 1½ in. After raking the mortar joints, there was nothing left to be done but remove the shoring, replace the brick where the needle beams had been and repair the earth. When we left, the owners were pleased, we were pleased, and the architects coming by to view the results were dumbfounded. ☐

W. Whitie Gray is a designer and builder in Shelbyville, Kentucky. Photo by the author.

Drawings: Bob Goodfellow

Replacing Rotted Sills

It's a dirty job, but somebody's got to do it

by George Nash

The heavy clay soil of northern Vermont is notorious for its poor drainage. Before the era of the backhoe and dump truck, foundation walls were usually backfilled with the soil taken from the cellar excavation. If this happened to be gravelly soil, then the dry-laid fieldstone foundation walls would remain in place. If not, they would inevitably begin to heave inward.

Another problem with these dry-laid foundation walls became apparent each spring as the water table rose, or especially after a heavy rain; water washed into the cellar through the cracks between the stones.

Heavy equipment and transit-mix concrete allow present-day renovators to remove a failed foundation and replace it. Carpenters of an earlier generation did not have this luxury. In the attempt to shore up a heaved wall or to prevent water infiltration, they would often pour a sloped concrete wall directly against the old stone; sometimes on the inside, but more typically on the outside. This "buttress" wall would sometimes extend to the bottom of the foundation, but it would often end wherever the ditch diggers felt was deep enough.

The bulky, spalling buttress wall was the first thing I noticed about the house that Will Leas and Lisa Dimondstein hired me to help

renovate. The house had begun life as a hunting camp some 50 years ago. Over time the camp had been tinkered with and remodeled until it was almost a regular house. The Dimondsteins were following a long tradition when they decided to give the house a facelift and upgrade its energy efficiency. Leas had discovered and repaired a section of rotten sill along one wall the previous year and suspected that there might be more decay behind the mildewed clapboards on the remaining walls.

Finding fault—Structural rot is not always apparent. When probed with an awl from the cellar side, the timber sills felt as solid as new wood. There was no evidence here of rot caused by a dank, unventilated cellar. On the outside, however, the bottom edge of the siding was punky where it slipped behind the top of the buttress wall. I was hoping that a sim-

When probed with an awl from inside, the sills pictured above felt solid, but mildew and signs of decay on the clapboards outside suggested otherwise. The concrete wall, used to buttress the old stone foundation, had no flashing or drip cap on top of it, so water seeped behind the wall and into the sills, joists and studs.

ple flashing installed over the concrete and up under the first course of clapboards might be all that was needed to halt damage.

We inserted flat bars under the edge of the second course of siding, loosened the nails and removed the first clapboard. Like a vampire shrinking from the noonday sun, the freshly exposed sheathing board virtually crumbled into compost as it was revealed. The next clapboard was removed, and yet another. Still the decay continued upward, joining a vein of rot that had begun under the window sills. I was beginning to wonder what had held those clapboards on the wall.

With a nail-eating carbide blade in the circular saw, I sawed along the bottom edge of the sixth course, removing all the siding below the window sills. Feeling like a surgeon probing a malignant cancer, I removed the sheathing boards. What remained of the timber sill would have made an excellent medium for growing mushrooms. The decay had progressed into the ends and bottom edges of floor joists that rested on the sill and continued up into the bottom of the wall studs (photo above).

Surprises such as this are what make renovation work so stimulating—and so difficult

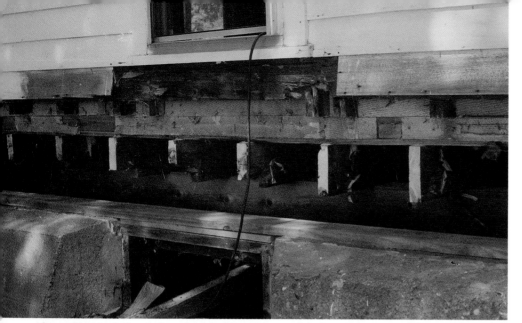

After cutting back the studs and joists (above) to a point where there was solid wood, the author capped off the old stone foundation with mortar and nailed down a pressure-treated 2x10 mudsill.

Rebuilding (above) involves a lot of improvising based on the configuration of the original framing, the extent of the decay and the materials at hand. Here the author added doubled sole plates to the stud wall, a 2x10 rim joist to cap the joist ends, a 2x6 on edge under the joists and blocking.

To prevent future rot, the author blocked water access by installing lead flashing between the sheathing and the concrete wall (below). Lead conforms well to the irregularities in concrete and lasts indefinitely. However, exposed lead is a health hazard, so the flashing had to be painted.

to estimate. To protect myself against financial ruin, I had long ago learned to stipulate in bids and contracts that any decay discovered in the course of a job would be repaired as an extra at cost plus. The extent of rot or insect damage can seldom be determined until walls are ripped apart and the bones of the house exposed. Here was a case where a barely noticeable lesion—the punky first course of siding—concealed lethal structural decay.

The irony of all this is that the damage and subsequent repair work could have been avoided if a drip cap or simple flashing had been installed when the buttress wall was poured. Why this was not done eludes me. Perhaps it was ignorance or laziness, but I have seen many such walls over the years, and except for a desiccated bead of caulk between clapboard and concrete, nothing protected this problem zone.

The buttress wall had been poured directly against the siding, forming an exquisite water trap. The old building paper soaked up moisture like a paper towel and held it against the sheathing. Ventilation was discouraged by the painted siding, which was relatively rot-resistant red cedar. A more ideal environment for decay-producing fungi would be hard to build. Thus the rot grew inward, first through the sheathing boards, then into the framing. The sills were hardest hit because they rested on masonry, which tends to draw water.

Structural support—Once the rot had been exposed, we had to determine how to support the structure while the sills were removed and replaced. Most of the rotted sills that I've replaced have been on timber-frame houses. And the salient feature of the timber frame, at least from a structural point of view, is concentrated loading. Unless it carries the floor joists or girt, removing a portion of sill between posts is not hard because there is little or no load on it. But where the sill supports a post, the entire load carried by that post must be relieved before the sill is removed. At times this can get tricky.

The situation is much easier with a stick-frame structure. Here the load is distributed along the entire length of the sill. Now one might suppose that this would complicate things, but since the actual portion of the load at any given point is quite small, rather large sections of sill and attendant framing can be removed with impunity. The web of framing, siding, sheathing and interior finish also help to distribute the load and support itself so long as some portion of the wall is left to bear on the foundation. An adjacent section of wall will often support the corner of the building, while the sill directly under the corner is removed, which is not always the case with timber-framed walls. I am continually amazed by how much sill can be removed and how little support is required to maintain the structural stability of a stick-framed house.

Of course, it is wise, in either case, to err on the side of caution. Experience will guide you, but cracking the interior wall finish or exploding a window is not a particularly gratifying way to learn.

This particular house was a bit unusual. The hand-hewn 8x8 sill beams had obviously been salvaged from an older structure. These supported rough-sawn 2x4 studs toenailed directly to the sill. The floor joists ran perpendicular to the gable wall and were also supported by the sills, so the roof load was separate from the floor load. That meant there would be less of a problem supporting the walls while the sills were removed.

We maneuvered a 16-ft. 8x8 timber into the cellar through the window opening and hung it from ropes just under the floor joists. This way we didn't have to worry about the timber crashing down on our heads while we positioned the jacks and uprights. We kept the timber far enough back from the sill that we could work on the sill from inside if necessary. I use hydraulic jacks if I'm actually lifting something, but here I was merely supporting the weight of the floor, so I used several screw jacks and 4x4 posts under the timber.

In with the new—Once the floor load was supported, the sill could be removed about 12 ft. at a time (half the length of the wall) before we had to reposition the jacks and timbers. The inside portion of the sill was still solid, so

I sawed it into bite-sized portions with a reciprocating saw. The pieces were easily pulled free with a prybar. The nails securing the studs to the sill had long since rusted away. To avoid splitting the bottom of the floor joists, which were mostly sound and nailed with 30d spikes, I cut them free with a nail-cutting blade in the reciprocating saw.

The dry-laid stone foundation was uneven and covered with dirt and debris. I sprayed the stones with water from a hose and wire-brushed them clean. Then I capped them with mortar, troweling the surface level to the top of the buttress wall, eliminating the watertrap. We drove 20d galvanized spikes through a 2x10 pressure-treated mudsill, then set the sill on the wet mortar so the nails would anchor it. The mortar was left to set up until the next day before we proceeded.

I squared the ends of the floor joists (top photo facing page), making allowances for a new rim joist flush to the outside edge of the new sill. An additional pressure-treated 2x6 on edge supports the underside of the joists, replacing the timber sill (drawing below). This left a gap between the top of the mudsill and the bottom of the rim joist, which I filled in with a horizontal 2x4 on edge and a series 2x4 blocks (middle photo facing page and drawing below) to provide nailing for the sheathing

boards. Once the joists were supported, I sawed off the studs above the rot and then installed a pair of sole plates to support them. For additional rot protection, we coated all exposed edges of existing framing with Cuprinol #10 Wood Preservative (Darworth Co., 50 Tower La., Avon, Conn. 06001).

The stud cavities were refilled with fiberglass batt insulation. Fortunately for us, the walls had not contained loose-fill insulation, which would have made quite a mess. Had it contained loose-fill, I would have plugged the cavities with rolled-up batt insulation to prevent the loose fill from spilling and then blown in new material after sheathing the walls.

Shim, sheathe, flash and finish—In a perfect world, the new 1-in. rough-sawn sheathing boards would have lined up flush with the old. But the old sheathing varied in thickness, and I found myself using ¾-in. stock in some places and furring it out with the remodeler's most useful tool—the cedar shingle. Also, the new straight sill didn't line up exactly plumb to the old irregular wall. A straight-edge held vertically over each stud established the amount of shimming required to align the old wall with the new sill before applying sheathing boards. I stapled up a layer of resin-coated building paper to seal the boards against air infiltration (a high-tech house wrap, such as Tyvek or Typar, would have been better, but I only needed a little and couldn't get a partial roll).

To make sure that no more water would get in under the siding, I installed 8-in. wide lead flashing (bottom photo facing page). Lead is ideal for this purpose because it conforms to every irregularity in the concrete and is flexible enough not to tear or split. It lasts longer than galvanized steel or aluminum, and it is cheaper than copper. Federal Housing Authority regulations prohibit exposed lead where it can be touched by animals or people (chimney flashings are okay, for instance), so Leas had to paint the metal. He used metal primer and enamel from Rust-Oleum Corp. (11 Hawthorne Parkway, Vernon Hills, Il. 60061). I sealed the flashing to the concrete with a bead of Geocel acrylic copolymer (Geocel Corp., P. O. Box 398, Elkhart, Ind. 46515). This is an excellent choice wherever dissimilar materials are to be joined because it is extremely flexible over a wide temperature range, and it's very sticky. Finally, I plugged the nailholes in the original siding with latex painter's caulk before renailing.

Repair and replacement of rotted sills is a highly idiosyncratic procedure. Improvisation and extrapolation from previous experience must guide you to the best approach. Take time to visualize the downward flow of the loads, the connections of the frame and what each member is carrying; it will become obvious where support is critical and when. □

George Nash is a builder and writer who lives in Wolcott, Vermont. Photos by the author.

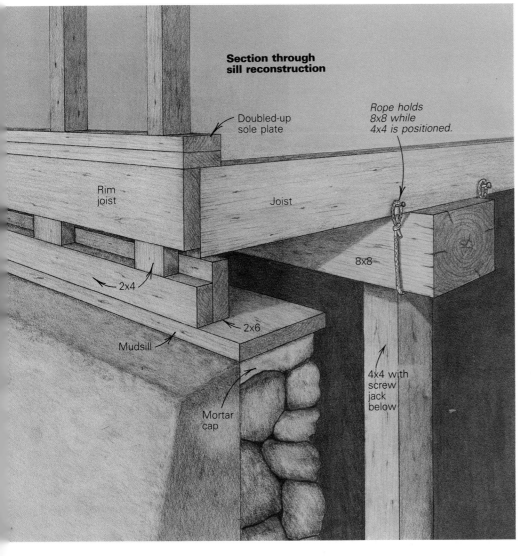

Section through sill reconstruction

Doubled-up sole plate

Rope holds 8x8 while 4x4 is positioned.

Rim joist

Joist

2x4

8x8

2x6

Mudsill

Mortar cap

4x4 with screw jack below

Saving the Old Daggett Place

Every inch from foundation to ridge was either repaired, rebuilt or replaced

by Kevin Ireton

Built early in the 20th century, the balloon-framed addition, with its bulky dormers, overpowered the 18th-century timber frame it joined.

The new owners bought the rundown Daggett property, just south of Cornwall, Connecticut's village green, to save it for posterity. They hired renovation contractor Will Calhoun to make some cosmetic and mechanical improvements and to salvage as much of the place as possible, figuring that they would sell the house soon after the work ended. But during the first few weeks of the project, two things happened. First, Calhoun discovered that cosmetic repairs would not suffice. And second, the historical significance of the house began to assume a palpable weight.

Reverend Daggett—During the early part of the 19th century, missionary zeal was widespread in New England, and it extended not only to the American Indians, but also to the "heathens" of Africa, Asia and the Pacific Islands. In 1817, Cornwall's Foreign Mission

Among the surprises uncovered during the renovation was damage from powder-post beetles. Whole sections of timbers (such as the one above) had to be replaced.

School was established to convert natives from these cultures to Christianity and train them to serve as missionaries to their own people. But the school was closed in 1826 because the people of Cornwall decided that such training was best done in the field, rather than in a quaint New England village—a conclusion reached shortly after two of the natives married local women.

Rev. Herman Daggett was principal of the Foreign Mission School for most of its brief existence. More than 160 years later, it was his name that the new owners of the house found carved among the clenched nails on the inside of the tiny attic door.

Dilapidated hodgepodge—Edward Starr's *A History of Cornwall, Connecticut*, (Tuttle, Morehouse and Taylor Co., 1926, out of print) refers to a house "which Mr. Daggett made

Photos this page: Will Calhoun

over from a barn." It was a 24-ft. by 30-ft. chestnut timber frame, built in the late 18th century. Rev. Daggett bought the property and converted the barn to a house in 1817. Over the next hundred years, the house passed through a variety of owners, but the basic structure remained largely unchanged. Then in 1907, Alfred and Delia Catlin bought the place and turned it into a boarding house called "Honeysuckle Cottage." They added windows, cut a pair of dormers into the south roof and built a 21-ft. by 30-ft. balloon-framed addition on the north side. So anxious were the Catlins for more space that they extended the addition far enough north to integrate a small shed into the house.

Unfortunately the huge balloon frame, with its own bulky dormers, overpowered the original house (top photo, facing page). And worse, all the work done at this time was done very poorly, with no consideration for structural integrity. The house had all the problems typical of 19th-century framing (see *FHB* #6, pp. 36-38). To accommodate the new windows, intermediate posts supporting girts in the original frame had been hacked off and the windows inserted with no framing around them. An 8x8 plate had been sawn through in four places to make room for the dormers. The 6x6 rafters above had also been cut, but no header was added, and the rafter simply hung from the sheathing. By the time Calhoun and his crew got to the place, the sections of roof outside the dormers drooped like the wings of a tired bird and were 4½ in. lower than the section between the dormers.

The original central chimney had been demolished, and the debris was heaped in the crawl space. A cellar had been dug under one section of the frame without reinforcing the fieldstone foundation—someone had simply dug down three feet below the stone. Constant flooding over the years had eroded the dirt walls, and the local fire department had pumped out the cellar five times the previous year. Although it was newer by 100 years, the balloon-framed addition was in no better shape. This wasn't the sort of work that prompts people to lament that "they don't build them like they used to."

"When we arrived," Calhoun said, "the house and outbuildings looked like soft sculpture. Gravity and weather were clearly reclaiming them, sending them back to the earth. The eaves and shutters sagged. The front door moaned and scraped as we pushed it open."

For the first few weeks, Calhoun and his crew poked tentatively at the old structure, adhering to the original plan of minimal work and quick resale. But each new corner they opened exposed new problems. According to Calhoun, "We arrived at a point where the scope of the project had been altered so severely that the owners had to reconsider where our efforts would take us." It was a great relief to Calhoun when the owners decided not to sell the house, but instead, to keep it as a weekend retreat. "This meant

major changes in the level of quality we would look for," Calhoun said. "It meant we could consider the owner's comfort and tastes as they applied to every detail of the house. Building for an individual is a far more satisfying process than building for an anonymous mass market."

Full-scale demolition—After the change in plans, the first thing Calhoun did was to rent a dump truck. The second thing he did was to help the crew tear down the entire balloon-framed addition. The demolition, like all the subsequent phases of the project, was a collaborative effort. Everybody got involved in the grunt work so that it was over quickly. They stripped the original structure down to the frame. A sturdy construction stair made the many trips between levels easier—and safer.

In addition to being open just two days a week, the local landfill required that all plaster, glass, plastic and paper debris be separated from wood and metal. So the plaster demolition became a separate operation. They had to tear it off, break it up, shovel and broom it into wheelbarrows, then cart it to the dump truck parked against the house. From the second and third floors, they sent the plaster down a plywood chute propped in the back of the truck. After several days of red eyes and congested chests, the crew gained new respect for hard hats, goggles, respirators and hearing protectors. Before they were done, they had hauled more than 50 heaping dump-truck loads to the landfill.

Despite the grueling days when plaster dust clung to sweat-soaked skin and ground between clenched teeth, Calhoun claims, "There was real pleasure in the demolition. Part was the sheer physical joy of ripping something apart that required little thought. But there was also the pleasure of discovery. We found old skirt hoops, a musket tamper, tobacco tins, a Chinese coin. We had to know when to stop acting like barbarians tearing down a house and become thoughtful archeologists." Calhoun carefully marked and stored anything that might prove useful later.

Foundations and the flying buttress—The next order of new business was to pour footings under the fieldstone walls where the cellar had been excavated. Calhoun and his crew dug out two-foot sections one at a time and poured the concrete in increments using a three-sided plywood form. Any stones that fell during the process were simply mortared back in place after the concrete had cured. The crew also cleaned and pointed all the fieldstone and poured a floor for a new furnace and hot-water tank.

Everybody pitched in to form a bucket brigade to clear debris from the crawl space. From the outside, the foundation showed massive granite blocks and looked sound. But once the crawl space was cleared out, everyone was surprised to find that the blocks were sitting on an unmortared rubble stone foundation. Working in dark, cramped

quarters, the crew hosed off the stones and painstakingly tuck-pointed every one. The final touch was a double layer of polyethylene and 4 in. of crushed stone spread over the floor of the crawl space. Despite the subsequent complaints of the subcontractors about working in the cellar and crawl space, conditions there were a vast improvement over what they had been. While all of this was going on, a backhoe was brought in to excavate, and a block-wall foundation was laid for a new addition where the balloon frame had been.

Along with the shoddy workmanship, water and insects had also taken their toll on the chestnut frame. So with the foundation in shape, it was time to repair rotted sills and eaten-away posts (bottom photo, facing page). The crew replaced whole sections of timbers in some places and spliced in patches elsewhere. They removed sections of bad wood by making a series of kerfs with circular saws and then chiseling out the waste. If the damage ran deeper, they made another series of cuts a few inches inside the first, and then built up a patch with staggered layers of pressure-treated 2x8s.

To get the weight off the sills and posts while repairing them, a site-built rig nicknamed the "flying buttress" was used. Made with 2x4s and two pairs of ¾-in. plywood triangles, the flying buttress was slipped around a post about two ft. above the sill and held in place with plenty of duplex nails. The base of the triangle created a cantilever to the side of the post, and a screw jack could then be set up to take the weight off the post (top photo, p. 110).

Avoiding the shiny-penny look—Ilse Reese, an architect from nearby Sharon, Conn., did all the initial design work, including floor plans and elevations. Reese designed a new single-story addition that was only half as wide as the old balloon frame. She wanted the original structure to dominate the elevations.

Following the owners instructions to "avoid the shiny-penny look," Reese carefully avoided unifying the exterior, which could have made it look like a new house. Instead, she cultivated the rambling, eclectic appearance of subsequent additions to an older house. For instance, she broke up the roof lines between the old shed (now the mud room) and the new addition and kept the decidedly uncolonial dormers on the main house. Reese also called for completely different eave designs on the shed, the addition and the house.

Up on the roof—Framing the new addition on a new foundation with new lumber came as a welcome relief to Calhoun and his crew. But the work went quickly, and they were soon up on the south roof of the main house, contending with the structural havoc wrought by the dormers. They completely rebuilt the section of roof below the dormers and jacked up the drooping sides as much as possible. Then they strung lines from eave to ridge over each rafter and measured the deflection every two ft. along the string. These measurements were used to cut long tapered shims from 2x stock, which were then nailed onto the rafters, creating a single roof plane.

After nailing solid sheathing in the valleys to provide support for the copper flashing, they strapped the entire roof with 1x4s, 5 in. o. c. and set about nailing on 30 square of cedar shingles. With the 9-in-12 roof pitch they needed scaffolding, but Calhoun didn't want to use standard roof brackets because they can damage shingles and leave a trail of nail holes behind. Instead, the crew built their own brackets that hooked over the strapping further up the roof (photo below left). Once comfortably ensconced on their nailing benches, the crew lined up the shingles along a straightedge hung from a string and nailed them home. They flashed the chimney and the dormers with copper and capped the ridges with cedar.

After finishing the roof, Calhoun strung heavy copper wire along both sides of all the ridges. Although he knew it might be nothing but superstition, he had heard that the solution created by a mix of rainwater and copper will make a cedar roof last longer. According to the Red Cedar Shingle and Handsplit Shake Bureau (515 116 Ave. N. E., Suite 275, Bellevue, Wash. 98004), what the copper really does is to keep the shingles clean by preventing the growth of fungus.

Underexposed siding—Long before the advent of fiberglass batts and rigid foam, people shoveled snow against the sides of their houses as insulation. Although it helped keep the house warm, it was hard on the siding. So carpenters started decreasing the exposure of clapboards around the bottom of a house. Calhoun decided to do this on the Daggett house. He laid out the story pole so that the first course of cedar clapboards shows only two inches to the weather. From there the exposure grows ¼ in. with each course until it reaches 4 inches, where it remains all the way to the eaves (top photo, p. 113). The owners chose a soft grey/green stain for the siding to help the house blend with the grass, trees and stones.

Plain-vanilla trim—Among the salvage that Calhoun had collected during the demolition was a section of patched and broken wainscotting. Made of wide boards, run horizontally and beaded along the edge, it couldn't be reused, but served as a clue to the original character of the house. Calhoun extrapolated all the trim details from this one element, adhering at the same time to the owners' admonition to keep the interior "bone simple" like "plain vanilla."

The owners wanted stained woodwork, so Calhoun decided to use sugar pine, which is straight-grained and very stable. Although it tears a bit when machined, sugar pine is easy to nail and work by hand. All the trim was milled on site using a tablesaw fitted

The builders used the "flying buttress" above to help them repair the sills and posts. Its plywood edges were slipped around the post and attached with duplex nails. Cantilevered off to the side, the base of the triangular-shaped rig provided a place to set a screw jack and take the weight off the post. Not wanting to damage the cedar shingles with standard roof brackets, the crew built brackets that hooked over the strapping further up the roof (photo below). In preparation for the copper flashing, the valleys had to filled in with solid sheathing.

Photo: Will Calhoun

In the design of the kitchen cabinets pictured above, Calhoun departed from the style of the house. He wanted to keep the design spare to enhance the panoramic view. Instead of frame-and-panel doors, the cabinets have flush doors with breadboard ends. Calhoun's first requirement when designing the mantel (photo below) was that he be able to comfortably rest his elbow on it. The restrained but elegant mantel was built entirely on site with flat stock and applied moldings made with a molding cutter on a tablesaw.

with a molding cutterhead. The baseboard is a 1x6 with a simple ogee cut in the top edge. The three horizontal boards that make up the wainscot have a delicate quirk bead along one edge and are capped with a scotia molding and chair rail. Window and door casings are plain 1x4 except for that same quirk-bead design, which loops around the inside edge.

Rather than miter the corners of the window and door casing, Calhoun decided to use butt joints, which were typical of the period when the house was built. The quirk bead on the inside edge still had to be mitered, though. Side casings could be done with two cuts on a miter box, but the joint on the head casing had to be cut entirely with a handsaw.

Calhoun and crew boxed in all the exposed beams of the timber frame, in part to hide the damaged areas that had been repaired, but also because it was in keeping with the period of the house (in contrast to today's timber frames, where the beams are planed smooth, the joinery is cabinet quality and the frame is celebrated). Eighteenth-century frames were rough-hewn, and the joinery was purely functional. It was a mark of distinction if you could afford to cover your beams with trim.

Although Reese had laid out the floor plans and cabinet elevations in the kitchen/dining area, the actual design of the cabinets fell to Calhoun, and here he departed from tradition, rejecting a frame and panel design. By keeping the cabinet design spare, Calhoun could enhance the panoramic view created by the solid bank of casements along the east wall. The drawer fronts are absolutely plain, The cabinet and pantry doors are flush, solid pine doors with breadboard ends (top photo, p. 111). It is a testament to sugar

Reverend Herman Daggett had been the principal of Cornwall's Foreign Mission School. Finding his named carved on the attic door (directly above) helped convince the new owners not to sell his old house but rather to renovate it for themselves. In the top photo you can see the windows to the right of the chimney that follow the line of the staircase to the second floor. Inside, the open L-shaped staircase (photo on facing page) comes as a surprise in a house full of small cozy spaces.

pine's stability that two years after their construction, none of these doors shows any sign of warp or twist.

The open L-shaped staircase in the central hall comes as a surprise in a house full of intimate spaces (photo, facing page). The stairwell is open to the rooflines, with natural light and delightful views provided by a divided-light door at the bottom and three windows along the ascent. Anchored soundly into the floor joists, the plain newel posts are composed of 2x stock wrapped with four pine boards, mitered along their length and capped with beaded finials made to Calhoun's design by a local turner. The store-bought balusters were dovetailed into the oak treads, making a very stout balustrade.

When he designed the living room's fireplace mantel and its flanking bookshelves, Calhoun's first requirement was a mantel shelf on which he could comfortably rest his elbow. Calhoun's design was influenced by drawings

in J. Frederick Kelly's *Early Domestic Architecture of Connecticut* (Dover Publications Inc., 1963). That's where he learned that fireplace walls were the place where colonial builders traditionally flaunted their skills.

Calhoun's design for the Daggett house mantel is very restrained (bottom photo, p. 111), but in its simple context it commands attention. The construction of the mantel is simpler than it looks. Flat stock was nailed in place and moldings were applied to it. The frame and panel effect was created with a very delicate molding, just ¼ in. thick, that was mitered to form squares and rectangles. Even this molding was made on the tablesaw with a molding cutter. After the profile was cut into the edge of larger stock, the thin molded edge was ripped off.

The beaded boards running horizontally above the mantel were laid out so that the beads line up with the shelves on either side. The bookshelves are fixed rather than adjustable and made of 5/4 sugar pine, captured by dados cut into the uprights.

Upstairs, Calhoun retained the orginal wide-plank pine flooring. The bedrooms are clipped by the rafter lines and have a cozy, sleep-late feel. The original attic stairway was hauled to the landfill, and access is now through a pull-down stair in one of the bedrooms. But Calhoun didn't forget about the old attic door. It's hung like a painting on a wall in the upstairs hallway. You won't find anything when you open it though, except of course, a crude inscription that reads: "Herman Daggett, 1820" (small photo this page). □

Kevin Ireton is an associate editor with Fine Homebuilding.

New Life for the Adelman Barn

A glass curtain wall and details inspired by history

by Louis Mackall

A renovation is frequently a conservative thing, as it was in this case. The owners, Bob and Merril Adelman, were quite happy with the existing structure, a 48-ft. long barn attached to their house (the house itself had, until 1947, been a barn; see photo above). Their need was simply to make it usable in the Connecticut winters. Where there were screens over raw openings, we added windows. We added a door with stairs out to the yard, and a cupola for light. Much of the rest involved adding insulation and a new floor. No new interior walls were added; the Adelmans wanted one big room. The trick was doing all this without erasing the patina of age on the inside.

At the outset, it was decided to leave the underside of the gambrel roof untouched so that it could be exposed to the interior. We added 5/4 by 4-in. sleepers, insulation and a new shingle roof on top. This required in-

creasing the fascia depth and fooling around with rigid insulation, but there was no other way that wouldn't have erased one of the most charming aspects of the barn: the interior finish. Where new framing was added to build the cupola, old lumber and old boards for sheathing were used wherever the work would be exposed to view from the inside.

A floating glass wall—The end of the barn had been more or less open for many years, and I wanted to keep the openness (but not the drafts). I was loathe to fill it with conventional windows because of the way their bulky frames would overpower the barn timbers and obstruct the view. The solution, built by Breakfast Woodworks, was to float the window two inches outside the original timber frame and treat it much like a curtain wall (top photo, facing page). The muntin layout was worked out on tracing paper laid over a

measured drawing of the barn end so that timbers and muntins would be synchronized.

We decided to use ⅜-in. insulating glass. The dimension of the muntins was determined by the need to conceal the sealed edges of the glass. We determined that ½-in. deep rabbets would do it (drawing, p. 116). The goal always is to keep the muntin as thin as possible; in this case it's 1⅜ in. thick. We chose the profile to provide enough depth so that the wall would be strong, and chose teak because it required no finish, no maintenance and its color related well with the other parts of the barn. For insurance, though, we applied ⅜-in. by ¼-in. brass flat stock to the interior face of each muntin (photo, p. 116). The strips were fastened to the muntins with Phillips-head brass screws. Among other things, this allowed us to erect the muntins in three sections while maintaining continuity across the joints.

After the wall was up, we tied it into the

Barn again. The main portion of the Adelmans' barn was turned into a house in 1947, and the second, smaller portion covered by this article was renovated recently (photo above). Though a cupola was eliminated in the first renovation, it reappeared in the second. The gable end of the smaller barn features a window wall that draws light indoors; the original timber framing of the barn supports the gable. The remodeling included only the second floor of the barn, leaving the first floor open as an unfinished storage area. Stairs angle up to the entry door (photo right) in order to avoid existing plantings. The Adelmans open the cupola windows in the spring, as the weather warms; hot air is exhausted naturally as cool air is drawn in through lower windows. In the fall, cupola windows are closed for the season.

From *Fine Homebuilding* (Spring 1991) 66:60-63

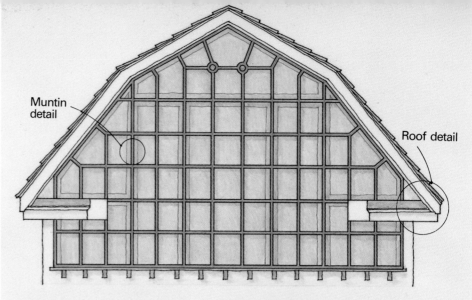

barn with brass stand-offs screwed to the existing timber frame. These stand-offs allowed us to accommodate differences between the barn frame and our new, straight window wall. The weight of the wall was carried on a separate teak sill anchored with small brackets to the barn. After the muntins were secured, the wall was glazed (photo facing page).

A golden crown of light—Building anything is exciting. I wondered about why this is so for some time and concluded that by building things, we participate in the age-old experience of birth, new life, and all that that means. There is a moment in each project, and indeed in each part of the project, during which that feeling is strongest. For the curtain wall, it was when large sections were assembled on the shop floor, and the wall began to assume the power at which the drawings hinted. For the project as a whole, however, this moment for me was when I first saw the cupola (photos, p. 115).

I had not been to the site for a few weeks. I walked in and of course looked up at the new work; it put a smile on my face that lasted a long time. I recommend cupolas if you enjoy getting high off framing lumber, glass and shingles. Cupolas are as close to pure spirit as one finds in a building.

Satisfying details—One true test of a successful renovation comes when you stand back to look at it. We found this one unusually satisfying, and on reflection, I think there are several reasons. First of all, the look of new wood shingles simply can't be beat. Too, the rake and drip molding came across nicely (drawing right). I had forgotten the visual damage aluminum drip edges have done to the average eave. For this project the builder, Dennis Doyle of Weston, Connecticut, had knives ground to match the existing molding. Molding makes a most wonderful fullness at that important line where the building leaves off and the sky begins. Doyle brought an unusual attention to every aspect of the work, and it shows—we were very lucky to have him on the case.

And there are a couple of likable details at the cupola. One was the angled transition between it and the main roof, and the other was the crisp overhang. But one of the most important elements marking the success of this project came from features given to it by the original builders. The barn had a distinct presence from the time it was first built, as well as strength and a certain scale that is not easily had in this age.

One never quite knows how such a project will turn out, or where it will lead. When things go well, the result is almost always more than anyone would have imagined, because, I suppose, it has had our hearts for a while. □

Louis Mackall is a practicing architect and president of Breakfast Woodworks, Inc. His office and shop are in Guilford, Connecticut.

Detail of window muntin

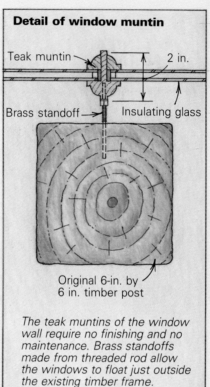

Teak muntin

2 in.

Brass standoff

Insulating glass

Original 6-in. by 6 in. timber post

The teak muntins of the window wall require no finishing and no maintenance. Brass standoffs made from threaded rod allow the windows to float just outside the existing timber frame.

Detail of roof

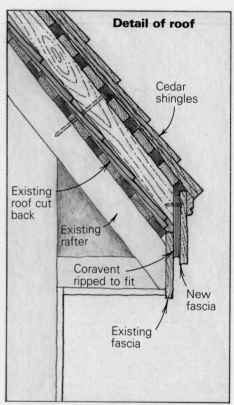

Cedar shingles

Existing roof cut back

Existing rafter

Coravent ripped to fit

New fascia

Existing fascia

Brass flat stock screwed to the inside of the window muntins (photo above) stiffens the gable-end expanse of glass (photo right). The owners loved the old barn's ceiling, so insulation and a new roof were added above it.

Wood-Infesting Insects

All about termites, carpenter ants and powderpost beetles

by Phil Pellitteri

Finding a fly in your soup is an insult, but finding termites, carpenter ants or powderpost beetles in your home, colonizing the timbers and chewing the wood, is a call to arms. These six-legged critters drive the average person to drastic and often expensive measures. Every year damage from termites alone costs Americans over one billion dollars. Some of that money is spent for insecticides, some for replacing damaged wood and some for aspirin to quiet the headache you get when you total the bill. The sad truth is that many homeowners—and builders—rush into needless or overly expensive treatments because they do not understand wood-infesting insects.

Termites—Termites are the sneakiest and most destructive of the three insects discussed here. They are serious structural pests because they feed on the cellulose found in wood. There are over 50 species of termites in the U. S., but the species known collectively as subterranean termites (*Genus Reticulitermes sp.*) accounts for more than 95% of all termite damage. Subterranean termites nest only in the ground, but will readily travel 30 or 40 yards from the nest to above-ground feeding sites.

The hot spot for termite problems is the Gulf coast region from eastern Texas to South Carolina. Moderate damage is seen in a band from California to southern Vermont, and activity is infrequent along a line from the Pacific Northwest to Maine.

All termites are social insects that live in colonies. Subterranean termites have two distinct forms: winged and unwinged. Called swarmers or reproductives, winged "kings and queens" are up to ½ in. long, dark colored and can easily be confused with winged carpenter ants. But ants have a constricted waist, elbowed antennae and wings of unequal length (drawing, p. 120). Winged termites, on the other hand, have thick waistlines, wings of equal length and straight or curved antennae (drawing right). Close up, the antennae look like a string of beads. The other form, worker termites, are ¼ in. long, wingless, eyeless, soft-bodied, white insects that are sterile (photo right). Workers avoid light, so are rarely seen in the open.

When a termite colony matures (that takes from 2 to 6 years), large numbers of winged individuals will emerge during the daylight, often after a rain. The most common sign of an infestation is a swarm of winged termites con-

gregating on windowsills or near other light sources. After the swarm disperses, the king and queen will find a nest site under a rock or in the soil and begin raising young (called nymphs). The nymphs mature into large-jawed soldier termites, which defend the nest, or into workers, which feed and care for the queen and young, build the nest and forage for food. Colonies can include hundreds of thousands of termites (reproductively mature males and females can develop from wingless nymphs).

The three critical needs of a termite colony are high humidity (moisture), a constant food source of wood or cellulose, and protection

from long periods of freezing weather. Although carpenter ants can hibernate, termites must continue to feed and be active throughout the winter. Because they are cold-blooded creatures, severe cold prevents termites from feeding above ground in unheated situations.

In the northern states termites did not become a building problem until the 1920s. The advent of central heating put wood in close contact with heated soil and gave termite colonies a year-round food source. Nesting in the soil keeps the colonies well-insulated and provides the needed humidity. Buried wood, tree stumps and fence posts all provide ter-

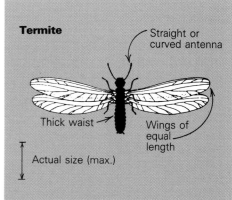

Termite

Straight or curved antenna

Thick waist

Wings of equal length

Actual size (max.)

Although they nest only in the ground, subterranean termites will forage a great distance looking for warm moist wood to feed on. Winged termites (top photo) are the kings and queens, also called swarmers. They are up to ½ in. long and can be distinguished from carpenter ants by their thick waists and wings of equal length. The worker forms (above) are ¼ in. long., wingless, eyeless, soft-bodied, white, sterile insects. They avoid light and so are seldom seen in the open.

mites with below-ground food sources, but termites will feed above ground if conditions are right. Termites are highly attracted to odors given off by decaying or wet wood.

When feeding on wood above ground, termites will often construct mud-like shelter tubes to protect themselves from temperature extremes, desiccation and enemies. These tubes are made of soil, wood and salivary secretions, and can be repaired quickly if damaged. Termites do not always need to construct tubes; cracks in cement slabs, any direct wood-to-soil contact, or hollow concrete blocks allow termites direct and hidden access to structural wood without leaving any visible tubes. The placement of stair carriages, wooden posts or partition walls in a basement before concrete is poured invites problems and makes the infestations hard to detect.

Termites leave little active sign on the outside of the wood they infest. Tapping infested lumber with the handle of a screwdriver will produce a dull hollow sound. Water stains or other signs of moisture problems may appear on the surface. If you probe the infested wood with a sharp screwdriver, you will find many small chambers (called galleries) that may or may not be crawling with small white insects. Damage is usually greatest in softer spring wood, and the gallery walls will be coated or spotted with a mixture of digested wood and soil that looks like dried oatmeal (photo below right).

When looking for termites outdoors, examine the foundation for shelter tubes coming from the soil. Look closely at areas such as attached porches, sidewalks and connecting patios that provide confined or hard-to-see spaces where termites can work up into the home. Check window and door frames, too. Indoors, probe or carefully sound door and window trim, baseboards and wood flooring. Do not overlook cracks or expansion joints in the foundation, and pay extra attention to places where utility pipes enter the foundation. If the house is built on a crawl space, you need to go into the crawl space and look for tubes on chimney bases, piers and along the beams and joists. Any standing water or leakage problems should be noted and corrected.

Preventing damage—Termite problems can be prevented through sound design and some common sense. In simple terms this means denying termites access to food, moisture and shelter. All wood-to-soil contacts should be eliminated including details such as trellises, stair carriages and fence posts. The grade level should be at least 6 in. to 8 in. below the top of the foundation or the siding, which will force termites to leave visible shelter tubes over the foundation and will make detecting them easier. In crawl spaces, there should be 18 in. of clearance between floor joists and soil and 12 in. between floor beams and soil. The use of metal termite shields to cap masonry walls forces termites out into the open and prevents the colony from working up through concrete blocks into the home.

Remove all wood, including concrete form boards and other debris containing cellulose, from under and around the house. Do not bury scrap wood or paper on the property during or after construction. Remove all stumps from underneath and around the foundation. Using scraps as fill under porch steps is a common and costly mistake. Fill cracks, voids or expansion joints and openings in the foundation with either cement grout or roofing-grade coal-tar pitch. Termites cannot eat through concrete, stone, metal or tar, but they will exploit any cracks or holes they find.

Polyethylene vapor barriers and proper foundation vents will prevent moisture buildup and lessen the potential for attracting termites. Any wood in contact with the soil should be pressure-treated lumber, which is impervious to termites. Some woods such as foundation-grade California redwood, all-heart Southern tidewater red cypress and very pitchy Southern pine have some natural resistance to subterranean termites and may also be used.

Controlling termites—Because termites nest in the ground, it's virtually impossible to find their nest and treat it directly. But placing a protective envelope of poisoned soil around the foundation of a house creates a barrier that will stop the termites. Chemical treatment of the soil before construction is far less expensive, allows for more accurate and efficient application of the chemicals and is less disruptive than the procedures used in treating existing structures. When building a home in a termite-prone area, *insist on a chemical pretreatment* before foundations, footings or slabs are poured.

Once a home is built, the problem is how to get the pesticide between the soil and the home's foundation without leaving any gaps. These chemical treatments require specialized drills, pressure injectors and pressure-generating pumps with high-volume tanks. Application rates run from 2 gal. to 4 gal. of mixed spray per 10 lineal feet of foundation, and drill holes through concrete slabs are spaced as close as every 12 in. Proper treatment is a real art, and improper treatment can contaminate the home or well water. When dealing with termite problems in existing structures, the best advice is to call in the services of a state-certified professional pest-control operator.

There have been major changes in the chemicals used for termite treatment in the last two years. For the past four decades, chlorinated hydrocarbon insecticides such as chlordane have been used to protect structures. Chlordane-treated soil prevented termite infestations for as long as 35 years. But concerns over potential health hazards associated with chlordane have resulted in the suspension of its use as of April 1988.

There has been a flood of new termiticides (insecticides that kill termites) in the last two years, and new products will continue to come on to the market. Only one formulation of one chemical, chlorpyrifos (Dursban), is available to the general public to use as a termiticide. Sold as Ortho's ORTHO-KLOR Soil Insect & Termite Killer (Chevron Chemical Co., P. O. Box 5047, San Ramon, Calif. 94583-0947), the use of this chemical is restricted by federal law to the directions on the label; it cannot be used indoors.

In general the new chemicals have fewer odor problems, and unlike chlordane, they can be cleaned up with detergent, deactivated if needed with relative ease, and seem to pose fewer environmental threats. Some seem to repel the termites rather than kill them. Disadvantages such as shorter residual (the term "residual" refers to how long a treatment will continue to work) and the lack of data

Termites can totally devastate the interior of the wood they infest, while leaving little active sign on the outside. In the 2x4 pictured above, you can see termite galleries (tunnels) coated with a mixture of digested wood and soil that looks like dried oatmeal.

on their long-term efficacy suggest that we can no longer assume treatments will last 20 to 30 years.

Some alternative methods of control are being looked at quite seriously. Parasitic nematodes that kill termites are commercially available, but the degree of control achieved so far has been disappointing. Dr. Glenn Esenther, retired entomologist from the U. S. D. A. Forest Products Research Lab, has been working with cardboard bait traps, which are placed in the ground to draw termite workers away from the infested structure. Once accepted as a food source by the colony, these traps can then be baited with a poison or collected and destroyed on a weekly basis. This is a slow system, but it's a viable alternative and is useful in structures that, for one reason or another, cannot be treated with insecticide. Other research efforts are exploring the possibility of using toxic elements, heavy metals or antibiotics mixed with food baits to poison the colony. Some of these systems are a few years away from the marketplace, but they do offer new and unique ways of fighting the battle.

If you do need to call in professional help, get estimates from two or three services. Be wary of excessively low or high bids, or companies that claim to have secret formulas. Ask about what chemicals they plan to use and why they have selected them. Professional companies should also advocate changes to the house (fixing leaks or lowering the grade around the foundation, for example) and moisture control along with their chemical treatments. Do not be rushed into treatment. Termites work slowly, and a few weeks' delay in treating them will not result in significant damage.

Carpenter ants—Carpenter ants (genus *Camponotus*) are found throughout the U. S., but are generally more of a problem in the Northeast, Midwest and the Pacific Northwest. Most medium to large black, or black and red ants seen on sidewalks or in the home are carpenter ants. They nest in the ground, in dead trees, in firewood, and sometimes, if conditions are right, they will nest in the home, especially in weakened or water-damaged wood. But unlike termites or powderpost beetles, *they do not eat wood*. Carpenter ants feed on protein sources, such as other insects, or on sweets. In many situations the ants may even be considered beneficial because they indicate moisture problems in the home, and this moisture poses a far more serious structural threat than the ants themselves.

There are a number of different species of carpenter ants, but they are similar in appearance. Workers range from ⅛ to ½ in. long, and queens are just under an inch in length. All carpenter ants have a constricted waist and elbowed antennae (drawing left). Carpenter ants have only one segment or node on their waist-like petiole, and in profile, their thorax is rounded. They have a tiny circle of hairs on the tip of the abdomen. Other ants (the ones that don't nest in wood) are smaller, lighter in color, have an uneven thorax, lack

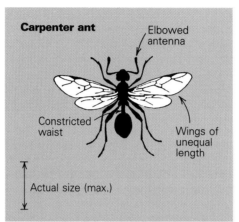

Carpenter ant — Elbowed antenna — Constricted waist — Wings of unequal length — Actual size (max.)

The winged forms of carpenter ants are the kings and queens (photo left). Their appearance indicates that the colony is at least three years old. If found indoors, or seen during the winter, swarms of winged carpenter ants tell you the colony is nesting inside. Carpenter ants do not eat wood, but they will use their mouths to remove it when creating their nests. Unlike termites, carpenter ants keep their galleries (photo below) very smooth and clean. The coarse debris removed to create the nest is shown in the inset photo.

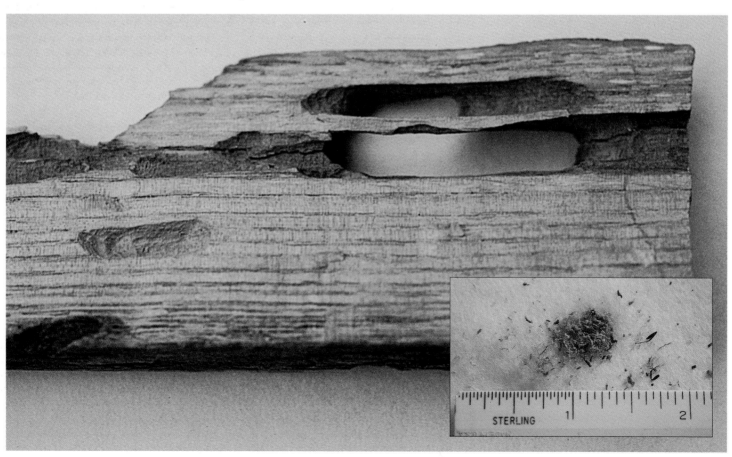

the circle of hairs on the tip of the abdomen or have two nodes at the petiole.

Newly fertilized queen carpenter ants will tear off their wings and search out a nesting site. Having selected or excavated a small cavity in the ground or in wood, the queen will seal the entrance and lay 15 to 20 eggs. Eggs hatch into grub-like larvae (all ants develop in stages—egg, larva, pupa, adult—just like butterflies). The queen feeds the legless larvae with fluid secreted from her mouth. It takes from two to ten months for the larvae to develop, spin silken cocoons and emerge as wingless worker ants. Carpenter-ant queens suffer very high mortality during this early nesting phase, and over 90% of the queens fail in rearing this first generation and establishing a nest.

The workers that emerge from the first brood take on the duties of collecting food, enlarging the nest and tending the young. Only the queen is capable of laying eggs, and new larvae are helpless and dependent on the workers for nourishment. Adult worker ants seen outside the nest will be from ¼ in. to ½ in. long and are all wingless, sterile females.

During the first three to five years, the colony will grow from the single queen to about 2,000 to 3,000 individuals. Once a colony reaches this size it develops the winged males and females (kings and queens) for the first time (top photo, facing page). Outdoors during the spring, and indoors at any time of year, from 20 to 400 winged individuals will emerge from the nest and swarm. The swarm tells you that the colony is at least three years old, and if found indoors or seen during the winter, means the ants are nesting inside.

When nesting in wood, carpenter ants construct irregular galleries that run with the grain of the wood. They remove wood with their mouths and kick it out. Unlike termites, carpenter ants keep their galleries very clean and smooth (bottom photo, facing page). Over time most of the softer wood will be removed, and the timber will look a bit like Swiss cheese. Carpenter ants also nest in other soft building materials, such as foam insulation.

Worker carpenter ants will forage a good distance from the nest (40 to 50 yds.), looking for food. A carpenter ant's diet includes sweets, plant juices, honeydew (a sugar secretion from aphids), other insects, honey, meat scraps, grease, fats and even pet food. Once a food source has been located, a worker will communicate the information to the rest of the colony and recruit other workers to help. This explains why a dish of food left out overnight or unclean plates left in the dishwasher may be crawling with black ants the next morning.

Control and treatment—The best long-term solution to a carpenter-ant problem is to find and treat the nest. Once the queen has been killed, the colony has no chance of surviving. The inital step in locating the colony should be to ask yourself the following questions: Where have the ants been seen? How many ants per day are seen? Are the ants associated with food? Are any ants seen in the winter months? Is any firewood stored indoors? Have I ever had any water problems in the house? Have I seen any swarms, and if so, where were they?

If more than five to ten black ants are seen in the house every day or large black ants are found active inside during the winter, then carpenter ants are probably nesting indoors. Spraying every baseboard inside the home may seem to get results because the ants are repelled by many insecticide sprays, but unless the nest is contacted by the treatment, the ants will reappear.

Carpenter ants can sometimes be heard "chewing" on wood, or they will expel coarse sawdust and debris from the nest. There are often small fragments of insects, foam and other debris mixed in (inset photo, facing page). If you think you know where the nest is, spot treat that site once with any registered ant or roach-killing insecticide and see what happens. Diazinon (Spectracide), chlorpyrifos (Dursban), carbaryl (Sevin), and propoxur (Baygon) can be bought at most hardware or garden stores. Placement into the nest is more important than what you use.

If small numbers of black ants start to appear as the air warms up in spring, but the ground is still cold, the nest is most likely along an outside wall. Carpenter ants, like all insects, are cold-blooded, and if the temperature drops below 50° F, they cannot move. Large numbers of ants found indoors in January may come from firewood stored indoors or from a nest located inside the building.

During indoor inspections your best bet in looking for the nest is to look for moisture problems. Carpenter ants do best when the moisture level is above 15%. Wood affected by water seepage from clogged gutters, leaky roofing, condensation problems, contact with soil, poor ventilation or weather is prime nesting territory. Check for nest sites in areas with small voids, too, such as hollow-core doors, delaminating plywood or in large wooden beams that may have pre-existing voids.

Outdoor nesting ants are most troublesome in the spring. Old tree stumps, firewood piles or trees with dead branches or heart rot may be the main nesting site. Carpenter ants will also nest in lawns or bare soil. Look for sawdust, piles of shredded wood, or piles of soil mounded outside the nest. As indoors, treat the nest directly to eradicate it.

For small numbers of ants filtering into the house from outdoors, finding the nest may not be practical. Spraying a 2-ft. to 10-ft. swath around the outside of the foundation during the spring or summer (a barrier treatment) will usually discourage carpenter ants from coming inside. Treat ground nests with dusts or granules. Keeping garbage cans clean, washing food scraps from dishes and not leaving pet food sitting out for extended periods will cut down on ants being drawn indoors.

Baits have not been very effective in controlling carpenter-ant problems. Either the ants refuse to feed on the bait, learn to avoid the bait or are killed before they can bring the poison back to the nest. New products are being developed that look promising, however. An antibiotic bait called abamectin is currently awaiting approval by the EPA and may be available in the near future. Current plans call for it to be sold only to professional pest-control companies. Effective baits will eliminate the need to find the nest, but they will take two to six weeks to work.

Do you need to call in professional help? It depends on how much you hate the ants. As discussed, the ants should not be a structural concern, but some people just do not like sharing their breakfast table with six-legged critters. Some pest-control companies will drill between every stud, door sill and window frame and also treat the outside foundation. This is labor-intensive, expensive ($400 to $1,200) and uses a large amount of pesticide. By treating everything in site they hope somehow to hit the nest. This can be an effective approach, but is analogous to rabbit-hunting with a tank. Remember that spot-treating the nest directly is just as effective.

Powderpost beetles—Powderpost beetles are from the beetle family *Lyctidae*. In the U. S., lyctids are second only to termites in their destruction of wood (top right photo, next page). The name "powderpost" comes from the extremely fine, flour-like fecal matter, called "frass," that is pushed out of infested wood by emerging beetles (bottom right photo, next page). Because the dust-like powder is loose in the feeding tunnels, it may continue to sift out long after the adults have emerged and even after the infestation has died out.

Adult powderpost beetles are small (⅟₁₂ in. to ⅕ in. in length), elongated, flattened, reddish-brown to black in color, and when viewed from above, their heads are visible (drawing, next page). Adults are attracted to light and often appear at windowsills in infested rooms. Lyctids are generally brought into buildings in wood that contains their eggs or larvae. There are six common species in the U. S.

Powderpost beetles attack only hardwoods and prefer porous wood, such as ash, oak,

For more information:

National Pest Control Association
8100 Oak St.
Dunn Loring, Va. 22027

The Bio-Integral Resource Center
P. O. Box 7414
Berkeley, Calif. 94707
—*Publishes information on environmentally sound pest management, including "Least Toxic Management of Termites and Other Wood-Damaging Organisms" ($11.95).*

Your county or state extension agent is another good source of information.

mahogany, hickory, maple, walnut, bamboo and wicker (photo facing page). In nature they attack old, well-seasoned wood. Almost all of the attack will occur in the sapwood. Oak firewood, two to four years old, is a common source of infestation in the home. Indoors, powderpost beetles may be found in hardwood flooring, rough-sawn timbers, plywood, barnboard and hardwood articles, such as tool handles, crating, furniture and picture frames.

An infestation begins when the female deposits her eggs in the surface pores of the wood or crawls into old adult emergence holes and deposits the eggs. Eggs hatch within 10 days, and larvae tunnel through the sapwood, usually following the grain.

In the southern U. S. the larval stage may be completed in as little as two months, but it normally takes 9 to 11 months in the northern U. S. As the larva matures, it chews to within $\frac{1}{8}$ in. of the surface of the wood and prepares a small chamber. Adults will emerge two to three weeks later and are commonly seen in April and May. The emergence holes are round, $\frac{1}{32}$ in. to $\frac{1}{8}$ in. in diameter (bottom left photo), and there are large quantities of frass packed at the surface. Mature larvae are curved wormlike, cream-colored grubs, less than $\frac{1}{5}$ in. long.

Lyctids will not lay eggs in sapwood with a starch content of less than 3%, and the higher the concentration of starch the better they thrive. Powderpost beetles can live in wood

with a water content of between 8% and 32%. Because green wood is commonly about 50% water, attacks are generally confined to partially or wholly seasoned wood. The greatest lyctid beetle activity is found in wood with a moisture content between 10% and 20%.

Infestations die out on their own as conditions change in the wood. Over time the starch content in sapwood will naturally decline, so that wood becomes less susceptible to attack. The most seriously damaged structures are unheated buildings, which tend to have increased moisture and humidity.

Controlling powderpost beetles—There are four methods of controlling powderpost beetles. If the infested wood can be easily re-

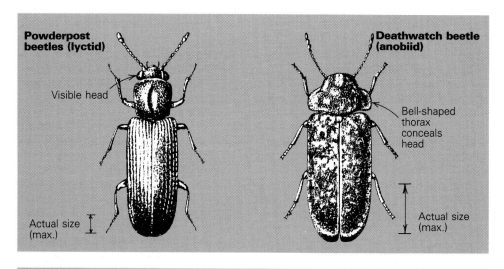

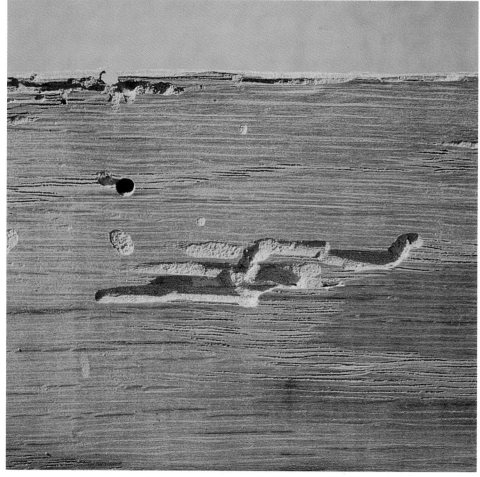

Powderpost beetles are second only to termites in their destruction of wood. Adults (top photo) range in size from $\frac{1}{12}$ in. to $\frac{1}{5}$ in. in length, and in color from reddish-brown to black. The name powderpost comes from the extremely fine, powder-like fecal matter called frass (photo above) that is pushed out of wood by emerging beetles. Emergence holes of powderpost beetles range from $\frac{1}{32}$ in. to $\frac{1}{8}$ in. in diameter. Note the tunnels filled with fine wood dust (photo left).

moved—one piece of oak baseboard or flooring, for instance—this would be the preferred method. Small articles, such as an antique tool or a picture frame, may be heated in a kiln or placed in a freezer where rapid temperature change does most of the killing. Rapid temperature change is not 100% successful, though, and obviously, some valuables cannot withstand the chilling or heating process.

If the infestation is widespread, fumigating may be called for. Methyl bromide is the preferred chemical because it will kill all life stages including eggs. This is an expensive treatment that needs to be handled by a professional pest-control company, and the cost must be balanced against the cost of replacing the wood. Proper fumigating will kill all insects present, but does nothing to guarantee or prevent the wood from reinfestation. Infested lumber can also be fumigated under a tarp. Small articles or furniture can be treated in a fumigation vault or chamber.

Painting or sealing the wood will prevent it from becoming infested if all pores are plugged, but it will not control an ongoing infestation by itself. Adult females will use existing emergence holes as a way of getting back into the wood (unless you've somehow managed to plug them all), and once inside, they can find pore spaces in which to lay their eggs.

The final treatment alternative is to treat the surface of the infested wood with an insecticide. By placing a thin layer of chemical on the outer surface, adults and larvae that come into contact with the treated surface will be killed, but any larvae living deep in the wood will not be affected. This surface treatment helps to prevent reinfestation and over time will "bleed out" the population. The infestation will remain active for some time after treatment, and even if the adults are killed upon emerging, they still produce exit holes.

Proper coverage is also of great concern with surface treatment. Spraying the outer surface of baseboards or the top surface of flooring leaves the undersurface of the wood untreated and gives the beetles continued access to the wood.

At present there are only a small number of materials registered for surface treatment of powderpost beetles indoors. Two formulations of chlorpyrifos (Dursban), some of the new termiticides and a formulation of silica gel/pyrthrum are labeled for wood-infesting beetles. In the past some formulations of pentachlorphenol were used, but they are no longer available for indoor treatment of existing structures.

Chemicals can be sprayed or painted on infested wood. Formulations with oil or petroleum solvents as carriers do a better job of penetrating the wood surface than do water-based materials. One of the major problems is that the best formulations for treating wood inside buildings are not available to the homeowner. Either you must hire a professional or settle for the shorter residual formulations. Read the labels carefully for proper use.

Anobiid beetles—There are over 260 species of deathwatch beetles (family *Anobiidae*) in the U. S. Several species attack and reinfest seasoned wood, and they are commonly lumped in with the powderpost beetles. Attacks often start in cold, unventilated crawl spaces and spread to other parts of the house. Anobiids attack the sapwood of both hardwoods and softwoods, and can extend into the heartwood. In nature, these beetles breed in old, dried limbs of trees.

Anobiids range from 1/10 in. to 1/2 in. in size and are usually reddish-brown to grey in color. They have a distinctive hood-like bell-shaped thorax, which conceals the head when viewed from above. Adult females lay up to fifty eggs in the cracks in wood or in old emergence holes. They prefer rough-sawn lumber, and the females may be inhibited from laying eggs on smooth or finished wood.

Anobiids have a high moisture requirement. Their eggs will not hatch at humidity below 60%. Larvae (immature beetles) are greyish-white wormlike grubs with black jaws. Larval development may take from one to ten years or more, depending on the species of beetle and the nutritional content of the wood. There are documented cases of anobiids taking 25 years to emerge from pieces of furniture.

The obvious sign of an infestation is the accumulation of powdery frass and tiny pellets found underneath infested wood. Fresh powder is bright and light-colored like freshly sawn wood. Small 1/25-in. long oval pellets will fall from infested channels or old emergence holes. These pellets will give the frass a gritty quality and will be loosely packed in the tunnels. This powder will not be as fine as that left by the lyctid beetles. If all the frass appears yellowed and partially caked on the surface where it lies, the infestation has died out. Emergence holes will be round and from 1/16 in. to 1/8 in. in diameter.

It normally takes 10 or more years for the number of beetles to become large enough for the infestation to be noted. As mentioned earlier, high-moisture conditions in wood are more attractive to adults and allow for shorter generation times. Old unheated buildings, livestock housing and homes with an earthen basement or damp crawl space are most susceptible to attack. Wood with a moisture content of 13% to 30% is needed for survival. Anobiids are much more likely to infest old lumber and wood than are the other species of wood-infesting beetles.

Controlling anobiid beetles—The control options for anobiids are much the same as they are for the powderpost beetles, but moisture plays more of a role in the beetles' environment. Proper vapor barriers and increased ventilation in crawl spaces are *very important*. Where excess moisture is a problem, the first step is to correct the cause. It does, however, take wood a long time to dry out, and reducing moisture may not be enough to control an infestation.

Infestations should be checked closely to be sure the beetles are still active. If structural wood has been heavily attacked, it may have to be replaced. Probe the infested wood with an ice pick to assess damage. Remember that much of the attack will be confined to the sapwood, and if much of the beam is heartwood, it may not be susceptible to further attack. Chemical sprays such as Dursban TC can be used, or the building can be fumigated. For fumigations, methyl bromide is the product of choice because it kills all life stages. Fumigation has no residual so it will not prevent further infestations. □

Phil Pellitteri directs the insect diagnostic lab of the Cooperative Extension Program of the University of Wisconsin at Madison. Photos by the author.

Powderpost beetles attack only hardwoods like the piece of beam pictured above. They prefer porous woods with a high starch and water content.

Wood-Destroying Fungi

What they look like, and what they mean to remodelers

White-rot fungi.

by Terry Amburgey

Throughout the world it's possible to find wooden structures that have given centuries of service. Frequently, however, wood-frame buildings suffer extensive decay damage within a few years of construction. Why do some structures provide hundreds of years of trouble-free service while others require continual maintenance and repair? The answer lies in design features and construction practices that trap moisture within structures, resulting in the action of insects or fungi that can disfigure or destroy a building.

In another article in this book, Phil Pellitteri described wood-destroying insects (see pp. 118-123). In the following pages, I'll describe the other half of nature's wood-destruction team: fungi. With a few clues to identifying deteriorating wood, you'll be that much closer to repairing it.

Know thine enemy—A fungus is a primitive plant that has no leaves and does not produce chlorophyll; it gets nutrients from sources of organic matter. Wood-destroying fungi, like other living organisms, require oxygen, moisture, a food source and favorable temperatures in order to thrive. Different families, genera and species of fungi have varying requirements, and the conditions that encourage the production and germination of reproductive spores (seeds) are not necessarily the same as those for optimum growth. In other words, fungi may grow through a piece of wood under conditions that are too harsh for them to colonize it in the first place. That characteristic makes fungi easy to acquire but tougher to eliminate. Of all the factors that in-

fluence the growth of fungi, moisture is the easiest to control in structures.

Three principal types of fungi inhabit wood: mold, sapstain and wood-decay fungi. It's a vicious circle and a remodeler's nightmare: moisture promotes fungi, fungi increase wood permeability, permeability allows moisture to enter the wood and that encourages the growth of more decay fungi...

Mold and sapstain fungi—Mold fungi produce pigmented spores on the wood surface, which may be black, green, blue, brown or yellow. Sapstain fungi produce blue to gray discolorations that occur as wedge-shaped areas going across the growth rings (photos facing page). Fungi of both groups utilize the readily available nutrients found in specialized storage cells of sapwood and cause the degradation of these cells. The result of this colonization and degradation of storage cells is an increase in the permeability of the wood (its capacity to absorb moisture), but these fungi have little *direct* effect on wood strength. Rather, it's the increased permeability that causes additional problems with wood. Increased permeability

It's a vicious circle and a remodeler's nightmare: moisture promotes fungi, fungi increase wood permeability, permeability allows moisture to enter the wood and that encourages the growth of more decay fungi...

may lead to a higher wood moisture content that promotes the growth of decay fungi.

Mold or sapstain fungi aren't exactly benign, however. They are often the culprits when house paint becomes discolored—either type of fungus can grow on or through a paint film when enough moisture is present (this is particularly true on shaded portions of the house). Contrary to the effects of these fungi on solid wood, the strength of composition-wood products (particleboards, OSB, fiberboards and the like) is significantly reduced when colonized by mold and sapstain fungi. This is because much more end grain is exposed within these products and because they include a larger percentage of sapwood. A further danger presented by mold fungi is their ability to make some people just plain sick. Hundreds of thousands of airborne spores are produced by mold fungi, and some of the spores are proven allergens. Given the proper conditions, infestations of these fungi may result in the buildup of spores on air-conditioner filters, decaying organic matter in crawl spaces and in upholstery, as well as on wood.

Mold and sapstain fungi grow best at temperatures between 75° F and 80° F, and they cannot colonize wood whose moisture content is below 20% (wood in a properly constructed home seldom has a moisture content above 15%). They are unable to colonize lumber that has been properly kiln- or air-dried and remains dry, but they can enter the end grain of freshly cut logs and lumber, or lumber that has become wet. Freezing temperatures simply slow the colonization; as temperatures pick up, activity resumes. When

From *Fine Homebuilding* (February 1992) 72:64-66

temperatures are between 50° F and 100° F, unseasoned or otherwise wet wood may be colonized within 24 hours because spores are constantly in the air. This is why most lumber to be air-dried commercially is first dipped in preservative chemicals. If you plan to air-dry unseasoned wood, the idea is to keep air flowing around it. Elevate the pile above the ground and don't let weeds grow around or beneath it. Sticker each layer, and if you want the boards to dry straight, be very sure to line up each row of stickers so that weight is transferred directly to the ground. I'd recommend that you place the stickers every 18 in. or so.

Despite similar growth requirements, mold and sapstain fungi differ in the way they disfigure wood. Mold fungi have colorless hyphae (the threadlike strands that comprise the body of a fungus) but produce green, yellow or black spores that discolor the wood surface; this discoloration can be removed by bleaching or light sanding. With sapstain fungi, on the other hand, the pigmented hyphae create a penetrating stain that permeates the sapwood in wedge-shaped areas across the growth rings; the stain cannot be removed by sanding or bleaching.

Actively growing mold or sapstain fungi are signs of a moisture problem that may lead to decay if left uncorrected. Inactive or dried growths of these fungi may indicate that the wood was colonized before being cut into lumber or during seasoning, was inadequately seasoned when installed, became wet after seasoning but before use, or had some other moisture problem (such as exposure to a plumbing leak) at one time. In any case, inactive growths are no cause for concern. How do you know if the growth is inactive? One way is to check the wood with a moisture meter; if the moisture content is below 20%, the fungi are inactive. Most people can feel moisture levels above 20%, so if the discolored wood feels dry, the fungi are probably inactive.

Wood-decay fungi—Brown rot, white rot and soft rot are three classes of fungi that are categorized according to the type of decay they cause. Wood decayed by brown-rot fungi (bottom photo, following page) is brown and crumbly and breaks into small cubical pieces; the strength of the wood decreases rapidly as decay proceeds. Most of the damage to structures caused by fungi is caused by brown-rot fungi.

Wood decayed by white-rot fungi (photo facing page) often assumes a bleached appearance, has black lines throughout the bleached area and feels spongy. The strength of the wood decreases gradually, with little loss in strength occurring during the early stages of decay. White-rot decay fungi usually colonize hardwood species (oak, maple and others).

Wood decayed by soft-rot fungi appears superficially like brown rot, but the affected wood softens gradually from the surface inward. Characteristic cavities (invisible to the naked eye) are produced within the wood cell walls. Soft rot occurs primarily in situations where wood maintains a high moisture content over a long

Sapstain fungi.

In any case, inactive growths are no cause for concern. How do you know if the growth is inactive? One way is to check the wood with a moisture meter; if the moisture content is below 20%, the fungi are inactive. Most people can feel moisture levels above 20%, so if the discolored wood feels dry, the fungi are probably inactive.

Mold fungi.

period of time, such as in contact with soil.

Wood-decay fungi can also be separated into groups according to the manner in which they colonize wood. The differences between them are the differences between opportunism and invasion. No wood-decay fungi can colonize wood that is below the fiber saturation point (about 30% moisture content). Some types of decay fungi colonize only when some event such as a roof leak brings wood to the fiber saturation point. Other types, however, take matters into their own rhizomorphs.

Water-conducting wood-decay fungi (improperly called "dry-rot" fungi) can wick water from wet portions of the wood to dry portions through rootlike strands known as rhizomorphs (center photo, facing page). Decay begins when the previously dry portions of the wood reach the fiber-saturation point. By this means, water-conducting, wood-decay fungi

can rapidly spread throughout a house, *provided the source of moisture, often an earthfilled porch, is maintained*. But if you cut off the moisture, you stop the invasion.

The primary water-conducting wood-decay fungus in the United States is *Poria incrassata*. This organism occurs throughout the southeastern United States and, rarely, as far north as Canada. In Europe, *Merulius lacrymans* is the primary water-conducting decay fungus. This fungus also occurs in the United States and causes some damage to houses in the northern portions of the country. Both of these fungi cause a brown-rot type of decay.

Principles of decay prevention—Wood decay can be prevented by following four simple principles: build with properly seasoned wood, keep wood dry, avoid contact between wood and soil and use preservative-treated wood if contact with the soil or other sources of moisture cannot be avoided.

Because wood-decay fungi cannot colonize and decay wood that has a moisture content of less than about 30%, it is recommended that wood used in construction have a moisture content of below 20%. This will provide a margin of safety. Air-dried wood has a moisture content between 6% and 24%, depending on the atmospheric conditions prevailing in the area where it is being dried. Kiln-dried wood has a moisture content of 6% to 12%.

Any design feature or construction practice that permits wood, especially wood joints, to get wet periodically increases the chances of decay and should be corrected. A roof overhang of at least 18 in. is adequate in most areas to protect house siding, windows and doors; rain seepage is a principal factor leading to decay in these components. A roof overhang of 30 in. or more may be needed in areas of high rainfall. Vents in foundation walls, roof eaves and roof gables prevent moist air from accumulating in crawl spaces and attics. Drainage of the building site to permit water to drain away from the house will aid in reducing water accumulation under a house. The application of polyethylene soil covers also helps. Maintaining the caulking around windows, doors, bathtubs and sinks prevents water from accumulating in walls. Paint decreases the likelihood of water penetrating the surface of wooden components, though it does not prevent water seepage into joints.

Wood in contact with the soil soon absorbs sufficient water to raise its moisture content above the fiber-saturation point. Also, many wood-decay fungi (including water-conducting decay fungi), as well as termites, are present in the soil. Earth-filled porches and patios are perhaps the most hazardous building structures in this regard. Foundations are used in part to elevate wood above the soil; earth-filled porches bring the soil back to the wood.

The term "treated wood" means wood to which a fungicide or an insecticide has been applied by brushing, cold soaking, hot soaking or by pressure treatment. Further, the preservative formulations may be applied in water or a variety of organic solvents ranging from light mineral spirits to heavy oils. Most "wood preservatives" offer protection from both decay fungi and insects, while others contain only a fungicide or an insecticide. Some contain a water repellent. Each of these types of treatment is useful for certain purposes, and each has its limitations. Brushed-on preservatives are quite effective in preventing wood-surface discoloration caused by the growth of mold and stain fungi, as well as the colonization of window and trim joints by decay fungi.

Preservatives added to paints and other finishes have proven to be very useful in decreasing the microbiological deterioration of the finishes. Dipping or soaking wood in preservative compounds is used extensively to protect millwork items such as windows and doors from surface discoloration and decay that often occurs at the joints of untreated units. This

Condensation-induced fungi.

No wood-decay fungi can colonize wood that is below the fiber saturation point (about 30% moisture content). Some types of decay fungi colonize only when some event such as a roof leak brings wood to the fiber saturation point.

Water-conducting, wood-decay fungi.

Brown-rot fungi.

method is also effective in treating wood siding, and the service life of dip-treated fence posts is greater than untreated ones. In general, pressure-treated wood is much more effective than the other types of treatment in preventing attack by fungi and insects and should be used in all portions of wooden structures where the hazard of decay is high. The use to which the wood will be put determines the type of preservative formulation to use. In general, wood pressure-treated with waterborne preservatives, such as chromated copper arsenate (CCA), is recommended for use in or around habitable spaces.

Prevention of condensation—I said earlier that keeping wood dry is the key to eliminating colonization by fungi. But many people forget that moisture doesn't enter wood only when it rains. Conditions highly favorable for decay development exist in many homes as a result of the condensation of moisture within walls and floors (photo top left). This condensation is caused by warm, moist air passing into the walls or floors and coming in contact with studs, sheathing or some other surface that is cooler than the dew point of the warm air. As the air is cooled, it can hold less water vapor, and the excess water is deposited on the cool surface.

In cold and temperate climates, cold-weather condensation can be prevented by placing moisture barriers on the warm side (inside) of insulated walls and ceilings. Most condensation problems occurring in warm, humid regions, such as the Gulf Coast area of the United States, are associated with air-conditioning. The most serious of these problems occurs in wood-framed floors of houses with a crawl-space foundation when inside temperatures are not maintained below about 75° F. These problems can usually be prevented by increasing the air circulation by using fans and by decreasing the atmospheric humidity of crawl spaces through adequate ventilation, soil drainage, soil covers, fans or mechanical dehumidification. Theoretically, such warm-weather condensation should also be prevented by placing a moisture barrier on the warm side (outside) of insulated walls. But research has shown that a moisture barrier installed directly under wood siding may lead to a serious accumulation of moisture within the siding. Evidence suggests that walls in hot, humid climates will be relatively safe if they are reasonably permeable to water vapor. When decay occurs in rather broad areas not associated with a specific source of water (such as a plumbing leak), the problem is either water-conducting decay fungi or conventional decay fungi growing on wood that has been wetted by condensation. In the latter case, the fungal growths will feel powdery or stringy. With decay caused by water-conducting fungi, the growths will feel leathery and often can be peeled off in sheets. □

Terry Amburgey is professor of forest products at Mississippi State University, Mississippi State, Miss. Photos by author.

INDEX